Participation, Responsibility and Choice

CARE & WELFARE

Care and welfare are changing rapidly in contemporary welfare states. The Care & Welfare series publishes studies on changing relationships between citizens and professionals, on care and welfare governance, on identity politics in the context of these welfare state transformations, and on ethical topics. It will inspire the international academic and political debate by developing and reflecting upon theories of (health) care and welfare through detailed national case studies and/or international comparisons. This series will offer new insights into the interdisciplinary theory of care and welfare and its practices.

SERIES EDITORS

Jan Willem Duyvendak, University of Amsterdam
Trudie Knijn, Utrecht University
Monique Kremer, Netherlands Scientific Council for Government Policy
 (Wetenschappelijke Raad voor het Regeringsbeleid – WRR)
Margo Trappenburg, Utrecht University, Erasmus University Rotterdam

PREVIOUSLY PUBLISHED

Jan Willem Duyvendak, Trudie Knijn and Monique Kremer (eds.): *Policy, People, and the New Professional. De-professionalisation and Re-professionalisation in Care and Welfare*, 2006 (ISBN 978 90 5356 885 9)

Ine van Hoyweghen: *Risks in the Making. Travels in Life Insurance and Genetics*, 2007 (ISBN 978 90 5356 927 6)

Anne-Mei The: *In Death's Waiting Room. Living and Dying with Dementia in a Multicultural Society*, 2008 (ISBN 978 90 5356 077 8)

Barbara Da Roit: *Strategies of Care. Changing Elderly Care in Italy and the Netherlands*, 2010 (ISBN 978 90 8964 224 0)

PARTICIPATION, RESPONSIBILITY AND CHOICE

Summoning the Active Citizen in Western European Welfare States

Edited by
Janet Newman
Evelien Tonkens

AMSTERDAM UNIVERSITY PRESS

Cover photo: © Mikkel Ostergaard/Hollandse Hoogte

Cover design: Sabine Mannel, NEON graphic design company, Amsterdam
Lay-out: JAPES, Amsterdam

ISBN   978 90 8964 275 2
e-ISBN 978 90 4851 343 7
NUR   741

Contents

Acknowledgements

It is without any doubt one of the most gratifying experiences of academic work to collaborate with colleagues in shared projects of research and writing, both in one's own Department and across the globe. When we met for the first time on such an occasion at the University of Amsterdam in 2006, it was immediately clear to both of us that we wanted to cooperate around our shared interests in the intersection of new modes of governance, citizenship, public service provision and gender. We agreed it would be even more inspiring to invite some other colleagues across Europe to join us. This book is the result of that ambition.

We want to thank all the authors for sharing our enthusiasm, not only by writing such wonderful texts, but also by participating in the academic workshop we organised in Milton Keynes in 2009 to discuss the first draft of the chapters. This book was possible only thanks to all their interesting and empathetic comments on each other's texts and on the themes of the book as a whole; this book is not just a collection of articles on a common theme but a book in which the chapters are logically related and build on each other.

We also want to thank the editors of this series for providing the opportunity for this cooperation and for their critical, supportive and inspiring comments on the text. We are grateful to the Open University in Milton Keynes for financing the workshop, and to Sarah Batt for taking charge of its practicalities. Lastly, we highly appreciate the various forms of assistance we received during the process of writing and editing from Tim Visser, Martine Buijs and particularly Anne Brouwers.

Janet Newman and Evelien Tonkens
August 2010

1 Introduction

Janet Newman and Evelien Tonkens

New formations of citizenship occupy a central place in the modernization of welfare states across Europe and beyond. A range of governmental and political projects swirl around the remaking of citizenship: the
restoration of national identity, the responses to the challenges of social
cohesion in a globalising world and the attempt to reinvent relationships
between people and the state. But at the centre of these struggles are
notions of the 'active' citizen: one who is no longer dependent on the
welfare state and who is willing to take a full part in the remaking of
modern societies. The active citizen is invited, cajoled and sometimes
coerced to take on a range of responsibilities for the self, for the care of
others and for the well-being of communities. S/he is offered a range of
opportunities to participate in a devolved and plural polity as well as to
exercise choice in the expanding marketplace of care and welfare services. And s/he is expected to take up opportunities for self-development
and paid employment in order to contribute to national projects of survival and success in a globalising world. While there is now an extensive
body of work on the encouragement of citizens to be active in the labour
market, our focus is on three related but distinct dimensions of activation that focus respectively on:

- '*choice*' in the marketplace of welfare services;
- extended *responsibility* for individuals, carers, families and communities; and
- '*participation*' in service delivery, policymaking, governance and the
  polity.

These three comprise a new policy focus on 'active citizenship' in many
nations – a focus that transforms older meanings of citizenship and that
seeks to incorporate (or at least rework) older struggles.

The paradoxical rise of active citizenship

How can we understand this rise of policies directed towards the active
citizen? On the one hand, it can be argued that this is a triumph of the
new social movements of the later decades of the 20th century. The women's movement, movements of patients and carers, disabled people's
movements and the gay liberation movement, amongst others, all
claimed more citizens' rights, both in terms of the redistribution of
power and resources and in terms of recognition and voice. Three

themes can be discerned. Firstly, the movements all have in common a demand for participation in (and often the transformation of) politics and policymaking, wherever power is exercised. Secondly, there is a demand for recognition of the political and public aspects of what were considered private issues, such as sexuality and caring.

Thirdly, there is a demand for more autonomy and choice: for the ability to shape one's own life, to be recognised as an independent person rather than a dependent subject. There are valid reasons to argue that active citizenship can be considered a response to such claims, and as such represents the crowning achievement of the work of new social movements. Many issues that a few decades ago were considered private and thus hardly issues of public deliberation have been brought into the public domain. Governments have come to recognise the importance of citizen participation and choice, and some now acknowledge the political importance of care. 'Choice' and 'empowerment' have often become seamlessly coupled, as in new policies on disability and elder care in some countries in Western Europe. New issues as well as new topics have been included as issues of public importance, and citizenship itself – its inclusions and exclusions as well as its rights and duties – has become the focus of extended political attention.

From a different perspective we might suggest that active citizenship is not the triumph but rather the ultimate disowning or even devouring of social movements. The term active citizenship itself is an invention of policymakers, and the ideals of social movements, it can be argued, have been appropriated and adapted for policy purposes, leading to new strategies of responsibilisation or incorporation. That is, the idea of active citizenship is used to discipline rather than liberate and empower citizens (Cruickshank 1990). For example, participation as a right and a form of empowerment may be transformed into participation as a duty in the service of policy aims. Policymakers try to activate as many citizens as possible in order to manage tensions emerging from the transformation of welfare states: those of providing higher-quality care with lower budgets, of responding to concerns over crime by devolving responsibility for the management of social control to 'communities', or of promoting healthy lifestyles in a climate of growing healthcare costs. Citizens' demands for inclusion are being remodelled as duties to be included and to include others. And while social movements sought to render so-called private issues public in order to extend rights, transform politics and enhance their power, these same private issues are now the object of ever more intensive state intervention and state control. For example, government policies now seek to stimulate unpaid care, to mould ideas on sexuality, to shape behaviour on parenting, diet and exercise, and to seduce or even coerce citizens into volunteering (Jones 2003).

Moreover, government policies have reworked the claims for choice, transforming it from a collective issue and as such an issue of solidarity, to an individual consumer issue. Now all are expected to make the best choices for themselves, regardless of others and, if need be, even at the expense of others. As such, government policies can be viewed as transforming choice from a right to a duty; citizens sometimes have to choose between goods and services in order to fulfil their citizen duties as 'demand steerers', punishing bad-quality service providers by rejecting or withdrawing from their services and rewarding good quality by choosing these services. Governmental promotion of active citizenship thus draws on the success of social movements and other struggles, recognising the capacities and competencies that marginalised and disadvantaged groups offer and utilising these in new policy framings.

But which of the two perspectives on active citizenship sketched here makes most sense? Can active citizenship be regarded primarily as co-opting political claims for voice or empowerment? Is it thus stolen from those struggling for expansive conceptions of citizenship? Or does it crown three decades of efforts of new social movements to ensure participation and choice and to politicise the personal? This question, we suggest, cannot be answered at an abstract level: we need more nuanced accounts of how different forces and pressures come together in particular places, services and struggles. We also need to uncover the experiences of citizens themselves as they negotiate the identities that governments seek to bestow on them. That is, we need detailed empirical research of the kind offered by this volume. Here we draw together contributions from Germany, the Netherlands, France, the UK, Norway, Finland and Italy, countries chosen because they demonstrate the range of reform trajectories in Western Europe and allow in-depth analysis of the issues that arise at the interface of different political projects and programmes.

The contributors trace the emergence of new formations of 'active' citizenship, setting these in national historical, political and cultural contexts. They examine what happens as struggles 'from below' meet new governmental discourses in the context of the reform of welfare services. They suggest ways in which diverse policies, enactments and meanings of active citizenship interact in specific sites. And many of our contributors also draw on detailed ethnographic research with service users, carers and citizens, thereby offering data on citizens' own meanings and practices of active citizenship. In doing so, they point to shifting experiences and identifications, to the changing relationalities of care, and to the transformation of professional/user relationships.

Gender is particularly significant in each of these dynamics: in selecting the themes of responsibility, participation and choice we have been particularly concerned to identify their implications for women as citizens, whether as service users, providers, carers or activists (though where we deal with care, our focus is on social care rather than childcare). Gender has also informed our methodologies; several chapters have used ethnographic work to capture the everyday experience of citizens and have preferred grounded analysis to grand theory, including that of welfare regimes but also mainstream theoretical work on citizenship. Our volume privileges gender since our focus is primarily on the institutions of social welfare and the gender settlements on which these were founded. However, such settlements were often inflected through colonial projects and national(ist) programmes of expansion and renewal. They are also based on forms of solidarity that assume homogenous, rather than heterogeneous, populations. Such settlements are now of course profoundly contested, and it is these contestations that are in part producing the struggles we are concerned with in this volume: struggles that cannot, we argue, be contained within specific nation states.

The aims of the volume, then, are:
- To analyse the ways in which policies on active citizenship encounter and are overlaid on citizenship struggles within specific nations, regions or sectors;
- To explore ways in which notions of choice, participation and responsibility are being translated and enacted in particular sites and services;
- To explore how new relationships and identifications are negotiated by citizens, professionals, carers, activists, consumers, residents and others;
- To suggest frameworks and perspectives that open up the politics of active citizenship to critical analysis, with a particular focus on theories of the politics of public and private relationships and acts, and on the contribution of feminist analysis.

The first two aims are delivered through the country-based chapters that follow, and are reviewed in chapter 10. Chapter 11 explores the remaking of relationships and identifications, with a particular focus on professional-user relationships, while in chapter 12 we review our theoretical contribution to the wider politics of active citizenship. In the remainder of this introduction we develop a little further our three core concepts; highlight the importance of situating studies of active citizenship in the context of wider citizenship struggles and claims; and set out the contours and contributions of a multinational approach.

Key concepts

Choice

Choice has been a long-standing claim of many citizens burdened by dependent relationships with state services. The introduction of consumerist models of participation in a marketplace of public and private goods can be viewed, in part, as a response to long-standing struggles by service users for more flexible and accessible models of service delivery – albeit struggles that are now largely becoming de-collectivised and de-politicised as the focus shifts to the individual, choice-making citizen-consumer. Citizens are being invited to view themselves as market actors, expressing choice in a new marketplace of public and private goods (Sulkunen et al. 1997). However, many 'free choices', it can be argued, are not so free, as in practice there are no realistic alternatives, or the choices to be made are too complicated and unforeseeable to be attractive (Schwartz 2003; Swierstra & Tonkens 2002, 2005).

Consumerism is usually associated with the individualisation of agency, stripping it from collective or solidaristic associations; it privileges choice while marginalising issues of voice. This makes it highly attractive to some modernising governments, offering a means of both de-collectivising social and welfare provision while at the same time promising both the empowerment of disadvantaged groups and new routes towards a fair society (Clarke et al. 2007; Clarke & Newman 2008; Newman & Vidler 2006). However, a range of literature now focuses on the significance of agency expressed through the exercise of consumer power, with consumerism seemingly offering new ways of expressing solidarities and exercising political power both within and beyond the polities of individual nation states.

For example, Hajer (1997) considers claims that the public, by exercising choices that move in the direction of a better environmental quality of life, produces new environmentally oriented policy discourses and gives manufacturers an incentive to improve technologies that protect the environment. Sassatelli (2007) traces both the ways in which traditional consumerist organisations and other social actors – environmental groups, fair trade organisations, organisations concerned with ethical finance, organic food and many others – are framing consumer action in more political terms. In the context of this volume, we might point to struggles on the part of older people, disabled people and people with learning disabilities – each has opened up consumerism as a route to empowerment for groups traditionally dependent on a malignant combination of professional and bureaucratic power.

In this volume, these two faces of consumerism are scrutinised. When, where and under what conditions might we view consumerism as individualising or as having the potential for collective agency? And might there be other framings of 'choice' that might be significant? For example, in what context might choice invoke ethical and moral, rather than market-based, judgements?

Responsibility

The tendency to stress active citizens taking responsibility for their own and each other's welfare and for community well-being is a second pillar of the new care and welfare order (Garland 2000; Paddison et al. 2008; Ilcan & Basok 2004). Notions of the active citizen bring into view forms of activity that have tended to remain invisible and unrecognised, part of the informal – and highly gendered – economies of care provision, neighbourhood participation and community self-organisation. Processes of responsibilisation seek to extend these unpaid activities and to open up new areas of both individual and collective responsibility. The idea of the responsible citizen – caring for others, nurturing and protecting communities and engaging practically in a whole range of projects – draws on highly gendered conceptions of the capacities of family, civil society and community.

The reshuffling of public and private in today's appeal for active citizenship is a key theme of this volume. One might argue that the successful slogan of the women's movement – 'the personal is political' – has been turned upside down: government policies promoting active citizenship in fact demand that citizens take more responsibility, particularly for those issues that were first put on the agenda to be recognised as public by social movements. Now that they have been recognised successfully, governments tend to throw these successes back to citizens, with the more or less implicit message that, yes, these are indeed important topics, so we will from now on see to it that you go ahead and broaden your scope of personal responsibility to include these issues too: to live a healthy lifestyle, to care for your neighbours, to behave in a sexually responsible manner. As such, the notion of active citizenship encompasses the enlargement of citizen responsibility in a range of social spheres (much broader than labour-market activation policies, to which most attention has been paid in the academic literature on active citizenship).

Participation

Conceptions of active citizenship invoke issues of agency, politics and power. Active citizens are invited to deliberate on policy options or service developments, or to contribute to an ever-expanding array of new governance and partnership bodies. Such modern conceptions of the citizen participating in the polity draw on – but also transform – older republican conceptions of citizenship. Feminist scholarship had criticised the narrow conception of agency inherent in republican traditions (voting and other forms of participation in the formal polity), drawing attention to the importance of participation in the 'politics of everyday life', and broadening notions of both citizenship and of politics (Lister 2003). Such politics potentially widen the social inclusion of groups whose citizenship status has been problematic, transforming children, disabled people and others from the 'objects' to the 'subjects' of political agency (Lister 2007).

Citizens are thus invited to engage in a range of opportunities to participate in community-based, policy-related service or governance decisions. We are witnessing a proliferation of deliberative forums such as citizens' panels, citizens' juries, service user consultations, governance boards and evaluation projects. Governments are also turning to web-based and other technologies to expand opportunities for participation. This turn to collaborative governance has diverse origins (Barnes et al. 2007; Pollit 2003), bridging concerns about the health of civil society, the decline of trust between governments and people, the performance of services and problems of social exclusion. It thus offers different images of citizenship rights, duties and responsibilities (Doheny 2007; Jenson & Philips 2001).

Citizenship struggles

The three discourses traced in the preceding section are not imposed onto a static and settled formation of European citizenship. Rather, they are overlaid onto existing patterns of contestation and struggle over the boundaries to, and meanings of, citizenship. In the next paragraphs we set out some frameworks that offer ways of conceptualising some of the dynamics of struggle taking place at the interface between 'active' and 'activated' forms of citizenship. Our starting point is Marshall's pivotal work (1950) depicting a long march of liberal democratic citizenship through civic, political and social rights, with each stage of this evolution producing a thickening of the concept. This evolutionary framing of citizenship carries an implicit notion of natural development, rendering invisible the struggles that led to the expansion of rights and rendering citizens as the passive receivers of benevolent state reforms, patiently waiting to be served. It masks, that is, the struggles that produced a progressively more inclusive and substantial institutionalisation of citizenship. Such struggles – on the part of workers, women, migrants and a range of social movements – mean that citizenship remains one of the most contested images in the political lexicon (Lister 2003).

Newman and Clarke (2009) suggest that citizenship struggles can be understood as expansive or transformational. Expansive struggles focus on questions of access and inclusion to a more or less public realm of citizenship rights and entitlements. Transformative struggles seek to re-make the relationship between the public realm and the 'private' realm of personal and domestic life, and to challenge structured forms of domination and subordination. Many social movements had a significant role in transforming the meanings and practices of citizenship, changing the public domain itself rather than simply demanding access to it and a voice within it, and in the process changing the boundaries between what are deemed to be public, private and personal matters.

Feminist politics and scholarship in particular has challenged the separation of a public world of citizenship and justice from the personal world of relationships and care, noting how such a separation has bracketed care and other contributions to social well-being from wider public recognition (Daly & Lewis 2000; Lister 2003; McKinnon 1989; Uberoi 2003). Responses to this challenge include the attempt to expand a 'feminist ethic of care' from the private to the public domain (Tronto 1993; Sevenhuijsen 1998) or to link issues of care to dimensions of social justice (Lister et al. 2007; Barnes 2006). In practice, transformative and expansionist citizenship claims can easily be entangled, for example in struggles around care.

Both expansionary and transformative struggles may be subject to processes of co-option or retrenchment, thereby turning active citizenship from a citizen's demand into a governmental strategy. Expansive struggles may be subject to attempts on the part of dominant political projects to accommodate radical demands for access through a form of normative universalism (Duggan 2003). This has certainly been the case where social movements, disability rights movements and forms of community activism have been co-opted in the political projects of making new images of the active citizen, being potentially stripped of their radicalism in the process (Marinetto 2003).

The distinction between expansive and transformative is related to another pair often contrasted in citizenship debates: redistribution versus recognition. Though the vocabulary differs, the idea of citizenship as an issue of redistribution fits well with Marshall's message that citizenship is an evolution of rights, with the emphasis in his view on socio-economic rights to be guaranteed by the welfare state. The distinction between redistribution and recognition in citizenship struggles was added by feminist scholars (Fraser 1995; Fraser & Honneth 2003; Lister 2003; Young 1990). A focus on redistribution as the principal means of addressing inequality, it is argued, privileges class-based inequalities to the neglect of other dimensions of differential access to power and resources. It also offers a narrow view of the person as producer and consumer of resources, neglecting other capacities and needs.

The concept of recognition directs attention towards the extent to which particular groups have access to cultural and symbolic resources, the extent to which their voices and contributions are recognised and the extent to which disadvantaged groups are afforded dignity and respect (Young 1990; Sennett 2003). The distinction between recognition and respect has been challenged (Lister 2004, 2007; Phillips 2003), and Fraser (2008) herself adds a third dimension, variously designated as participation and representation, to the couplet of redistribution and recognition. Nevertheless, the distinction between redistribution and recognition still offers a helpful way of engaging with the transformations associated with the emergence of active citizenship in public and social policy.

JANET NEWMAN AND EVELIEN TONKENS

While the development of welfare states had largely been founded on class-based claims for redistribution, in the second half of the 20th century and beyond they became the focus of extensive – and sometimes competing – claims for recognition as women, lone parents, black and minority ethnic groups, asylum seekers, 'sans papiers', lesbians and gays, disabled people, mental health service users, older people and others demanded political and social rights. These claims varied considerably, reflecting the history of the oppression of and struggle by particular groups. But across these diverse movements we can see the emergence of claims for more 'voice' (the capacity to influence treatment by welfare institutions) and in some cases more 'choice' (the capacity to live independent lives). We can also see the emergence of claims for greater recognition of the skills and capacities that citizens brought to their encounters with welfare institutions, challenging the 'knowledge-power knot' of professional power (Clarke et al. 2007; Kremer & Tonkens 2006). The expertise and voice of 'ordinary' citizens now claims a legitimate space in both welfare interactions and the wider polity.

The current (often called neo-liberal) transformation of welfare states and its stress on active citizenship is tending to subordinate claims for redistribution. This draws on at least two dominant policy tropes: the idea that class-based inequalities have largely been resolved in modern European states, and the idea that pressures of global economic restructuring now challenge the sustainability of welfare states. Each of these brings issues of recognition to the fore. The shift of responsibility from state to civil society and community, and thus to active citizens, draws on claims for recognition on the part of a range of constituencies, including faith-based groups, black and minority ethnic associations, self-help groups and alternative forms of provision. Yet if the claim for recognition leads to the devolution of responsibility, can we understand that as recognition? Is it indeed empowering? Or is it merely a matter of retrenching political responsibility (Schram 2000)? Again: is active citizenship disciplining and/or empowering, or is there some other way of framing this question?

The extent to which we can see a fit between claims for recognition and welfare state restructuring is one of the questions we raise in this volume. We anticipate that this relationship will be played out in very different ways in specific sectors and services, and in different welfare states. We do not wish to offer overly simplistic – and conspiratorial – interpretations of history, but instead want to draw attention to the idea that active citizenship is not just a new set of policy discourses but draws on already embedded resources and claims.

We also do not wish to suggest that claims for recognition are now being tidily resolved through the elaboration of new welfare discourses. This is far from the case. Access to civic and political rights remains highly contested, and indeed struggles are intensifying as responses to patterns of inward migration in western European welfare states produces new categories of partial and conditional citizenship, as security concerns challenge long-standing civic and political rights, and as new discourses of transnational citizenship emerge (Dwyer 1998; Dryzek 2006; Fraser 2008).

At the same time, the welfare settlements that inscribed social rights and thus worked at redistribution – albeit partially and differentially – are rapidly becoming unravelled in many states. Not only does this produce new patterns of activation, it also leads to a range of coercive policies and strategies directed towards non-citizens, marginal citizens and disruptive citizens (see Flint 2009; Ruppert 2006; Neveu, this volume).

The contribution of multinational study

This volume has contributions from a range of European researchers. As such, it takes forward previous comparative work, e.g. that of Siim (2000), who contrasted forms of politics and agency in France, Britain and Denmark from feminist perspectives, and the study by Lister et al. (2007) exploring gendered citizenship across Europe (see also Bellamy et al. 2004; Lewis et al. 2008). The concepts of active citizenship that we address in this volume – those of choice, responsibility and participation – each draw on forms of agency represented, to different degrees and in different ways, in particular national histories and traditions of citizenship. But while recognising the significance of national formations, ours does not set out to be a comparative project.

Rather, our focus is on how different meanings of active citizenship collide, intersect and perhaps stand in tension with one another within – and across – nations. In unravelling contested meanings, several contributors refer to common typologies of citizenship: for example, that distinguishing between socio-liberal, communitarian and republican ideals of citizenship, each of which may be unevenly aligned with newer neo-liberal rationalities. Such categories map unevenly onto theories of welfare regimes, long the focus of extensive critical engagements. Feminist scholarship in particular has continued to highlight the contested relationship between work and care, challenging Esping-Andersen's class-based typology of welfare regimes in order to accommodate the state-family nexus and the gendered divisions of work (Lewis 1992; Lewis & Ostner 1994; see also review in Lister et al. 2007).

We find these 'ideal types' of citizenship or of welfare regimes less than helpful for our purpose, since what is at stake are highly dynamic political processes that reshape and rearticulate these idealised formations. The divergent origins and enactments of active citizenship mean that the figure of the active citizen is complex, condensing often contradictory trends and embodying different forms of agency. Instead, we explore active citizenship as a *travelling idea* that is translated and enacted in plural ways not only in nations but also in regions, localities and sec-

JANET NEWMAN AND EVELIEN TONKENS

tors, and that is inflected through transnational processes of migration and care. When the contributors met together to discuss first drafts of their chapters, we began, inevitably, to have comparative conversations: how similar were the two Nordic cases? Might we be able to find parallel processes of reform in Germany and the Netherlands, both historically shaped by pillarised systems of welfare provision? How might the 'Latin' countries of Italy and France be contrasted with northern European states? Was the UK an 'outlier' or was the so-called 'Anglo-Saxon' model permeating other reform programmes?

But in trying to have such conversations we kept stumbling across the different apparent meanings of our key words. We had moments of discovery and excitement – 'Oh, *that's* what you mean' – as we began to explore different inflections and usages of our core concepts, and to highlight linguistic slippages (where translation did not quite work) and silences (where a word just did not translate). We became fascinated by problems of translation, especially where particular languages did not have a suitable word (see for example the footnote in Vabø's chapter on the lack of fit between the English language concept and existing Norwegian concepts).

We became aware of terms that may not translate: for example the idea of 'practical citizenship' in the Netherlands did not translate readily into the English lexicon of citizenship terms, though all of the things it denotes were containable in the idea of 'responsible citizenship' or 'care'. We also became aware of the different usages of key terms associated with welfare reform in different national, regional and local contexts: the idea of 'contractualisation' in Norway was very different from that in Germany, but so too was it in different regions of Italy. Similarly, participation in the chapter from Finland was explicitly tied to the participation of service users, whereas in France it denoted the participation of '*les habitants*' of specific localities. In some countries (e.g. France), the concept of active citizenship is not present as an explicit policy focus. In others (Germany), it is available but not strongly mobilised in policy: as Kuhlmann notes, there is no exact parallel of the English language term 'active citizenship', while the German term *Staatsbürgerschaft* (state citizenship), specifying formal rights and duties, has no exact parallel in the English-speaking world. But in other countries it is 'imported,' co-opted or appropriated to pursue particular political projects.

This took us to a realisation of the importance of *translation*. This points not only to the problem of linguistic translation but also to the significance of agency in translating travelling ideas in ways that fit or promote change in specific contexts. The idea of translation highlights the creative and dynamic ways in which actors seek out, interpret and enrol ideas of active citizenship in new settings. It does not just denote linguistic processes; translation is emerging as a theoretical approach to understanding the flow of policy ideas across borders. The more usual concepts of policy transfer or diffusion tend to conceptualise policies as rather static objects that can move across boundaries without losing their coherence. The idea of translation, in contrast, focuses on the flows, processes and movements at stake in the process of policy development and learning. Attention shifts to the local settings in which ideas are translated, mediated and adapted (e.g. Czarniawska & Sevon 2005; Lendvai & Stubbs 2007; Sahlin-Andersson & Engwall 2002).

This makes comparative analyses that rely on policy texts and/or the study of governance arrangements alone problematic. The country-based studies in this volume have drawn on a wide range of data that enables different perspectives to be brought into the analytical framing of active citizenship, including data on spatial differences within nations, on the elaboration of new citizenship discourses in specific sectors, on citizenship mobilisations and struggles, on professional mediations and on the experience of citizens as providers, users, consumers, carers and participants. These offer multiple spaces of translation – spaces in which meaning is made and in which different meanings potentially collide and are actively negotiated. Furthermore, as several contributors to this volume have argued, active citizenship draws on much older traditions of citizenship, so one puzzle was to try to identify what was 'new' about their usage in the context of state reform processes and welfare state 'modernisation'.

Our approach, then, does not view active citizenship as a global imperative that is enacted in path-dependent ways. It has to be understood as plural – as a set of notions, images and concepts that swirl around in the political landscape and in policy texts. It is a concept whose meaning is never fixed; rather it is subject to particular translations and attempts to fix its meanings as it is enrolled and mobilised in a multiplicity of political and governmental projects within and beyond the nation state. This means that ours is not a comparative project; indeed, we want to distance ourselves from the long tradition of comparative work on welfare states and in social policy more generally. In particular, we want to avoid conceptualising the contributory chapters as 'case studies' whose differences and similarities can be mapped using existing typologies of welfare regimes. Not only would this flatten some of the differences within specific national settings, but it would also offer little help in identifying what might be common themes and dynamics. Context does of course matter, both historically and spatially, but there is now an extensive critique of the mapping of nations into groups corresponding to distinct welfare regimes (Lister et al. 2007; Ostner, forthcoming). In addition, contemporary processes of governance have been associated with significant projects of 'rescaling' the nation (Newman & Clarke 2009: chapter 2; see also Anttonen & Häikiö, De Leonardis, Neveu, and Vabø in this volume). This volume, then, can be situated in emerging critiques of the 'methodological nationalism' that has tended to characterise comparative work (e.g. Chernilo 2007; Dale 2009; Deacon 1997; Yeates 2005

JANET NEWMAN AND EVELIEN TONKENS

and other work on global social policy). There are of course different national routes to active citizenship (e.g. French republicanism versus German corporatism; Nordic universalism versus UK neo-liberalism). But as we show, nations are not just contexts that shape the meanings of citizenship in path-dependent ways but are actors who mobilise concepts and resources in particular political projects. Political projects 'involve more or less coherent efforts to bring ideas, interests, people and power together' (Newman & Clarke 2009: 22; see also Dagnino 2007, cited in chapter 8 in this volume). Such projects do not correspond to nation states or welfare regimes: they may transcend nations, or may be specific to particular regions or sectors within them. Nor do they map on to particular political parties, and indeed are not confined to the actions of politicians; they enrol civil servants, the professions, municipalities, NGOs, protest groups, campaigners and indeed academics. And as we will see in the chapters that follow, different political projects are likely to co-exist within specific nations, producing contradictions and tensions, and perhaps ambiguities and spaces of agency.

The structure of the book

The first two chapters offer studies of the politics of reform in continental European nations as the imperatives of modernisation confront established welfare regimes and embedded formations of citizenship. Ellen Kuhlmann, in chapter 2, shows how current government policy on healthcare in Germany is driven by a political project of enhancing provider and purchaser competition in the context of the squeeze on healthcare finance. Citizens are invited to be 'government's little helpers' in challenging institutional and professional power. However, this meets a strong culture of entitlements, derived from the legacies of the Bismarckian notion of public responsibility coupled with communitarian values. This mitigates the impact of neo-liberal market rationalities on the German healthcare system. Furthermore, health insurance organisations and other stakeholders (including powerful 'citizen professionals') translate and mediate policy shifts. Kuhlmann uses the idea of 'patchy activation' to suggest tensions between different discourses of citizenship and the constraints placed on the new agenda of choice.

Evelien Tonkens' chapter on the Netherlands (chapter 3) also highlights the limits placed on the project of installing neo-liberal market rationalities by communitarian ideas of citizenship. She shows how the democratic movements of the 1970s paved the way for the elaboration and recognition of 'voice'. However, from the 1980s, the withdrawal of state responsibility for welfare provision was linked to delegating responsibility to citizens. In asking why the communitarians won despite the power of patients' and other social movements, Tonkens points to the coincidence of embedded values of solidarity and the newer discourses of responsibility and community: responsibility both appeals to governments (as a way of delegating problems and achieving cost reductions) and to citizens themselves (as a way of challenging individualism and achieving social cohesion).

We then move to the ways in which Nordic welfare states are inscribing new norms of active citizenship in contexts marked by strong public values and rights-based citizenship cultures. Both chapters focus on services for older people, and both show strong evidence of a continued emphasis on a socio-liberal form of citizenship. However, in the case of Finland (chapter 4) Anneli Anttonen and Liisa Häikiö suggest that current reforms in elder care are driving a shift from social citizenship to active citizenship. They show how the idea of universal protection is being challenged by the imperative to reduce the costs of institutional care through a double process of devolution: the first from the state to municipalities, the second from the state to individuals and their families. As such, strong central institutions are giving way to consumerist and market-based models. They also show how unpaid carers can bring a critical discourse into their negotiations with municipalities responsible for care, but how this voice is becoming individualised as consumer logics displace collective citizenship norms.

Mia Vabø, in chapter 5, traces the evolution of norms of active citizenship in Norwegian elder care through the era of welfare expansion – an era of radical decentralisation – and the new era of rationalisation, regulation and consumerism. While the focus in chapter 4 was on unpaid care and active citizenship, here the primary focus is on consumers, but again attention is drawn to the uneven articulations of rights-based discourse and new norms of active citizenship. Vabø tells the story of the Norwegian elderly revolt of the 1990s and the later emergence of a campaigning organisation fighting for improvements in elder care. She also draws on empirical research to highlight some of the paradoxes of the consumerist turn in social policy and the inequalities that may result. The current modernisation agenda seeks to align the discourse of citizens as rights-holders with a discourse of citizens as discriminating and active consumers. Alignment is made possible since both share a language of entitlement; however, deep antagonisms remain.

The chapters by Newman and De Leonardis show how political projects intersect in different services and places within the nation state. In chapter 6, Janet Newman traces the intersections of choice and participation in healthcare; of consumerism and responsibility in social care; and participation and responsibility in local governance. Each is linked to governmental projects of reform, and each is subordinated to the overarching political projects of equipping the UK with a workforce able to meet the challenges of global competition and of reducing reliance on the welfare state – both enacted through labour-market activation strategies. However, the tensions between the different reform strategies and the conceptions of citizenship they summon up are, she argues, mediated through a number of different practices. Most simply, they may be – as in the case of Norway – met by resistance or refusal on the part of citizens. They may also be the focus of creative processes of translation, in which dominant discourses and political imperatives are re-shaped by professional and organisational actors. And they may be displaced (and thus depoliticised) through new technologies of governance and through processes of spatial devolution.

Ota De Leonardis (chapter 7) traces the impact of divergent contemporary political projects in two regions of Italy. These are contrasted, initially, with the political projects of the 1970s whose exhaustion heralded a move from 'politics' to 'policy' as the framing of active citizenship, and from political participation to civic involvement. But she resists the framing of such moves in terms of either the success of earlier activist claims or their incorporation and neutralisation. Rather, her two contrasting studies – one in a region with a strong culture of public service provision, the other in a region characterised by a neo-liberal reorganisation of welfare – are used to highlight the impact of local political projects within a devolved system, especially their impact on the most disadvantaged citizens.

Catherine Neveu takes up these themes of delegation and devolution in the context of France (chapter 8). She begins from one of the political projects of the 1970s – that of reconstructing social cohesion in derelict neighbourhoods through citizen participation – and traces this through to a dominant conception of the public of public participation as *les habitants*: residents of a specific territory called on to contribute their local knowledge and experience in projects of improving services and contributing to local governance. In contrast, she suggests, a number of public participation schemes now seek to transform *les habitants* into more detached citizens through new pedagogies of citizenship. These different evocations and summonings of the public cannot be collapsed into a general notion of republican citizenship. As Neveu argues, they designate different political projects which are in tension with each other, giving rise to different logics of active citizenship: a logic in which social movements and 'the state' are seen as opposing each other and a logic in which they are viewed as collaborating as partners.

Shifts in conceptions of participating citizens are also traced in chapter 9 by Marian Barnes, who analyses the politics of care movements in the UK. The movement, she suggests, has had considerable impact in terms of the recognition given to the carer role in public policy and in terms of specific policies designed to support and 'empower' carers. However, she also highlights tensions between the different notions of responsibility elaborated in government policy and by carers, and suggests ways in which the consumerist image of citizenship that dominates the discourse fails to reflect the relational, moral and ethical perspectives on care held by carers themselves. The governmental move towards collaboration and partnership with carers may be subordinated to the consumerist project of enhancing choice and autonomy for service users. Despite the success of the carers' movement, care itself – as an expression of citizenship – remains undervalued.

This brief review illustrates some of the diverse political projects associated with active citizenship: the goals of enhancing citizen engagement in the polity (through participation) tend to be associated with different projects than, say, the goal of enhancing market choice. These may be more or less skilfully articulated, but such articulations are always likely to become unstuck, revealing the tensions and schisms they sought to elide. It may well be that some political projects become dominant, and there is now an extensive literature on the roll-out of neo-liberal market rationalities as a dominant trend. But this does not mean that others disappear: rather they continue to circulate as discursive and practical resources that others mobilise in order to resist dominant tendencies, to offer alternative projects of reform or to enact in professional and organisation mediations.

Together, these contributions raise key issues that are examined in three cross-cutting thematic chapters. Chapter 10 reviews the contributions of this volume to understand responsibility, participation and choice. In relation to each concept – or 'keyword' – we highlight its contested meaning, trace its evolution in policy discourse in particular countries and review the data from our contributors on the experiences and perspectives of citizens themselves. The chapter then suggests the significance of ways in which these different discourses are being articulated, and the inclusions, exclusions and inequalities that may result from dominant formations. Finally, it returns to the issue of the relationship between social movement claims and new policy discourses, arguing for a nuanced and situated analysis of the relationship between discourse and social agency.

The final two chapters review the contributions of the volume as a whole to some of the aims we set out earlier in this chapter. Chapter 11 explores the impact of active citizenship on professionals and other workers. We suggest three different regimes of professionalism that shape the interaction between providers and consumers in different ways, trace the impact of changing landscapes of power on traditional conceptions of the professions and explore ways of conceptualising professionals as both active and activated citizens. Chapter 12 reviews the contributions of this volume analysing the politics of active citizenship. It explores the public/private boundary and dynamic around four relationships: state/market; collective/individual; public/personal; and personal/political. Each of these offers a way of understanding the shifting politics of welfare reform, but the focus on the relationship between public, personal and political opens up issues brought into visibility by feminist politics and scholarship. We review the resources on which a feminist project of researching active citizenship might draw and identify issues for future research.

References

Barnes, M. (2006), *Caring and Social Justice,* Basingstoke: Palgrave Macmillan.

—, J. Newman and H. Sullivan (2007), *Power, participation and political renewal: Case studies in public participation,* Bristol: Policy Press.

Beckett, A.E. (2005), 'Reconsidering citizenship in the light of the concerns of the UK disability movement', *Citizenship Studies,* 9 (4): 405-421.

Bellamy, R., D. Casiglione and E. Santoro (2004) (eds.), *Lineages of European Citizenship,* Basingstoke: Palgrave.

Clarke, J., and J. Newman (2008), 'What's in a name? New Labour's Citizen Consumers and the remaking of public services', *Cultural Studies,* 21 (4-5): 738-757.

—, J. Newman, N. Smith, E. Vidler and L. Westmarland (2007), *Creating Citizen Consumers: Changing publics and changing public services,* London: Sage.

Cruickshank, B. (1990), *The Will to Empower: Democratic citizens and other subjects,* Ithaca: Cornell University Press.

Czarnawska, B., and G. Sevón (2005) (eds.), *Global Ideas: How ideas, objects and practices travel in the global economy,* Copenhagen: Liber and Copenhagen Business School Press.

Dagnino, E. (2007), 'Participation, citizenship and democracy: perverse confluence and displacement of meanings', in C. Neveu (ed.), *Cultures et Practiques Participatives: perspectives comparatives,* Paris: L'Harmattan, 353-70.

Dale, R., and S. Robertson (2009), *Globalisation and Europeanisation in Education,* Oxford: Symposium Books.

Daly, M., and J. Lewis. (2000), 'The concept of social care and the analysis of contemporary welfare states', *British Journal of Sociology,* 51 (2): 281-98.

Deacon, B. (1997), *Global Social Policy: International organisations and the future of welfare,* London: Sage.

Desforges, L., R. Jones and M. Woods (2005), 'New Geographies of Citizenship', *Citizenship Studies,* 9 (5): 439-451.

Dobson, A. (2003), *Citizenship and the Environment,* Oxford: Oxford University Press.

Doheny, S. (2007), 'Responsibility and the Deliberative Citizen: theorising the acceptance of individual and citizenship responsibilities', *Citizenship Studies,* 11 (4): 405-420.

Dryzek, J. (2006), *Deliberative Global Politics: Discourse and democracy in a divided world,* Cambridge: Polity.

Duggan, L. (2003), *The Twilight of Equality,* Boston, MA: Beacon Press.

Dwyer, P. (1998), 'Conditional citizens: welfare rights and responsibilities in the late 1990s', *Critical Social Policy,* 18: 493-517.

Flint, J. (2009), 'Subversive subjects and conditional, earned and denied citizenship', in M. Barnes and D. Prior, *Subversive Citizens: Power, agency and resistance in public services,* Bristol: Policy Press.

Fraser, N. (1995), 'From redistribution to recognition? Dilemmas of justice in a 'post socialist' age', *New Left Review,* 212: 68-93.

— (2008), *Scales of Justice: Reimagining political space in a globalizing world,* Cambridge: Polity.

— and A. Honneth (2003) (eds.), *Redistribution or Recognition? A political-philosophical exchange,* London: Verso.

Garland, D. (2001), *The culture of control. Crime and social order in contemporary societies*, Oxford: Oxford University Press.

Grundy, J., and M. Smith (2005), 'The politics of multi-scalar citizenship: the case of lesbian and gay organizing in Canada', *Citizenship Studies*, 9 (4): 380-409.

Hajer, M. (1997), *The Politics of Environmental Discourse*, Oxford: Oxford University Press.

Hobson, B., J. Lewis and B. Siim (2002) (eds.), *Contested concepts in gender and social politics*, Cheltenham: Edward Elgar.

Ilcan, S., and T. Basok (2004), 'Community government: voluntary agencies, social justice and the responsibilisation of citizens', *Citizenship studies*, 8 (2): 129-144.

Isin, E.F., and P.K. Wood (1999), *Citizenship and Identity*, London: Sage.

Jenson, J., and S. Philips (2001), 'Redesigning the Canadian citizenship regime: remaking institutions for representation', in C. Crouch, K. Eder and D. Tambini (eds.), *Citizenship, markets and the state*, Oxford: Oxford University Press.

Jones, P.S. (2003), 'Urban regeneration's poisoned chalice: is there an *Impasse* in (Community) Participation Based politics?', *Urban Studies*, 40 (3): 581-601.

Kremer, M., and E. Tonkens (2006), 'Authority, trust, knowledge and the public good in disarray', in T. Knijn and M. Kremer, *Professionals between people and policy*, Amsterdam: Amsterdam University Press, 122-136.

Latta, A. (2008), 'The ecological citizen', in E.F. Isin (ed.), *Recasting the Social in Citizenship*, Toronto: University of Toronto Press.

Lendvai, N., and P. Stubbs (2007), 'Policies as translation: situating transnational social policies', in S. Hodgson and Z. Irving (eds.), *Policy Reconsidered: Meanings, politics and practices*, Bristol: Policy Press.

Lewis, G. (2004) (ed.), *Citizenship: Personal lives and social policy*, Bristol: Policy Press.

Lewis, J. (1992), 'Gender and the development of welfare regimes', *Journal of European Social Policy*, 2 (3): 159-173.

— and I. Osnter (1995), 'Gender and the Evolution of European Welfare States', in S. Leibfried and P. Pierson (eds.), *European Social Policy: Between fragmentation and integration*, Washington: Brooking, 159-194.

—, T. Knijn, C. Martin and I. Ostner (2008), 'Patterns of Development in Work/Family Reconciliation Policies for Parents in France, Germany, the Netherlands and the UK in the 2000s', *Social Politics*, Fall: 261-286.

Lister, R. (2002), 'Sexual Citizenship', in E.F. Isin and B.S. Turner, *Handbook of Citizenship Studies*, London: Sage.

— (2003), *Citizenship: Feminist perspectives*, 2nd ed. Basingstoke: Palgrave Macmillan.

— (2004), *Poverty*, Cambridge: Polity Press.

— (2007), 'From object to subject': including marginalized citizens in policy-making', *Policy and Politics*, 35 (3): 437-455.

—, F. Williams, A. Anttonen, J. Bussemaker, U. Gerhard, J. Heinen, S. Johannson, A. Leira and B. Siim (2007), *Gendering Citizenship in Western Europe*, Bristol: Policy Press.

MacKinnon, C.A. (1989), *Towards a Feminist Theory of the State*, Cambridge, MA: Harvard University Press.

Marinetto, M. (2003), 'Who wants to be an active citizen? The politics and practice of community involvement', *Sociology*, 37 (1): 103-120.

Marshall, T.H. (1950), *Citizenship and social class*, Cambridge: Cambridge University Press.

Morris, J. (2005), *Citizenship and Disabled People*, London: Disability Rights Commission.

Newman, J. (2001), *Modernising governance: New Labour, policy and society*, London: Sage.

— and J. Clarke (2009), *Publics, Politics and Power: Changing the public in public services*, London: Sage.

— and E. Vidler (2006), 'Discriminating customers, responsible patients, empowered users: consumerism and the modernisation of health care', *Journal of Social Policy*, 35 (2): 193-209.

Orloff, A. (forthcoming), 'Gendering the comparative analysis of welfare state: an unfinished agenda', *Sociological Theory*.

Paddison, R., I. Docherty and R. Goodlad (2008), 'Responsible participation and housing: restoring democratic theory to the scene', *Housing Studies*, 23 (1): 129-149.

Phillips, A. (2003), 'Recognition and the struggle for political voice', in B. Hobson (ed.), *Recognition struggles and social movements*, Cambridge: Cambridge University Press.

Pollitt, C. (2003), *The essential public manager*, Berkshire: Open University Press.

Prokhovnik, R. (1998), 'Public and Private Citizenship: from gender invisibility to feminist inclusiveness', *Feminist Review*, 60: 84-104.

Robertson, S., and R. Dale (2008), 'Researching education in a globalising era: beyond methodological nationalism, methodological statism, methodological educationalism and spatial fetishism', in J. Resnik (ed.), *The Production of Educational Knowledge in the Global Era*, Rotterdam: Sense Publications.

Ruppert, E. (2006), *The Moral Economy of Cities*, Toronto: University of Toronto Press.

Sassatelli, R. (2007), *Consumer Culture: History, theory, politics*, London: Sage.

Schram, S.F. (2000), *After Welfare. The culture of post-industrial social policy*, New York/ London: New York University Press.

Schwartz, B. (2003), *The paradox of choice. Why more is less*, New York: Harper Collins.

Sennett, R. (2003), *Respect in an age of inequality*, New York: Norton.

Sevenhuijsen, S. (1998), *Citizenship and the Ethics of Care*, London: Routledge.

Sharma, A., and A. Gupta (2006) (eds.), *The anthropology of the state*, Oxford: Blackwell.

Siim, B. (2000), *Gender and Citizenship: Politics and agency in France, Britain and Denmark*, Cambridge: Cambridge University Press.

Sulkunen, P., J. Holmwood, H. Radner and G. Schulze (1997) (eds.), *Constructing the new consumer society*, London: MacMillan.

Swierstra, T., and E. Tonkens (2002), 'Klakkeloze keuzevrijheid. Kanttekeningen bij de dominantie van keuzevrijheid in hedendaags beleid' [Freedom of choice unlimited. Reflection on the dominance of the ideal of free choice], *Filosofie en praktijk*, 23 (2): 3-18.

— (2005) 'Kiezen als burgerplicht. Conclusies' [Choice as citizens' duty. Conclusions], in M. Hurenkamp and M. Kremer, *Vrijheid verplicht. Over tevredenheid en de grenzen van keuzevrijheid*, Amsterdam: Van Gennep.

Tronto, J. (1993), *Moral Boundaries*, New York: Routledge.

Uberoi, P. (2003), 'Feminism and the public-private distinction', in G. Mahajan and H. Reifeld (eds.), *The Public and the Private: Issues of democratic citizenship*, London and New Delhi: Sage.

Yeates, N. (2005) (ed.), 'Transnational Social Policy', Special themed issue of *Social Policy and Society*, 4.

Young, I.M. (1990), *Justice and the Politics of Difference*, Princeton: Princeton University Press.

2 Citizenship and healthcare in Germany

Patchy activation and constrained choices

Ellen Kuhlmann

As elsewhere in Europe, the politics of activation are gaining ground in Germany's public sector. Activation is especially advanced in labour-market policy but relevant in all areas of welfare governance, although in different ways. Citizens are increasingly expected to take on greater responsibility for managing the challenges of welfare transformations, thus playing the role of what might be viewed as 'government's little helpers'. As market subjects, they are expected to exercise control of public service and other providers in order to achieve greater cost efficiency and quality of services, and in turn gain greater choice of provision and voice in the policy process. These new roles provoke a number of tensions and uncertainties because the new policy discourse of activation does not sit easily with the institutional architecture of welfare provision. Nor can it be easily reconciled with traditional modes of citizenship in Germany, including the specific configuration of rights and responsibilities of individuals as citizens and service users, as well as those of the professionals who provide the welfare services. While new policy discourses of activation emerged within a matrix of marketisation, rights and responsibilities, there is no exact parallel of 'active citizenship', in its original Anglo-Saxon version, in the German policy discourse (see Bode 2008).

This chapter seeks to explore how the concept of active citizenship is framed by, and plays out in, a corporatist conservative welfare system using developments in healthcare in Germany as a case study. The aim is to highlight the tensions that render the creation of active citizenship a 'patchy enterprise' facing a number of constraints and uncertainties. This approach challenges the concept of policy convergence in welfare state analysis. It also departs from the evolutionary concept of citizenship as developed by Marshall (1963) and his followers.

Germany is an interesting case for exploring the uneven trajectories of active citizenship for a number of reasons. The German model of citizenship emerged beyond the notions of 'nation' and 'state'; it is strongly based on rights and entitlement dating back to early attempts to establish welfare services in the 19th century. The Bismarckian model pioneered welfare in Europe but in ways that granted citizens rights 'from above' (Turner 1990) in order to pacify the workers' movement. Interestingly, the German language does not even provide a word that captures the complex meaning of 'social citizenship' (Marshall 1963) in the Anglo-Saxon context. Indeed, the German term *Staatsbürgerschaft* ('state citizenship', specifying formal rights and duties) has no exact parallel in the English-speaking world (see for instance Aiken & Bode 2009).

To make things even more complicated, citizenship in its German version emerged as a community-centred rather than a state-centred approach. Lister and colleagues clearly highlight the historical trajectories that gave rise to this model; most important was the separation of nationhood and statehood in the 18th and 19th centuries that was reproduced after World War II and accompanied by strong pressures for overcoming nationalist identities (Lister et al. 2007: 25). The social movements from the 1960s onwards have added further pressures towards more participatory and empowering concepts of citizenship, while the reunification of western and eastern Germany has added new challenges of amalgamating two totally different systems (ibid. 2007: 61-62).

Within this context, healthcare provides a particularly interesting arena for exploring the constraints of activation and choice; more precisely, I will focus on clinical or medical care because Germany's care sector is highly fragmented and diverse in terms of both governance and organisation of care services. Germany has the oldest tradition of public responsibility for the provision of healthcare, the highest levels of choice for patients and well-established forms of democratic participation. In line with the rights-based model of citizenship, healthcare in Germany is informed by an 'entitlement culture' (Schunck 2000: 237; for an overview of welfare culture see Bode 2007). Consequently, active citizenship did not play any significant role until very recently. Why, then, is active citizenship becoming relevant in the German healthcare system and how does it play out? These questions will be addressed in this chapter.

My focus will be on two characteristics of the German system, namely choice and contractualisation. These are interesting examples, because in the current policy discourse, choice and contractualisation are strongly linked with New Public Management and neoliberal welfare markets; however, in Germany they are embedded in older concepts of welfare governance – such as entitlement – and nurtured by other discourses than marketisation and competition. Empirical material from a study into the modernisation of healthcare in Germany (Kuhlmann 2006) informs my analysis together with documentary analysis and the work of other scholars.

The chapter begins by placing citizenship in the context of the German healthcare system and current pressures for change. This is followed by an in-depth analysis of the transformations enhanced by recent attempts towards more active forms of citizenship. Focusing on contractualisation and choice, I explore the politics of competition from the different perspectives of institutions, providers and users. Finally, I highlight the uneven transformations of citizenship and conclude with some preliminary suggestions on how to advance citizenship beyond 'nation' and 'state'.

Placing citizenship in context: the Bismarckian architecture of healthcare governance and the pressures for change

The 'healthcare state' continues to shape the pathways of changing governance (Burau & Vrangbæk 2008; Greer 2008; Kuhlmann & Burau 2008; Newman & Kuhlmann 2007). I will therefore outline some basic characteristics of the German health system (for an overview, see Blank & Burau 2010; Moran 1999) and how they are linked with the concept of citizenship before moving on to contemporary challenges of activating citizens as market subjects.

At the turn of the 19th century, an emergent Bismarckian welfare system established, for the first time, compulsory social health insurance; a key goal was to improve the provision of healthcare for the working class (Bäringhausen & Sauerborn 2002). Based on a social insurance model, access to healthcare is not linked to citizenship but to membership of an insurance fund. Here, it is important to keep in mind that the system emerged when ideas of social citizenship and welfare were in a developmental stage (Marshall 1963). Thus, the German system developed along the lines of older concepts of citizenship that were linked to civil rights and entitlement.

Alongside the rights-based model of citizenship, the Bismarckian model embodies strong ideas of public responsibility coupled with communitarian values and family subsidy of care services. In terms of finance, this model draws on various different social contracts, the so-called *Solidarprinzip*: a generation contract where the productive generation secures welfare for younger and older generations; and a social contract based on the joint responsibility of employers and employees, and the coupling of fees with income. Accordingly, the finance of healthcare is nurtured by notions of class solidarity but more de-coupled from 'nation' and 'state' that are indicated in tax-funded systems.

What is, however, overlooked in this typology is a third form of social contract. This is the gender contract, based on a 'male breadwinner model' (see Lewis 2002) and women's responsibility for care work, both as professionals in formal institutions and as informal caregivers in the family and community (Burau et al. 2007). Thus, gender inequality has served as a hidden backbone stabilising the finance of healthcare for many years. This is, however, no longer sustainable and increasingly challenged by women's labour market participation and the attempts to professionalise both care work and the caring occupations. Together, these three forms of contract denote the form of contractualisation I address in this chapter.

The system is based on two institutional pillars, namely the sickness funds and the medical associations. These pillars are connected through a number of contractual arrangements that form the 'joint self-administration' of Statutory Health Insurance (SHI) (Bäringhausen & Sauerborn 2002; Blank & Burau 2010). In a recent review the SVR (Advisory Council on the Assessment of Developments in the Health Care System) stated: 'More than any other sector of the economy, the German health care system has a wealth of corporative elements' (SVR 2005: 9). The state has established the legal framework for collecting and distributing funds for healthcare, but the responsibility for administration and decision making is delegated to a network of public law institutions.

Within this model the sickness funds represent the interests of the users, while doctors represent the provider side. The joint self-administered bodies are charged with making decisions in the interest of the public. As such, the system relies on processes of delegation to bodies that represent different interests rather than on the active participation of citizens. This is true for both the service users and the majority of health professionals who are submerged within the bodies representing medical interests. The architecture of governance is stabilised by democratic features, including a system of public law institutions, collective representation of stakeholder interests and elections of representatives of the key regulatory bodies. However, the power of the medical profession is strong and more integrated into the regulatory architecture than in most other European healthcare systems (Kuhlmann & Burau 2008). In contrast, the position of the service users is weak and more detached from institutional powers, but free choice of providers is an entitlement and highly prized in terms of its cultural value.

The corporatism and multiple social contracts that nurtured the emergence of a Bismarckian model gained new significance as modes of governing healthcare after World War II, when the regulatory arrangements and institutional formations were shaped by external political demands for federalism and decentralisation to mitigate centralised state power. In a situation where notions of 'state' and 'nation' were deeply discredited and the concept of public (*Volksgemeinschaft*) saddled with the negative legacy of the Nazi state, the medical professions filled the vacuum. Doctors were thus able to expand their powers over the governance, organisation and delivery of healthcare services. For many years, doctors were the stronger element in the pillarised system. They defined the codes of contractualisation and dominated the processes of mediating the public interest (Kuhlmann et al. 2009); enjoying the highest levels of public trust, they were able to furnish government and governance with legitimacy.

It is interesting to note here the pressures for establishing models of 'governance without government' long before these demands were tacked on to a neoliberal agenda and the 'managerial state' (for an overview, see Clarke & Newman 1997; Newman & Clarke 2009). In the German context, the established model of contractualisation provided the backbone for both political renewal and service delivery in a situation where state power was discredited and democratic features had to be revitalised. Accordingly, the 'rise of contractualisation in public services' (Knijn & Selten 2006: 19) has an older tradition in Germany than the new managerialist regimes. This is in stark contrast to other European countries and, in consequence, contractualisation in its German version does not necessarily facilitate competition and activation policies in the same way it does in other countries. However, the traditional de-coupling of contractualisation from state power makes it a highly flexible concept that is open to transformations (see for instance Burau 2009; Sauerland 2009).

Specific pressures for remaking governance in Germany after World War II met with an overall trend in Western societies towards 'individualisation'. Within the context of a prospering economy, (western) Germany's health and other welfare services rapidly expanded and, in turn, allowed for greater choice of the service users, without promoting a more active stance of the users in the regulatory framework. Indeed, initially choice was much more linked to a 'happier' way of life after World War II rather than used as a policy concept – it was a means of welfare, consumption, freedom from state control, and universal social security.

More recently, the so-called 'third way' approach to welfare introduced a new agenda of choice that has stronger linkages with institutional change and active participation in decision making, thus enhancing further transformations in governance (Allen, Riemer & Hommel, 2006; Barnes et al. 2007). At the same time, the new agenda of choice clashed with both the taken-for-granted right of users to choose a provider, and with the high levels of clinical autonomy traditionally enjoyed by medical providers. In Germany the configuration of institutional arrangements and entitlements causes strong tensions with the figure of an active citizen acting as a rational, choice-making consumer in the new healthcare market. I explore these issues further in the following sections.

Corporatism goes to market: competition and constrained choices

The introduction of market elements and greater competition between purchasers and providers (as well as within these groups) are key elements of health reform in Germany (SVR 2003, 2005, 2007). It is important here to keep in mind that the main drivers for policy change are increasing economic problems and the need for cost containment caused by a number of external factors. On top of this, demographic changes due to a low fertility rate and an ageing population place new challenges on the generation contract, while high rates of unemployment further challenge the employer-employee contract as the cornerstone of SHI finance. Compared to economic pressures, democratic renewal and deliberative participation play a minor role, not least since the quality of care and access to services are already very high, including the entitlement to free choice of providers.

Due to economic pressures there was a need for transforming the contractual arrangements in Germany and redefining choice in ways that allow for greater control of providers and users as well as for stronger governmental interventions in the self-regulatory SHI system. Although recent changes in public institutions and the legal framework of healthcare mark an important step in Germany's health policy towards a more interventionist state and more active forms of citizen participation, they have not replaced the monolith of physicians' associations and SHI funds, nor undermined the classic corporatist delegation of responsibility to these institutions. Consequently, the idea of consumers taking on a direct role in controlling healthcare providers is less evident than in other countries where provider power is more separated from state power.

The 'meeting' of active citizenship with other modes of governing will be illustrated in greater detail by focusing in the next section on the role of active citizens in facilitating change, specifically in the system of financing healthcare, the place of the professions in the activation process and the citizen consumer as a choice-making subject.

Transforming healthcare finance: active citizens as facilitators of change

The coupling of social insurance contributions and salary makes healthcare expenditure highly visible but, at the same time, public control is limited with regard to funding and the provision of service. A falling income rate and high levels of unemployment in Germany directly impact on funding, thereby exerting constant pressure on the government to reduce expenditure. While funding increasingly draws on mixed sources, the employer-employee contract remains an important element and enjoys high currency in the population (SVR 2003).

In this situation, the introduction of free choice of sickness funds in the 1990s was meant to gain greater public control over the finance of healthcare through competition between sickness funds. However, the changes also mark a long overdue modernisation of both an encrusted administrative system and the long-standing division between blue and white collar workers (Klenk 2003). By contrast, the reforms did not significantly change the gender contract based on a 'male breadwinner' model, nor the family as the organising unit of welfare provision' (Lewis 2002). If one partner is entitled to membership of a SHI fund, the fund

ELLEN KUHLMANN

covers free healthcare for spouses who are not employed or otherwise in receipt of welfare benefits. These are usually, but not exclusively, women. Negative incentives towards women's labour market participation are thus embedded in the SHI model; in 2006 every fourth married woman in the western part and every twentieth woman in the eastern part held 'derivative entitlements' via a (predominantly male) breadwinner (Leiber & Zwiener 2006). While this model for many years guaranteed social health insurance for almost all citizens, at the turn of the 21st century the gender arrangements no longer fit with the patriarchal and paternalist model of organising social health insurance (Abels et al. 2009). Despite strong drivers for change, changing gender relations and women's efforts towards greater equality and participation are, however, marginal in the new discourse on active citizens.

We can conclude that the introduction of free choice of sickness funds opened the door for internal markets and competition in the SHI system. However, this reform did not significantly challenge corporatist governance and existing social contracts; this is true for the employer-employee contract as well as for the gender contract. Furthermore, it did not cause substantive change in the attitudes of citizens. The majority did not act as market subjects, exercising control by changing their sickness fund, even where they might have gained some financial advantage or benefit from other incentives. For instance, various polls in 2003 revealed the quota of 'changers' to be in the range of about three to ten percent (Braun & Streich 2003: 73). It is important to keep in mind that incentives are generally weak; opportunities for competition between sickness funds are constrained by a risk equation scheme together with the legal obligations of funds to deliver a clearly defined range of services (Social Code Book V). However, the missing 'enthusiasm' of citizens to shop around and choose the best sickness fund may also reflect that a discourse of competition does not easily replace an older discourse of solidarity (see Köppe et al. 2007).

In summary, this reform neither brought sustainable changes that would fulfil the hopes of policymakers to improve cost containment nor did it significantly improve voice and agency on the part of citizens (see Haarmann et al. 2010). Thus, the attempts to activate citizens as market subjects who could exercise control in the purchaser market did not meet with much success, although there may be incremental changes in the attitudes of citizens (for an overview, see Braun et al. 2008).

Strong pressures for transformations in the financing of healthcare persist, since the social contracts are no longer sustainable. This is the case for each of the social contracts described in the previous section: for the generation contract, the employer-employee contract and the gender contract, although the reasons in each case differ. In this context, active citizenship has come to enjoy high currency as a facilitator of change. Its appeal is especially strong in that it avoids the overt conflict that is likely to result from more direct governmental interventions in the SHI system. One proposed reform that was debated from 2000 onwards was the *Bürgerversicherung* – translated as 'citizen insurance'. This relied on the appeal to active citizens, freed from the constraints of social contracts and capable of maximising their individual benefit. The *Bürgerversicherung* was – and still is – an attempt to move towards a tax-funded system.

Although this model does not attempt to radically abolish the corporatist elements, it cuts into the social contracts underpinned by the *Solidarprinzip* (for an overview, see Nullmeier 2005; Strengmann-Kuhn 2005). In consequence, an appealing discourse of active citizens turned out to be constrained by institutional settlements and the meeting with other discourses; thus, the debates continue. As an intermediary solution, the so-called *Gesundheitsfond* was introduced in 2009 in an attempt to improve the distribution of scarce financial resources between purchasers and providers.

The changing finance of healthcare is an interesting case because it brings into view both the appeal of a new discourse of active citizenship and its limitations. It shows how more radical attempts to transform the employer-employee contract are difficult to establish and provoke stronger tensions with an older discourse of social solidarity and public responsibility for healthcare. Thus, it remains to be seen how the ongoing attempts to reform the system will turn out.

Citizen professionals: contractualisation and competition

The professions, especially medicine, are often perceived both as the counterparts of active citizens and as the 'objects' of new governance. However, professions are also part of the transformations in healthcare and are themselves subject to activation policies (Kuhlmann 2008). This is strongly linked to an introduction of competitive elements in a system of contractualisation (see Stuck et al. 2007). The 2000 Health Reform Act for the first time launched pilot projects on different ways of contracting, but studies suggest the projects have largely failed to contain costs or improve quality (Tophoven 2003).

Following this experience, further health reform acts introduced more complex strategies, including a number of incentives for organisational change and professional performance along with new forms of flexible contracting (see for instance Greß et al. 2006; Pfaff et al. 2003). Furthermore, some pilot projects introduced office-based generalists as gatekeepers, with take-up encouraged via financial incentives from the SHI funds (*Hausarztmodelle*). Participation is voluntary for both providers and users but the monopoly of collective contracting of the SHI physicians associations has been significantly relaxed.

Most recently, new forms of selective contracting with sickness funds gained ground, furnished with support from within the medical profession. These developments were nurtured by doctors' increasing dissatisfaction with their work conditions (Janus et al. 2007) but also by the attempts to reinstate their power in an increasingly competitive medical market. While collective contracting enjoys overall high currency, some groups also welcome more flexibility and choice in the system. In focus group discussions, doctors criticised their associations as 'encrusted'; women in particular complained about the hierarchical relationships to which they were subject (Kuhlmann 2006). Another problem is the dominance of specialists in the associations; generalists often feel they are not accepted as equal colleagues. Especially when it comes to budget allocations, the hierarchical relationship increasingly causes overt conflict (see for instance Ärztezeitung 2009).

Overall, we can increasingly observe that doctors actively participate in the transformations of healthcare, creating various new forms of contracting as well as collaborative networks at a local level. Doctors may support flexible contracting, but in practice they transform the initial intention of greater control over providers by building new alliances within the medical profession. As contracts are negotiated regionally and at community levels, doctors may merge and negotiate with sickness funds as a collective group. Thus, they catch 'two birds with one stone': they are capable of reasserting their powerful position within the SHI system *and* increasing individual flexibility and choice. This example highlights the fact that the new 'citizen professional' calls for individual choice without radically transforming the system of collective contracting (Kuhlmann 2006). Classic forms of collective representation of interests and new modes of choice and active participation through selective contracting are both relevant, and may serve to support the professional interests of doctors. The different modes of representing professional interests may cause tensions and do not simply translate into a uniform new model of contractualisation.

It is interesting to note here that a transformative potential of professionals as active citizens exercising control and participating in decision making is relevant within the medical profession but totally ignored when it comes to other professional groups, including nurses as the majority of the health workforce (Kuhlmann 2006). As with the gender contract discussed earlier, this provides another example of how the institutional governance arrangements shape the trajectories of active citizenship and may clash with the perspective of the health occupations striving for professonalisation and a more active role in the healthcare sector.

The citizen consumer: activation and constrained choices

Here I turn to a focus on the service users as the target of activation, and the emergent figure of a citizen consumer exercising market control. The existing system of democratic forms of participation and representation of interests through the SHI funds faced a number of transformations. At the institutional level the 2004 Health Reform Act extended the key regulatory body of SHI care, the Federal Commission, and subordinated other tiers of decision making. Representatives of user groups are now included on the new boards but remain 'second class' participants; they can raise their voice more directly but do not have equal rights when it comes to decision making (SVR 2005). It is interesting to note that the status of a user representative is legally defined and only open to those groups of users that have achieved (and accepted) high levels of formalisation of their groups. By contrast, the numerous self-help groups are more committed to an older discourse of empowerment and self-help and often resist the institutionalisation of self-help and voluntary organisations. Accordingly, they largely fall through the grid of the new modes of more active participation, or must move 'sideways' to get access through nomination as a delegate from an approved user group. This highlights how the discourse of empowerment developed in the medical counterculture and the women's health movement of the 1970s onwards may now be in conflict with the current transformations of participation and deliberative decision making (Abels et al. 2009).

The transformative potential of active citizenship and choice is even more complicated and limited when it comes to essential changes in the coverage of SHI care. What was a system of comprehensive coverage, equal access and high quality of services for all citizens is now increasingly limited. The overriding goal of cost containment has led to the exclusion of several services from SHI care. Co-payments by patients have been introduced and the users of healthcare services are burdened increasingly with additional out-of-pocket expenses; ongoing financial pressures may cause even more dramatic reductions in public services in future. So significant constraints of choice on the part of users are embedded in new health policies, and are likely to be exacerbated by the global financial crisis.

Moving from the institutional level to the micro level of decision making, in the German context the improvement of information is viewed as the key to 'activating' citizens to exercise their new role as experts and discriminating consumers (SVR 2003; for an example, see Wöllenstein 2004). Although these developments are accompanied by changes in medical ethics and challenges to the paternalism of doctors, choice is limited for a number of reasons. As other chapters in this volume have done, I want to highlight the importance of moving beyond policy analysis to consider citizens' own perspectives. Here empirical data from focus groups with patients working in self-help groups provide in-depth information on the perspective of the service user (for details, see Kuhlmann 2006).

First and foremost, the findings underscore that patients in Germany perceive choice as a taken-for-granted *right* and tend to view recent policy

ELLEN KUHLMANN

aims as a significant attack on such rights. User respondents strongly expressed the idea of their expertise over their own health and illness, and consequently were suspicious of any attempt to reduce the range of choices over either providers or the treatments available:

> But in the end it's up to me to decide and say, 'all right, perhaps it isn't scientifically sound, it's still not a standard, perhaps it's still being studied. But I choose this way quite consciously because it's my way... because I have faith in it, because I think it helps me. And so I should also have the possibility of using it myself. (self-help group member)

The findings suggest that 'choice' is a highly contested area and has a complex meaning for patients. They take the idea of self-responsibility seriously and are willing to exercise their new role as 'experts'. And they perceive the freedom to choose a provider and a treatment or diagnostic procedure as an important condition of self-determination and participation. Consequently, health policies aimed at tighter regulation of providers – like the disease management programmes and upgrading of generalists as gatekeepers – may clash with patients' demands:

> Of course, one hopes that they [DMPs] will improve quality. But my fear is that this is not their aim; that all possible kinds of interests lie behind them. Perhaps optimising costs. And everyone brings in their own particular interest, only we patients are hardly a part of it... I'm very afraid, and I'm very sceptical. (self-help group member)

Furthermore, users are highly ambivalent about and suspicious of policy proposals directed towards the standardisation of care, expressing fears that standardisation would reduce freedom of choice and neglect individual needs and wants. In this situation, patients form alliances with physicians to counteract health policy aims, and the system provides opportunities for both users and providers to bypass or outflank tighter regulation. For example, several patients in the focus groups reported that they would continue to contact a specialist directly where they perceived that the generalist was not competent to deal with their health needs. This counteracts the policy goals of introducing a gatekeeper system or even moderate forms like the Disease Management Programmes (DMPs) that aimed to improve care for chronically ill patients (Burau 2009; Pfaff et al. 2003).

Others participants in the group discussions rejected the idea of being directed to the hospital responsible for the region in which they live; instead they continued to contact the hospital of their choice, negotiating with the physician for permission to be treated there, despite the fact that this caused higher expenditures for the SHI fund. The findings highlight that patients take up their new role as discriminating consumers but in ways that depart from the intentions of government. Moreover, they are increasingly dissatisfied with health policy and direct their claims for improved choice to the government rather than to clinicians.

In summary, patients are included as new actors in the system of care without substantively changing the regulatory patterns based on physicians' associations and SHI funds. New healthcare models have had a positive impact on patient participation. But such developments tend to be viewed with suspicion. Patients feel themselves to be 'objects' rather than actors in the healthcare system. 'It makes you wonder what they are going to do with us,' or 'Once you're in a system like that, everything just takes its course' (members of self-help group). These attitudes clearly nurture dissatisfaction with government, while any positive effects of government policy on empowerment and participation are less clear. There are few, if any, signs that users are willing to act as market subjects and thereby limit provider power. Activating user participation and choice thus has the capacity to challenge health policy itself, while being highly compatible with provider power (see Newman & Kuhlmann 2007).

Citizenship as patchy enterprise: which way forward?

The embeddedness of citizenship in country-specific governance formations calls for a context-sensitive and dynamic approach in order to understand the negotiations of citizenship 'above and below the state' (Isin & Turner 2002: 5; see also Newman & Tonkens, chapter 1). This chapter has attempted to explore how new forms of active citizenship play out in a corporatist conservative welfare system, using healthcare as a particular case. I have investigated the figure of an active citizen as part and parcel of modernisation agendas driven by neoliberal market logics of competition but also shown how it is informed by other agendas. I have suggested a concept of 'patchy activation' to bring the fragmented, uneven and messy nature of citizenship into perspective and to highlight the constraints of current activation policies.

This concept of 'patchy activation' brings into perspective the tensions between different discourses of citizenship and the constraints of the new agenda of choice. Furthermore, I have argued for a dynamic approach that includes the providers and service users and takes the different dimensions of active citizenship into account, such as for instance the choice of providers on the side of the service users as well as the capacity to participate more actively in contracting on the side of doctors. Linking citizenship with more complex forms of governing and different sets of governance 'beyond government' in this way brings the politics of mediation into perspective. Elsewhere I have highlighted the linkages between citizenship and modernisation agendas in healthcare and introduced an approach on 'professions as mediators' between the state and the citizens (Kuhlmann 2006, 2008). Research from different countries underlines the connectedness of professional and state powers and the various ways of remodelling this relationship (Bertilsson 1990; Dent 2009; Kremer & Tonkens 2006; Kuhlmann & Burau 2008).

In the case of Germany my arguments highlight the ways in which the trajectories of active citizenship are shaped by cultural and institutional formations, and mediated through professional practice. This relates to the model of *Bürgerrechte* that emerged after World War II as a means of controlling state power, and to the rise of particular forms of network-based governance in which the state took a backstage position. My findings also highlight the fact that the corporatist system is based on the co-existence of user choice and producer power. This includes high levels of choice in clinical decision making for both doctors and patients alongside democratic forms of participation in the policy process through the representational role of SHI funds. In this situation, contractualisation and choice have gained specific meanings as mechanisms of mitigating state power rather than exercising market power.

The German model of citizenship clearly challenges the dominant approach to citizenship as an evolutionary development with cumulative benefits of legal, political and welfare rights (Marshall 1963). In contrast, the German case sheds light on the uneven transformations and tension of citizenship: a discourse of active citizenship is gaining ground as a facilitator of change, especially when it comes to provider and purchaser competition and new forms of healthcare finance, but meets with a strong culture of entitlement and a set of social contracts that follow a logic that is not based on the market.

Tensions are most obvious when it comes to the new agenda of choice. In stark contrast to the promises of choice, Germany's service users face a number of new constraints on choice, together with attempts to limit the choice of a provider and the coverage of SHI care. Unsurprisingly, they do not necessarily act as consumers exercising control of providers and purchasers, thus failing to play the role of 'government's little helpers'. On the contrary, as citizen consumers fuelled by activation policies, they hold on to the entitlement culture and they may now direct even stronger entitlement-based claims towards the government, including claims for more active participation in policymaking. They may also form alliances with doctors and eventually with other health professions. In sum, the new figure of an active citizen shows up in various shapes and may be fuelled by different interests, so the effects of activation policies are highly uncertain.

Finally, the German concept of citizenship not only tells a story of 'patchy activation' and 'constrained choices', it also highlights the role of professions in the governance arrangements which I would like to turn our attention to in a concluding remark. While the figure of an active citizen is primarily created as a uniform counterpart to the service providers, as a model it does not fit with complex network-based and partnership governance arrangements where professionals are part of the mechanisms of public control, including mitigating state power. A closer look at the professions as being part of the architecture of governance – the citizen professionals – may therefore help to better understand the variations of a common theme of active citizenship across countries and public sectors.

References

Abels, G., E. Kuhlmann and J. Lepperhoff (2009), 'Geschlechterpolitische Dimensionen von Gesundheit: Einleitung', *Femina Politica*, 18 (1): 9-24.

Aiken, M., and I. Bode (2009), 'Killing the golden goose? Third sector organizations and back-to-work programmes in Germany and the UK', *Social Policy & Administration*, 43 (3): 209-225.

Allen, P., and P. Riemer Hommel (2006), 'What are 'Third Way' governments learning? Health care consumers and quality in England and Germany', in *Health Policy*, 76: pp. 202-213.

Ärztezeitung (2009), 'Bayern Hausärzte versagen Fachärzten die Unterstützung', *Ärztezeitung*, 26 (March 2009): 4.

Bäringhausen, T., and R. Sauerborn (2002), 'One hundred and eighteen years of the German Health Insurance System', *Social Science & Medicine*, 54: 1559-1587.

Barnes, M., J. Newman and H. Sullivan (2007), *Policy, participation and political renewal*, Bristol: Policy Press.

Bertilsson, M. (1990), 'The welfare state, the professions and citizens' in R. Torstendahl and M. Burrage (eds.), *The formation of professions: Knowledge, state and strategy*, London: Sage, 114-133.

Blank, R.H., and V. Burau (2010), *Comparative health policy*, 3rd ed. Houndmills: Palgrave.

Bode, I. (2007), *The culture of welfare markets*, London: Routledge.

— (2008), 'Social citizenship in post-liberal Britain and post-corporatist Germany – curtailed, fragmented, streamlined, but still on the agenda', in T. Malby, P. Kennett and K. Rummery (eds.), *Social Policy Review*, 20.

Braun, B., and W. Streich (2003), in J. Böcken, B. Braun and M. Schnee (eds.), *Gesundheitsmonitor 2003*, Gütersloh: Bertelsmann, 71-84.

— et al. (2008) (eds.), 'Einflussnehmen oder Aussteigen? Theorie und Praxis von Selbstverwaltung und Kassenwechsel in der GKV', Berlin, edition sigma.

Burau, V. (2009), 'Negotiating reform at an arm's length from the state: Disease Management Programmes and the introduction of clinical standards in Germany', *Health Economics, Policy and Law*, 4 (4): 347-365.

Burau, V., H. Theobald and R.H. Blank (2007), *Governing home care. A cross-national comparison*, Cheltenham: Edward Elgar.

Burau, V., and K. Vrangbæk (2008), 'Global markets and national pathways of medical re-regulation', in E. Kuhlmann and M. Saks (eds.), *Rethinking professional governance: International directions in healthcare*, Bristol: Policy Press, 29-43.

Clarke, J., and J. Newman (1997), *The managerial state*, London: Sage.

Dent, M. (2009), *Patient choice and the medical profession: Choosing and trust in the NHS,* paper presented at the EGOS Colloquium, Barcelona, Spain, 2-4 July.

Greer, S. (2008), 'Choosing path in European Union health services policy: A political analysis of a critical juncture', *Journal of European Social Policy,* 18 (3): 219-231.

Greß, S. et al. (2006), 'Financial incentives for disease management programmes and integrated care in German social health insurance', *Health Policy,* 78: 295-305.

Haarmann, A., T. Klenk and P. Weyrauch (2010), 'Exit, choice – and what about voice? Public involvement in health insurance funds in corporatist welfare states', *Public Management Review,* 12 (2), 213-231.

Isin, E.F., and B. Turner (2002), 'Citizenship studies: An introduction', in E.F. Isin and B. Turner (eds.), *Handbook of citizenship studies,* London: Sage, 1-10.

Janus, K. et al. (2007), 'German physicians "on strike" – shedding light on the roots of physician dissatisfaction', *Health Policy,* 82: 357-365.

Klenk, T. (2008), *Modernisierung der funktionalen Selbstverwaltung. Universitäten, Krankenkassen und andere öffentliche Körperschaften,* Frankfurt/M: Campus.

Knijn, T., and P. Selten (2006), 'The rise of contractualisation in public policy', in J.W. Duyvendak, T. Knijn and M. Kremer (eds.), *Policy, people and the new professional,* Amsterdam: Amsterdam University Press, 19-33.

Köppe, S., F. Nullmeier and A. Wiesner (2007), 'Legitimationswandel des bundesdeutschen Sozialstaats', *Sozialer Fortschritt,* 56 (9-10): 227-236.

Kremer, M., and E. Tonkens (2006), 'Authority, trust, knowledge and the public good', in J. W. Duyvendak, T. Knijn and M. Kremer (eds.), *Policy, people and the new professional,* Amsterdam: Amsterdam University Press, 122-134.

Kuhlmann, E. (2006), *Modernising health care: Reinventing professions, the state and the public,* Bristol: Policy Press.

— (2008), 'Governing beyond markets and managerialism: Professions as mediators', in E. Kuhlmann and M. Saks (eds.), *Rethinking professional governance: International direction in healthcare,* Bristol: Policy Press, 45-59.

— and V. Burau (2008), 'The "healthcare state" in transition: National and international contexts of changing professional governance', *European Societies,* 10 (4): 617-631.

Kuhlamnn, E., J. Allsop and M. Saks (2009), 'Professional governance and public control', *Current Sociology,* 57 (4), 511-528.

Leiber, S., and R. Zwiener (2006), *Zwischen Bürgerversicherung und Kopfpauschale: Vorschläge für einen tragfähigen Gesundheitskompromiss.* WSI-Diskussionspapier, Nr. 146.

Lewis, J. (2002), 'Gender and welfare states', *European Societies,* 4: 331-357.

Lister, R. et al. (2007), *Gendering citizenship in western Europe: New challenges for citizenship research in a cross-national context,* Bristol: Policy Press.

Marshall, T.H. (1963), *Sociology at the crossroads,* London: Heinemann.

Moran, M. (1999), *Governing the health care state,* Manchester: Manchester University Press.

Newman, J., and J. Clarke (2009), *Publics, politics and power,* London: Sage.

— and E. Kuhlmann (2007), 'Consumers enter the political stage? Modernization of health care in Britain and Germany', *European Journal of Social Policy,* 17 (2): 99-110.

Nullmeier, F. (2005), 'Leistungsfähigkeitsprinzip und Generationengerechtigkeit als Legitimation der Bürgerversicherung', in W. Strengmann-Kuhn (ed.), *Das*

Prinzip Bürgerversicherung. Die Zukunft im Sozialstaat, Wiesbaden: VS Verlag, 51-66.

Pfaff, H. et al. (2003) (eds.), *Gesundheitsversorgung und Disease Management,* Bern: Hans Huber.

Sauerland, D. (2009), 'The legal framework for health care quality assurance in Germany', *Health Economics, Policy and Law,* 4: 79-98.

Schunk, M. (2000), 'Empowerment in pathways through care: A cross-national comparison of care delivery systems in Britain and Germany', in L.F. Heumann et al. (2001) (eds.), *Empowering frail elderly people,* Westport/Connecticut: Praeger, 223-237.

Strengmann-Kuhn, W. (2005) (ed.), *Das Prinzip Bürgerversicherung. Die Zukunft im Sozialstaat,* Wiesbaden: VS Verlag.

Stuck, S.A., M. Redaellia and K.L. Lauterbach (2007), 'Disease management and health care reform in Germany – Does more competition lead to less solidarity?' *Health Policy,* 80: 86-96.

SVR – Advisory Council for the Concerted Action in Health Care (2003), *Health care finance, user orientation and quality,* report summary in English, http://www.svr-gesundheit.de, accessed 15 July 2009.

SVR – Advisory Council for the Assessment of Developments in the Health Care System (2005), *Coordination and quality in the health care system,* report summary in English, http://www.svr-gesundheit.de, accessed 15 July 2009.

SVR – Advisory Council on the Assessment of Developments in the Health Care System (2007), *Cooperation and responsibility. Prerequisites for target-oriented health care,* report summary in English, http://www.svr-gesundheit.de, accessed 15 July 2009.

Tophoven C. (2003), 'Wandel der ambulanten Versorgung', in H. Pfaff et al. (eds.), *Gesundheitsversorgung und Disease Management,* Bern: Hans Huber, 87-94.

Turner, B. (1990), Outline of a theory of citizenship', http://www.nationale-denktank.nl/ *Sociology,* 24 (2):189-217.

Wöllenstein, H. (2004), 'Der informierte Patient aus Sicht der Gesetzlichen Krankenversicherung', *Bundesgesundheitsblatt,* 47 (10): 941-949.

3 The embrace of responsibility

Citizenship and governance of social care in the Netherlands

Evelien Tonkens

Active citizenship is a highly popular concept among Dutch policy-makers. Many ministries – ranging from education, health, justice and integration to the Home office – have policies for promoting active citizenship. Among local governments, civil society and public service organisations, active citizenship is a popular concept as well. It is by all means a buzzword, expected to provide a solution to difficulties that arise out of globalisation, individualisation and democratisation (Duyvendak et al. 2010). In the area of health and social care, a new law was installed in 2007 – the Social Support Act (Wet maatschappelijke ondersteuning or WMO) – in which active citizenship figures prominently.

The central aim of the WMO is to promote participation. It particularly stresses a communitarian idea of citizenship of taking responsibility for social care in your family and your community, both as a family member and as a member of the local community and civic organisations. This communitarianism is surprising, since the Dutch patients' movement was quite successful from the late 1960s onwards in promoting more republican and liberal notions of citizenship, stressing voice and choice respectively. How can we understand the late victory of communitarian notions of citizenship? What happened to voice and choice? In this article I will try to understand this communitarian victory by tracing the fate of responsibility, choice and voice in social care from the late 1960s onwards. I will also reflect on how it relates to views and patterns of care among Dutch citizens on the basis of my own empirical research on 25 care networks.

Late 1960s and 1970s: voice and autonomy as rights

In reconstructing the ideal of active citizenship in social care, and thereby the victory of communitarianism, we should start with the introduction of the law on health and social care, the AWBZ (*Algemene Wet Bijzondere Ziektekosten*, or General Law on Special Care Costs) in 1968. The WMO replaces the AWBZ in many respects, as we will see later on. Legal rights to social care services were firmly installed with the AWBZ. The law covered long-term social – back then often still residential – care for all Dutch citizens, who were automatically insured for it: the AWBZ was a collective fund. It was an extension of the health fund law (*Ziekenfondswet*) of 1941, the other legal coverage of medical services for which people with lower or medium incomes were automatically insured. Welfare services such as support from social workers were not included, but these were well subsidised from the 1950s onwards. The legal framework of the AWBZ was the main framework for social care. (By social care, we mean the broad range of care and support services for vulnerable groups such as the elderly and people with handicaps). It put patients in a safe position as legally entitled recipients of services – a position that would later on be qualified as merely passive.

The 1970s are well known for the spirit of democratisation of society, both in the Netherlands and in many other Western welfare states. This spirit also hit health and social care. Many new patients' organisations were set up during this period (Oudenampsen 1999). There was little need for patients' organisations to demand access to services as such, as access was already well established in the two laws that together guaranteed healthcare to all Dutch citizens: the health fund law and the AWBZ. While the health fund law covered the whole range of 'cure' services (mainly provided by hospitals and general practitioners), the AWBZ covered 'care' services, where cure is generally not expected; rather, the idea was that these AWBZ services are needed for a lifetime (see figure 1).

Figure 1 Changes in the legal framework for social care in the Netherlands

	1940s	1950-2000	2000s
cure	health fund law, 1941: entitlement to cure for low income (high income = private insurance)		health insurance law, 2005: universal entitlement to cure for all Dutch citizens
(long-term) care	Pillarised non-profit organisations	AWBZ, 1968: Universal entitlement to care	AWBZ continued but restricted; WMO, 2007: combination of parts of AWBZ and Welfare Law; no individual entitlements to services
support (welfare)	- (charity, subsidised by government)	welfare law (Welzijnswet), 1994: devolution of welfare services to local governments; no individual entitlements to services	WMO, 2007 (see above)

The Dutch patients' movement put most of its energy in liberal and republican notions of citizenship – in autonomy and voice respectively. In order to gain autonomy and self-development, it was deemed necessary to free patients from what were considered paternalistic and authoritarian professionals (Duyvendak 1999; Tonkens 1999). In practice, professionals and informal carers played an important role in promoting the ideal of patient autonomy. Professionals criticised *themselves* and their colleagues for being paternalistic and authoritarian. In the critical democratic movement in psychiatry – the so-called anti-psychiatry – for example, psychiatrists themselves played a leading role (Blok 2004). More generally, the anti-authoritarian mood was very strong in the Netherlands, as it was backed up and often instigated by the political elite itself. It was not just psychiatrists who criticised their own practice; also other members of the elite in politics, education, healthcare and elsewhere surpassed each other in self-criticism (Kennedy 1998; Hutschemaekers & Oosterhuis 2004).

Thus the democratisation of health and social care was from the start anti-professional. The main enemy of the patients' movement were healthcare professionals and their organisations, and to a degree also (informal) carers, as they were also charged with blocking patients' freedom and autonomy (Tonkens 1999). The government was not the main target, mainly because the government collected and distributed most of the money but did not control health and social care, as these were organised and managed by pillarised non-profit organisations. This situation of indirect power of the government continues today, although the WMO does give more responsibility to local governments, as we shall see later.

In addition to these demands for autonomy, the patients' organisations also started to voice demands for influence in health policymaking. They aimed to institutionalise the voice of the patients in healthcare practices (Oudenampsen 1999; Duyvendak & Nederland 2007). The government was highly responsive to these demands. Already in 1974, it responded by acknowledging patient's rights to participate in decisionmaking, though initially this had little practical consequence.

1980s: voice from right to duty

Participation in decisionmaking was again stressed in the first white paper of the national government on patient policy in 1981. During the 1980s, patients' demands for political influence were turned into practice: patients' organisations were admitted as members in decisionmaking boards both regionally and nationally. Without the voices and views of patients, policymaking could hardly be considered legitimate. Patients' organisations were also granted subsidies to improve the quality of their work. Their influence was backed up by various laws enforcing their voice in policymaking and in health and social care organisations

(Oudenampsen 1999; Trappenburg 2008). During the 1980s, patients' organisations were not only generously subsidised but were also given political influence in policymaking boards.

Why was this demand for a voice so successful? One reason of course is the spirit of democratisation mentioned above, which affected many areas of social life, including health and social care. It was felt that patients should be empowered to fight the necessary battle against paternalistic and authoritarian professionals.

Another reason is that the government also had a stake in delegating power to citizens. The Dutch government only had limited, indirect influence in this area, as health and social care were mostly provided by collectively financed, but privately run, pillarised organisations. With the rapid expansion of the welfare state between 1950 and 1980, the government gained more influence and responsibility particularly for the regional spread of services, but its power was still limited. Meanwhile, costs kept on rising and the government was held responsible – but also took responsibility – for cost containment. Around 1980, the dominant view was that the welfare state had expanded beyond its limit, resulting in a cost explosion that urgently needed restriction. But how were these rising costs to be contained? As the central government struggled with the predicament of assuming much of the responsibility but having limited power to reduce costs, it had an interest in making other parties partly responsible for cost reduction. Patients were a good candidate for this, not because they were expected to reduce costs but because they were needed to share responsibility for policymaking.

The idea that gained ground at this time was the notion that the government should withdraw. This ideal of government withdrawal gained popularity among policymakers from the 1980s onwards, not just in this area but also in other fields. Government withdrawal was embraced and promoted by thinkers across the entire political spectrum, a response to what was considered a crisis of the welfare state. While one would expect such a notion to be promoted by right-wing conservative thinkers and policymakers who are ideologically for a restricted government, the surprise now was that it was also promoted by left-wing intellectuals. The welfare state had granted liberal rights to services, but these were now considered to have a dark side: they created passive, calculating citizens rather than active, responsible citizens. The idea was that if the government withdrew and delegated responsibility back to citizens, they would become more active and responsible.

In the spirit of welfare policy critics such as Ivan Illich and Jacques Donzelot, Dutch intellectuals criticised welfare policies for disempowerment and medicalisation (Tonkens & Weijers 1999; Tonkens & Van Doorn 2001). The welfare state had promised to empower citizens and provide them with the necessary conditions for active participation in society, but the unforeseen result was that it had made them passive, lazy, calculative and helpless. These intellectuals thus supported the idea that the government must withdraw; this would more or less force citizens to recapture responsibility for their own lives.

So to which party should the government delegate more responsibility, considering the need to reduce costs and to withdraw? Not to professionals and their organisations, as these were so successfully attacked in the 1970s as both paternalistic and as big spenders, expanding the welfare state beyond need (Tonkens & Duyvendak 2003; Kremer & Tonkens 2006). A decade later the logical answer would have been 'the market', but this did not make much sense in the early 1980s as there was hardly a market to be found and corporate actors more associated with exploitive capitalism than with cost containment. So which party involved in health and social care should get the undesirable job? Patients! Who else but patients could be made co-responsible for painful measures aimed at cost reduction (Lomas 1996)? This idea first appeared in the central government's first white paper on patients' organisations, called *Patient Policy*, delivered in 1981. The paper promoted patients' voice, but not just as a right, as the patients' organisations had put it on the agenda. There was also a touch of a sense of duty here: patients should get more room but also more responsibility to take over from a retreating government.

So, apart from straightforward democratic motives, the government also supported patients' demand for voice because it fit their desire to make patients and citizens more responsible for the management and cost reduction of healthcare. The government thus promoted and subsidised patients' organisations in order to promote both patient's rights and patients' responsibilities. Patients' organisations welcomed subsidies and voice, since they saw these as extensions of their rights rather than their duties.

The concept of citizenship thus explicitly entered the scene by the end of the 1980s. It could be embraced by both government and patients' organisations, as it contains both rights and duties. The government asked the main advisory board – the scientific council for policymaking (*Wetenschappelijke Raad voor het Regeringsbeleid* or WRR) – for an idea of 'contemporary citizenship', which resulted in the first report on this topic in 1992. The report did put the notion of citizenship higher on the political agenda, but its plea for pluralism and neo-republicanism (later academically rephrased in Van Gunsteren 1996) did not have much influence.

The patients' movement also started to phrase its demands in terms of full citizenship. For active patients it was first of all a way to express rights: citizens have equal rights, regardless of illnesses or handicaps. Their health problems should not block their full participation in society. They should be able to live independent lives, move freely, make their own choices and be treated with respect, just like anybody else. Particularly the physically handicapped who were well organised and fit the ideal of articulate self-conscious right-seekers embraced this notion of citizenship. They welcomed it as a possibility to distance themselves from the negative identity and to claim the opposite: to stress that, despite their illness or handicap, they were also citizens just like other citizens, entitled to function as such and not be hampered by their illness or handicap (Duyvendak & Nederland 2007).

1990s: from rights to duties

Thus, during the 1980s, republican demands for democratic participation by the patients' movement were embraced by the coalition government of Christian democrats and right-wing liberals looking for ways to install responsibilities and duties (and reduce costs). During the 1990s, roughly the same happened with liberal rights to choice and autonomy. Republican duties to participate in deliberation about policymaking continued, but they were joined by duties to choose and be autonomous. Again, what were first claimed as rights (to autonomy and choice) were now twisted to become duties.

In line with what happened in many other Western welfare states, the 1990s saw the rise of neo-liberalism and the introduction of market language and market mechanisms in the public sector, including health and social care. Already in its 1981 white paper *Patient policy*, the Dutch government had discerned two roles: patients and consumers. In their role as patients, the white paper argued, they were entitled to the right to participate in decision making. This role was further institutionalised, not only in regional planning but also in care organisations, which were obliged to install clients' boards from 1996 onwards.

During the 1990s, increasing weight was put on the consumer role as the marketisation of health and social care gained importance. Consumerism was also attractive for the patients' movement, as it fit with the ambition to be more independent and autonomous. Consumers were deemed to be free, autonomous and independent, and were in no danger of being patronised: they are offered services on an equal footing. When faced with patronising professionals, the market provides consumers with an exit: they can simply exercise their freedom of choice and exchange the one service provider for another. With the rise of quasi-markets and market-oriented language in the 1990s, patients' movements embraced the notion of citizen-patients as consumers expected to 'steer' social services by choosing between competing services.

The Dutch patients' movement put much effort into positioning itself in terms of consumerism. In their role as consumers, patients were entitled to be informed in order to make their own choices (Trappenburg 2008; Oudenampsen 1999). The patients' movement demanded individual rights to better services, more individual consumer choice, and more control over what was offered to them. Personal budgets (*persoons-*

EVELIEN TONKENS

gebonden budgets or PGBs) were introduced in the 1990s as a means to strengthen this consumer role.

These two roles – of consumers and patients – became the pillars of the patients' organisations in the Netherlands. The regional as well as national umbrella organisations are thus called 'Dutch patients' and consumers' federation' (*Nederlandse Patiënten Consumenten Federatie* or NPCF), even though from the 1990s the term patient was generally relinquished and replaced by the term client or consumer in order to get rid of associations of passivity and to underline independence and choice.

Personal budgets were attractive for policymakers as well, as these reduced their responsibility to arrange services and get rid of waiting lists: they could simply delegate these problems to patients in the name of autonomy and choice. Choice and autonomy were such dominant ideals that no one criticised PGBs. From their introduction in the early 1990s they experienced explosive growth (Kremer 2006).

The government embraced choice and autonomy for patients, again not just as rights but also as a duty. The first sign of this was the government project 'Choices in Care' that had started in 1988, in which citizens were invited to discuss choices for cutbacks that would have to be made because of rising costs. Discussions were organised all over the country. If we need to make choices, the government asked all kinds of citizen groups, what choices do you deem best?

With the rise of marketisation in the 1990s, choice and 'demand steering' – the demand of patients steering the governance of services – became key terms. Patients choosing between insurance companies and healthcare providers: that should be the pillar of a marketised system. For this system to function, patients had to make choices. Efforts to move to full marketisation of healthcare failed during the 1990s but the language and the ideas of marketisation remained. The plan was reintroduced at the end of the century, this time with success, resulting in a new healthcare insurance law a few years later.

The concept of autonomy was also twisted more in the direction of duties during the 1990s, particularly for many mentally handicapped and psychiatric patients. They were strongly urged and sometimes even forced to leave residential institutions to live independently in shared regular housing or on their own in regular neighbourhoods, as this was presented as the best way to autonomy (Tonkens 1999; Verplanke & Duyvendak 2009).

Because the government had a stake in active patients taking on this responsibility, and because the patients' movement was well adapted to the new consumerist discourse and thereby remained an attractive partner for policymaking, patients' organisations were generously subsidised and given much room to voice their opinions and influence policymaking. All health regions had Regional Patients/Consumers Platforms (RP/CPs) consisting of representatives of patients' organisations, which were one of the leading partners next to regional and local government bodies and health insurance companies in writing regional white papers. In these white papers (*regiovisies*), the main policy lines were set out.

Organisations of professionals were generally not part of such deliberative procedures. Their position was still weakened by the earlier attacks on their paternalism and authoritarianism. They were still considered too selfish to be a serious partner in deliberation. Subsidies to professional organisations were not augmented in the same manner as patients' organisations; and in 2002 the Ministry of Health drastically reduced the budgets of most of these organisations – ironically just before a public debate on the reappraisal of professionals from 2003 onwards (Tonkens 2010; Tonkens et al. 2010). With the introduction of the WMO, the organisation of municipalities (VNG) had arranged a transitional period so that the effects of the new law in terms of cutbacks would only be felt a few years later (see Pierson 1996, 2002).

After 2000: community participation as duty

What happened to voice, choice and responsible participation during the past decade, when the WMO was proposed and accepted? Let's first look at the ideal of choice and patients as consumers, so cherished by the patients' movement in the 1990s. In the WMO, choice is restricted to a new practice of tendering of services, particularly home cleaning for elderly and handicapped people, and welfare services. If care organisations have to tender for contracts with the local government, it was argued, this would result in lower prices and more consumer choice. It did indeed result in lower prices but this was done by hiring lower and unqualified personnel, which received quite negative media attention: not augmented choice but decreased quality was the image that dominated. Moreover, this choice is basically a choice for the local government organising the tendering, hardly for citizens themselves. So choice is not an important pillar of the WMO, which makes it all the more astonishing that this law was accepted without much protest.

For one thing, the ideal of choice, active consumerism and 'demand steering' services were still present in governments' white papers. Citizens are too often 'captive customers' of services, because they cannot go to another service provider if they are not satisfied, while the service provider experiences few incentives to take the demands of service users into account, a white paper of 2002 argued (*Other Government*: 23). 'In order to strengthen the responsibility and influence of citizens and society', the introduction of demand steering was deemed necessary.

However, most of the enthusiasm about choice as well as the obligation to choose now focused on two areas of healthcare: personal budgets, and the curative part, mainly concerning hospitals. In cure, a new healthcare insurance law was introduced in 2005, replacing the older health fund law of 1941 (see figure 1). The new health insurance law was based on the idea of a marketised health sector, with private insurance companies competing for contracting patients and services. Citizen-consumers were expected to be 'demand-steering' agents, particularly in their choice of insurance companies, and by choosing the healthcare providers of their choice, supported by government's (sponsored) comparative information on their quality. The patients' movements gave continuous, virtually unconditional support to this new law. Also, the amount of people receiving personal budgets kept rising (Ministry of Health, Welfare and Sport, website 2010).

So why was choice not so central in the WMO and why was this law nevertheless accepted? Partly this was because choice became concentrated in different areas, as argued above, but it was possibly also due to the fact that citizens appeared to be less enthusiastic about the rights and duties of choice than policymakers and patients' organisations had hoped for. The official board of the patients' organisation, NPCF, remained enthusiastic about freedom of choice for patients. But this was not true of patients and citizens in general. In health, virtually everyone prioritised solidarity and equality over freedom of choice (SCP 2003; Burkestichting 2004).

Also in other areas, choice was less embraced than was hoped for. In the area of social security, for example, 75% of citizens have said they do not want to choose their own pension provider and prefer the current, obligatory system. Particularly those with a higher education dislike these choices, arguing that they take too much time (SCP 2003; Burkestichting 2004). Even the association of people with personal budgets, which calls itself Per Saldo and which had up to this point always been fighting for freedom of choice, tempered its enthusiasm. This association now argues that having a personal budget is a complex responsibility that cannot be easily managed and thus is not a solution for everyone. It has happened too often that organisations give people the responsibility for a personal budget without checking if they can really cope with it (website Per Saldo, visited 13 November 2009).

But choice is not just a right, it is also a citizen's responsibility, argued the Dutch Minister of Health Ab Klink recently. It is the responsibility of citizen-consumers of healthcare to choose carefully and consciously. Citizens should not simply expect that the quality of care of every service provider to be guaranteed: 'Those who simply presume that it [the quality of health care] is OK can get into serious trouble', he was quoted in a daily newspaper (Trouw 28 October 2008).

But when choice becomes a duty, it is much less attractive to citizens. To disentangle these complexities of choice as a right and/or a duty, we can distinguish *steering* choices from *empowering* choices. Steering choices are choices that citizens are forced/required to make in order to play their part in governing (marketised) social services. Empowering choices are those that are demanded by citizens themselves and that are offered with the aim of raising their quality of life (Swierstra & Tonkens 2002; Tonkens & Swierstra 2005). In order to limit choice as a duty, choice should always be accompanied by an attractive and high-standard default mode: an option that is automatically put into place when citizens do not want to choose or are not able to do so (Tonkens & Swierstra 2008). Citizens are probably much more enthusiastic about empowering choices than about steering choices, as the Social and Cultural Planning Bureau also hypothesised (SCP 2003), but the government does not seem to have made a distinction between the two.

The ideal of choice is not prominent in the WMO, but the notion of autonomy has some meaning here. There is also a role for autonomous citizens: citizens who arrange their own lives, who put together their own arrangements of help from a range of parties varying from family members to neighbours and voluntary organisations (and professionals if absolutely necessary). There is a lot of autonomy and self-management required, according to an empirical research on networks of carers and patients (Tonkens et al. 2009). Many people with mental or psychiatric handicaps who moved from institutions to the neighbourhood, where they were promised a caring community, end up very lonely, since they do not have the competences to actively manage their relations (Verplanke & Duyvendak 2009).

And what happened to the ideal of democratic participation, also quite strong in the recent history of the patients' movement? It is present in the WMO, but it is not a core issue. It is echoed in the WMO's legal obligation that local governments must give citizens a say one way or another, without exactly dictating how. This forces local governments to reflect on this issue and organise a board or some other form of participation. Often the existing elderly board and the board for the handicapped are put together. In this way the obligation is fulfilled and local governments can concentrate on other, more complex and demanding obligations.

Rediscovering civil society

How does the ideal of responsible participation figure in the WMO? From the beginning of this century, the idea of government withdrawal was again accentuated, but it gradually gained a communitarian twist. It was placed in the context of hopes for a flourishing civil society. Civil society was rediscovered as crucial for creating social care, social well-being and social cohesion. The rediscovery of civil society was partly a response to the idea that society had become over-individualised. Dutch citizens were reported to miss community orientation and social cohesion and to complain about other people being too selfish and egocentric. From the beginning of the century, they reported in questionnaires that they were happy about their own lives but unhappy about

EVELIEN TONKENS

society as a whole. As in many other comparable countries, there was a rising desire for community (Bauman 2001; Koenis 1997) that could not be addressed by bureaucrats alone: they needed civil society and its civic organisations and initiatives. Inspired by the American communitarian Amitai Etzioni, civil society could hopefully take on responsibilities formerly assumed by the government:

> Government needs to be more retrained in its interventions in areas in which civil society can be expected to pick up issues and set norms. (Etzioni 1993: 7)

However, this is difficult for government because – contrary to autonomous choosing citizens who need little more than information to exercise their autonomy and choice – civil society needs to be both left alone to develop by itself and to be stimulated, developed, nourished:

> The most important and probably also the most difficult task for the government will be tempering its own ambitions. It will have to focus most of all on creating conditions and on guaranteeing procedures... Modern government... needs to be more restrained in what it regulates, provide more room to citizens and organisations. (white paper *Different government* 2002: 6)

The next white paper on this issue two years later – *Exploring citizenship and different government* (*Verkenning burgerschap en andere overheid*) – puts even more emphasis on the responsibilisation of civil society and its citizens: it explicitly aims to render citizens together responsible for the provision and/or management of services that were previously considered government tasks. We need more reciprocity between government and citizens, the government argued. The relationship of citizens passively demanding services and government providing them should be more balanced. Reciprocity demands active citizenship:

> [It] demands that citizens do indeed contribute, which implies an active attitude from their side. Would citizens – as is more common in the classical idea – have the opinion that they do not need to do anything that is not prescribed to them in detailed rules and regulation, then it [the desired reciprocity] does not work. (ibid. 9)

Citizens should be 'held accountable on the basis of generally phrased norms and general rules of decent citizenship' (ibid. 11). The government wants to formulate a *charter for responsible citizenship*, according to the coalition agreement of 2007. But, fearing that it might not be welcomed but rather seen as paternalistic, the charter was to be formulated 'in dialogue with citizens – although the terms are already set by the government itself. Citizens should debate four themes: respect, orientation towards the future, engagement and efforts for society' (www.handvestburgerschap.nl) – the last two clearly a reference to communitarian values appealing to responsible participation.

The WMO can be seen as the crowning achievement of these developments. The ideal of active citizens taking individual responsibility for themselves and others is the core of this law. As the ministry of health, welfare and sports explains, individual responsibility is aimed at participation:

> The WMO is the result of broader policy, emphasising individual responsibility in healthcare... The aim of the Social Support Act is participation of all citizens to all facets of the society, whether or not with help from friends, family or acquaintances. (ministry of health, welfare and sport, website)

Cost reduction is once again an important impetus, too. Much of the firm legal framework that was already established in 1968 in the long-term care law AWBZ, in which individual rights were firmly rooted, is replaced by a much weaker legal framework in which there are no individual rights to services but merely an amount of money to be distributed among those who need it. While the AWBZ refers to individual legal entitlements, the WMO describes 'areas of achievement' for local governments in which they must prove to be active, without guaranteeing services to individual patients. What patients do or do not receive depends on the money available and on the local priorities in allocating that money. The move of care services from the AWBZ to the WMO also implies devolution from the national level to the local level: local governments are in charge of the WMO.

Active citizenship is put to the fore to fill the gap that arises as a consequence of this reduction in rights: informal care and volunteering is expected to jump in where gaps arise. The responsibility that the WMO wants to promote is thus the responsibility of carers and volunteers to help patients where paid care disappeared or will disappear in the near future.

This substantive reduction of rights was accepted with relatively little protest. Patients' organisations and local governments did raise some concerns, and many amendments were prepared in parliament in response to them, but few of these had a substantial impact on the core of the law itself. The only amendment that potentially has significant influence is the legal right to be 'compensated' for handicaps that limit one's participation in society, the so-called 'compensation principle'.

Informal and professional carers, two parties that could have protested and that have a strong position in other European countries, are politically and organisationally weak in the Netherlands. While in Norway and Finland, professional carers have regularly stood up to protect patients' rights (see chapters 4 and 5 in this volume), professional carers were positioned as enemies of patients in the Netherlands since the 1970s. In the three decades that followed, professionals were not in a position to

EVELIEN TONKENS

raise their voices, neither as experts nor as defenders of patients' interests. Thus, professionals were not in a position to speak for patients; doing so would have backfired: they are suspected of only acting out of self-interest and not putting all their effort into helping patients. If only they would work more efficiently, it was argued, there would be no problems.

A clear example of this was the reaction to the director of a nursing home who protested against the low quality of nursing home services in 2003. This director announced in public that he had introduced 'pyjama days' because of shortage of money and staff. This action was met with disdain, also by the LOC (*Landelijk Overleg Cliëntraden*), the clients' organisation of nursing homes: according to the LOC, this simply proved that the director was doing a bad job.

In recent years, however, there has been a major debate about this 'taming' of professionals in the public sector (Duyvendak et al. 2006, Noordegraaf & Steijn 2010). The core message of this movement was that professionals should be less imprisoned by bureaucratic regulations and should be allowed more discretionary power. This met with striking success, as it was reflected in the 2007 coalition agreement of the central government, which also makes a plea for 'more room for professionals' in the public sector. This ideological consensus has not yet been translated into policy, so in practice the position of professionals has hardly changed so far.

(Informal) carers' organisations are also not very powerful in the Netherlands when compared with, say, *Carers UK* (see chapter 9 in this volume). The problems that made this organisation powerful in the UK – the bad financial position of carers – was not nearly as deeply felt in the Netherlands, because care hardly affected their financial position. Being part of a male breadwinner household and working on average a few hours anyway, most of them did not enter poverty when entering informal care, and they still don't. A legal right to reduce one's working hours was one of the successes of the women's movement's demand for time to spend on care: employers must grant demands of workers to reduce their work week, provided there are no serious objections from the perspective of fulfilling their tasks.

As a consequence, the Netherlands has more women (and men, for that matter) working part-time than in any other country in the world. Almost half the Dutch workforce works part-time; the only country that comes close to this is Sweden, where 26% of the labour force works part-time. Dutch women in particular are part-time champions: 75 percent of them have part-time jobs, while 25 percent of the male Dutch labour force works part-time (Central Bureau for Statistics CBS, 22 July 2009). Elderly women, who are most often the ones providing informal care, do not participate much in the labour market. Moreover, the huge rise of personal budgets in the Netherlands since the mid-1990s, which has opened up the possibility for carers to be paid by personal budgets, has strengthened their financial position (Kremer 2006).

What these carers do demand in the Netherlands is to be valued. They want their contribution to society to be recognised and praised. In this, they side with a strong demand from the women's movement from the 1970s onwards, that care should be valued and women performing care should be acknowledged for their important contribution to society (Kremer 2007). The stress on citizens' responsibility for care and support in practice implies more pressure on women's time and energy as carers. This is not met with resistance as long as it goes hand in hand with recognition of the value of (women's) caring tasks as valuable social tasks that should be allowed more time and financial compensation. Caring for one's loved ones oneself is very much valued in the Netherlands (Kremer 2006).

Recognition of their importance is what they do get. The WMO pays tribute to the women's movement's demand for the recognition of the importance of care. The vice minister, who is a well-known, long-time feminist, appeals to these demands for the valuation of care:

> Volunteers and carers make an important contribution to the self-reliance and participation of others. And they contribute to the cohesion, to increasing involvement and the social coherence of our society. (vice minister Jet Bussemaker 2007)

With the WMO, the idea of government withdrawal leading to responsible citizenship was now explicitly phrased in terms of 'active citizenship':

> Volunteers and carers provide an example of 'active citizenship'. Participation in wide networks and the mutual involvement of citizens also have a wider positive effect. They contribute to strong social cohesion, to a stable society and to democracy... Carers and volunteers are actively involved citizens. (ibid.)

The vice minister proudly remarked that 'the Netherlands leads the way when it comes to the percentage of citizens who voluntarily devote their time and energy' (ibid.). Recent research shows, however, that volunteering has been declining since 1989 for all groups except those aged 65 and older (Dekker et al. 2009: 79). The pride with regard to volunteering can be seen as a plea for more volunteering. This plea for volunteering and mutual involvement also appeals to the feeling many Dutch people have consistently reported in surveys in this decade (SCP 2002, 2005): that they are happy with their own lives but unhappy with society. The WMO appeals to the desire for community and speaks the language of social cohesion. It promises a more caring, cohesive society.

So communitarian-style responsible participation, in the sense of taking personal and shared responsibility for the co-citizens in your family and the neighbourhood, is a key issue in the WMO. It is still linked to the ideal of government withdrawal, but the responsibility is now less delegated to individual citizens and more directed towards citizens' collectives, from (women in) families to (women in) neighbourhood collectives and civil society organisations.

Care networks

How does this ideal of communitarian-style responsible participation of the WMO work in practice? Research I recently conducted with two colleagues (Tonkens et al. 2009) on patterns of cooperation in 25 networks around patients with various ethnic backgrounds and with various kinds of illnesses or handicaps can shed some light on this. We held 75 in-depth interviews with patients, carers and professionals. Of the 25 networks analysed, only three fit the ideal of the WMO. In these *balanced networks* as we called them, there was a balanced combination of professionals, volunteers and informal carers. There were various professional and informal carers involved and sometimes volunteers as well. One central informal carer arranges and coordinates all care and volunteering. This central carer makes time schedules fit, coordinates, puts effort into the communication within the network, sees to it that there is back-up care when needed, and makes sure everybody involved feels appreciated. In order to be able to do all this, she has reduced her working hours, stopped working or in some other way adapted her job to her caring tasks. Towards volunteers and other carers, this central informal carer acts as a proper 'human resources manager'. She can be warm and comforting towards the patient and carers but also assertive and firm towards organisations. She perceives formal care as a fundamental right she is entitled to claim in the welfare state, and she does not hesitate to claim it. But she takes on the role of coordinating and controlling the situation of the patient, and if she considers the care provided by an organisation to be inadequate, she complains and claims her rights. She is bureaucratically competent, speaks Dutch fluently and is well acquainted with the rules, regulations and institutions, usually through a (former) occupation in healthcare services. And, as said, she is in the financial position to reduce her working week or to stop working altogether. It will come as no surprise that the members of these networks were native Dutch with a higher education.

The other 22 networks are less well attuned to the modernisation of welfare as embodied in the WMO. There are variations on either side, of leaning more on the family or on the professionals respectively. In what we called *family networks*, (mainly female) family members provide most of the care, while professional care may be additional but not vital.

Sometimes one family member, generally a woman, is performing all tasks. There is little or no discussion on how tasks can be divided, and she thus finds no support from other people. The whole idea of negotiation, either with family members or with professionals, is strange to her. So to her, the WMO simply means that access to care services becomes more difficult: services are less easily offered to her and she is not prepared to go after them, since she does not feel she is entitled to do so. She does not know the ways to find professional care and her family members do not support her in finding them, as they consider care a family's task. Most of these networks consist of migrant families of Turkish or Moroccan descent.

At the other end of the continuum, there are networks in which professional carers perform the bulk of the caring tasks, while (informal) carers merely take up additional tasks. These we called *professional networks* because professionals were the most important caretakers here. In this network, the professional carer, the (informal) carer and the patient all felt that professional care possessed a value of its own. Contrary to the dominant opinion in family networks, professional care was not judged as being of lesser quality than family care. Caregivers thus are not expected to perform all care themselves. These professional networks are also ill prepared for the WMO, as they often lack one central caregiver and are not prepared or able to coordinate and negotiate. They lack the capacities and the time to perform these roles, and they also assume the welfare state is there to support them in this. Carers in these networks do not expect much from their family or friends who, they argue, have their own lives and their own worries. They do have high expectations from the welfare state and professionals in it. Yet particularly those who care for patients with progressive or difficult and incurable diseases tend to feel disillusioned and let down. To do even more, to negotiate more, to be responsible for arranging and coordinating all care, as carers in the balanced networks do, is stretching their bows so far that there is a genuine risk of their bows breaking. These networks consist mainly of native and Surinamese Dutch. The WMO does not fit their views and lifestyles.

Thus, the WMO's modernisation of welfare, with more stress on informal care and cooperation among various partners, is best attuned and best accessible to those who need these services the least: those who are self-assertive, competent in dealing with bureaucracies, highly educated, speak the language well and can thus operate in balanced networks, and who can reduce their working hours. It is, however, ill-equipped for all other groups, though in varying degrees. It expects them to have capacities and views that they do not have and thus implicitly marginalises them.

De-responsibilisation

With the mounting stress on the importance of responsibilisation (in terms of active social participation and choice), attention is increasingly directed towards people who are (considered) not (to be) participating, people who live isolated lives inside their homes or fail to educate their children in such a manner that they are stimulated to be active participants. Failing participants – i.e., mothers with migrant backgrounds, migrant families, and people (predominantly men) with behavioural and/or psychiatric problems living by themselves – are all subject to outreach programmes, where social workers try to 'get behind the front door' to find social problems and offer social care and welfare while also using more enforcing policies, often in a carrot-and-stick manner. Social workers in some poorer areas go from door to door, visiting every household in order to find out what kind of problems are hidden 'behind the front door'. Domestic violence against women and children is one of the most prevalent problems these social workers come across, in addition to debt, educational neglect, illegal housing, the illegal growing of soft-drug plants and loneliness. This practice of social workers' visits reflects a more controlling and interventionist government, peeping behind front doors and taking children away from their parents much more often.

In these outreach programmes, we can see the co-occurrence of responsibilisation and de-responsibilisation: of making citizens more responsible while at the same time taking responsibility away from them. On the one hand, politicians and policymakers expect citizens to be responsible and treat them as if they already are responsible, arguing that to do otherwise would be paternalistic. On the other hand, citizens are treated as irresponsible and not capable of being left alone to do their own thing, and therefore responsibility is taken away from them. This approach is taken not only when they are still adolescents or when they are causing serious harm to others, but also again 'for their own good' when they have legally reached adulthood and are not causing harm to others.

There seems to be a tension between the responsibilisation implied in the active citizenship discourse and the simultaneous de-responsibilisation that it gives rise to. As responsibilities for active citizenship grow, so too does the tendency toward de-responsibilisation. Seeing them both in tandem, they seem to strengthen each other: the more emphasis policymakers put on responsibilisation, the more light will be shed on failures to expose such responsible behaviour, and the more this will give rise to both responsibilisation and de-responsibilisation. Thus these two tendencies seem to be each other's distorting mirror.

Conclusions

So how did the communitarian ideals of caring for your own family and your own community – so strong in the new law on social care and welfare, the WMO – come to be embraced in a country where the patients' movement had been so successful in demanding autonomy, choice and voice?

Voice, choice and autonomy were indeed acquired successfully by the patients' movement, but not only as rights. They were embraced by the government, too, because they could gradually be twisted: over the last decades, they were bent in the direction of duties. There are elements of autonomy in the WMO: the active citizen presupposed in it is not just a caring communitarian but also an autonomous, self-steering citizen capable of arranging and managing various kinds of formal and informal care. This is attractive for the patients' movement because it fits their self-image. It is less attractive for other, more vulnerable citizens who are not active in patients' organisations, as research indicates (Tonkens et al. 2009). But who voices these vulnerable citizens' needs? In other countries, such worries are sometimes expressed by carers' organisations or professional carers' organisations, but neither of these are very powerful in the Netherlands. They still have not fully recovered from the blows they received in the 1970s.

Responsible, communitarian participation is clearly the dominant motive in the WMO, as it was a way for the government to delegate problems of management and cost reduction to citizens. But it also seems to appeal to citizens. Responsible participation is also compelling for various groups of citizens. It was appealing first and foremost to the majority of Dutch people, who repeatedly report to be happy about their own lives but unhappy about (what they conceive to be) a selfish, over-individualised society. Communitarianism appealed to the desire for community cohesion. For carers and parts of the women's movement, the rhetorical value given to informal care was appealing. Responsible participation is backed up by the simultaneous movement towards deresponsibilisation: the state will intervene where the community fails to reach.

References

Bauman, Z. (2001), *Community. Seeking Safety in an Insecure World*, Cambridge: Polity Press.

Brink, G. van den, T. Jansen and D. Pressers (2005), *Beroepszeer. Waarom Nederland niet goed werkt*, Amsterdam: Boom/Sun.

Bussemaker, J. (2007), 'Getting (it) together. Policy letter: informal care and voluntary work 2008-2011', Vice minister Jet Bussemaker, 9 October 2007.

Blok, G. (2004), *Baas in eigen brein. Anti-psychiatrie in Nederland, 1965-1985*, Amsterdam: Nieuwezijds.

Edmund Burkestichting (2004), *Klagende burgers en politieke verandering. Voorwaarden voor hervorming van het zorgstelsel*, (brochure) The Hague: Edmund Burkestichting.

Etzioni, A. (1993), *The spirit of community. Right, responsibilities and the communitarian agenda*, New York: Crown.

Clarke, J. (2005), 'New Labour's citizens: activated, empowered, responsiblized, abandoned?' *Critical Social Policy*, 25: 447-464.

Coalition agreement between the parliamentary parties of the Christian Democratic Alliance, Labour Party and Christian Union, 7 February 2007.

Cruickshank, B. (1999), *The Will to Empower. Democratic Citizens and Other Subjects*, Ithaka, NY: Cornell University.

Dalrymple, T. (2001), *Life at the Bottom: The Worldview That Makes the Underclass*, Chicago: Irvan R. Dee.

Dekker, P., and J. de Hart (2009) (eds.), 'Vrijwilligerswerk in meervoud. Civil society en vrijwilligerswerk', Den Haag: SCP.

Doorn, J.A.A. van, and C.J.M. Schuyt (1978), *De stagnerende verzorgingsstaat*, Meppel/Amsterdam: Boom.

Duyvendak, J.W. (1999), *De planning van ontplooiing: wetenschap, politiek en de maakbare samenleving*, Den Haag: SDU.

— and T. Nederland (2007), *New Frontiers for Identity Politics? The Potential and Pitfalls of Patient and Civic Identity in the Dutch Patients' Health Movement*, Bingley: Emerald.

—, T. Knijn and M. Kremer (2006), *Policy, people and the new professional. Deprofessionalisation and re-professionalisation in care and welfare*, Amsterdam: Amsterdam University Press.

Duyvendak, J.W., M. Hurenkamp and E. Tonkens, (2010) 'Culturalization of citizenship in the Netherlands' in: Ariane Chebel d'Appollonia and Simon Reich (eds.), *Managing Ethnic Diversity after 9/11: Integration, Security, and Civil Liberties in Transatlantic Perspective* (New Brunswick, NJ: Rutgers University Press, Chapter 13, pp. 233-252

Foucault, M. (1977), *Discipline and punish: The Birth of the Prison*, London: Allen Lane.

Garland, D. (2001), *The culture of control. Crime and social order in contemporary society*, Oxford: Oxford University Press.

Jenson, J., and S. Philips (2001), 'Redesigning the Canadian citizenship regime: remaking institutions for representation', in C. Crouch, K. Eder and D. Tambini, *Citizenship, markets and the state*, Oxford: Oxford University Press.

Haar, M. van der (2007), *Ma(r)king Differences in Dutch Social Work. Professional Discourse and Ways of Relating to Clients in Context*, Amsterdam: Amsterdam University Press.

Hutschemaekers, G., and H. Oosterhuis (2004), 'Psychotherapy in the Netherlands after the second world war', *Medical History*, 48 (4): 429-448.

Jordan, B. (2000), *Social Work and the Third Way. Tough Love as Social Policy*, London: Sage.

— (2004), 'Emancipatory Social Work: Opportunity or Oxymoron?' *British Journal of Social Work*, 34 (1): pp 5-19.

Koenis, S. (1997), *Het verlangen naar gemeenschap. Politiek en moraal in Nederland na de verzuiling*, Amsterdam: Van Gennep.

Kearns, A. (1992), 'Active citizenship and urban governance', *Transactions of the Institute of British Geographers*, 17 (1): 20-34.

Kremer, M. (2006), 'Consumers in charge of care: the Dutch personal budgets and its impact on the market, professionals and the family', *European Societies*, 8 (3): 385-402.

— and E. Tonkens (2006), 'Authority, trust, knowledge and the public good in disarray', in Duyvendak, J.W., T. Knijn and M. Kremer (2006), *Policy, people and the new professional. De-professionalisation and re-professionalisation in care and welfare*, Amsterdam: Amsterdam University Press, 122-134.

— (2007), *How welfare states care. Gender, parenting and care in Europe*, Amsterdam: Amsterdam University Press.

Ministerie van Bestuurlijke Vernieuwing (2003), *Actieprogramma 'Andere overheid'*, The Hague. (http://www.minbzk.nl/@9320/programma_andere)

— (2005), *Verkenning burgerschap en andere overheid*, The Hague.

Ministry of Health, Welfare and Sports (2007), *Social Support Act* (www.minvws.nl/en/themes/social-support-act/default.asp).

— (2010), Personal Budget Facts and Numbers (http://www.minvws.nl/dossiers/persoonsgebonden_budget_pgb/feiten-en-cijfers-pgb/).

Noordegraaf, M., and B. Steijn (2010), *Professionals under pressure*, Amsterdam: Amsterdam University Press.

Pierson, P. (1996), 'The new politics of the welfare state', *World Politics*, 48 (2): 143-179.

— (2002), 'Coping with permanent austerity: welfare state restructuring in affluent democracies', *Revue française de sociologie*, 43 (2): 369-406.

Scholte, R. (2008), 'Burgerparticipatie in veiligheidsprojecten', in H. Boutellier and R. Van Steden, *Veiligheid en burgerschap in de netwerksamenleving*, The Hague: Boom Juridische Uitgevers, 223-242.

SCP (2003), *De meerkeuzemaatschappij*, The Hague: SCP.

— (2005), *Landelijk verenigd. Grote ledenorganisaties over ontwikkelingen in het maatschappelijk middenveld*, The Hague: SCP.

Swierstra, T., and E. Tonkens (2002), 'Klakkeloze keuzevrijheid. Kanttekeningen bij de dominantie van keuzevrijheid in hedendaags beleid', *Filosofie en praktijk*, 23 (4): 3-19.

Tonkens, E., and I. Weijers (1999), 'Autonomy, Care and Self-realization. Policy Views of Dutch Service Providers', *Mental Retardation: The Journal of the American Association on Mental Retardation*, 37 (6): 468-476.

Tonkens, E., and L. van Doorn (2001), 'Turning Rough Sleepers into Responsible Citizens. Third Way policies on homelessness in England and the Netherlands', *Renewal: The Journal of Labour Politics*, 3 (3): 142-151.

Tonkens, E., and T. Swierstra (2005), 'Kiezen als burgerplicht? Conclusies over de voorwaarden voor keuzevrijheid in beleid', in M. Hurenkamp and M. Kremer (eds.), *Vrijheid verplicht*, Amsterdam: Van Gennep, 207-217.

Tonkens, E., and J.W. Duyvendak (2003), 'Paternalism, Caught between Rejection and Acceptance: Taking care and taking control in community work', *Community Development Studies*, 38(1): 6-15.

Tonkens, E., J. van den Broeke and M. Hoijtink (2009), *Op zoek naar weerkaatst plezier. Samenwerking tussen mantelzorgers, vrijwilligers, professionals en cliënten in de multiculturele stad*, Amsterdam: Amsterdam University Press.

Swierstra, T. and E. Tonkens (2008) (eds.), *De beste de baas. Prestatie, respect en solidariteit in een meritocratie*, Amsterdam: Amsterdam University Press.

Tonkens, E. (2010), 'Civicness and Citizen Participation in Social Services: Conditions for promoting respect and public concern', in T. Bransen, P. Dekker and A. Evers (eds.), *Civicness in the Governance of Social Services,* Baden-Baden: Nomos.

Tonkens, E., M. Hoijtink and H. Gulikers (forthcoming), 'Democratizing Social Work: From New Public Management to democratic professionalism', in M. Noordegraaf and B. Steijn (eds.), *Professional under pressure,* Amsterdam: Amsterdam University Press, chapter 9.

Trappenburg, M. (2008), *Genoeg is genoeg. Over democratie en gezondheidszorg,* Amsterdam: Amsterdam University Press.

Wacquant, L. (2006), *Punishing the Poor: The New Government of Social Insecurity,* Durham, NC: Duke University Press.

Wilson, J. (2000), 'Volunteering'. *Annual review of sociology,* 26: 215-240.

4 From social citizenship to active citizenship?

Tensions between policies and practices in Finnish elderly care

Anneli Anttonen and Liisa Häikiö

In this chapter, active citizenship is discussed in relation to elderly care policies and informal care practices in Finland. Active citizenship, in the way that Janet Newman and Evelien Tonkens define the notion in the introduction of this book, composes the main conceptual frame for our analysis. We will demonstrate that the ideal of social citizenship is giving way to active citizenship. The ideas of participation, responsibility and choice shape political norms and objectives within the policy discourse on elderly care; but active citizenship is also manifested in the everyday practices of informal care. As we will show, informal carers of older people might, however, bring a critical voice into the discourse and practice of active citizenship. We will also trace major tensions between the emerging political discourse on active citizenship and how it is materialised in everyday care practices. This brings into view questions of justice and equality: citizens (i.e., informal carers) have very different resources at their disposal, and access to social networks shapes their capabilities to bear and share care responsibilities.

The chapter is structured as follows. We begin by setting the context for our study – public policy on care in Finland – then go on to describe and evaluate the official policy discourse on elderly care. We ask whether the idea(l) of active citizenship can be identified from the official policy discourse, and how far the three dimensions of active citizenship (participation, responsibility and choice) shape social care policy discourse and practice in Finland. We concentrate on elderly care arrangements at home and policies supporting these arrangements, since previous studies on informal care in Finland (see e.g. Anttonen, Zechner & Valokivi 2009) show how care provided by family members informally without pay or supported by payments for care schemes represents a strong political norm, leading to a new construction of care citizen (Ungerson 2004). In the third part, we focus on interviews with informal carers to find out how active citizenship discourse is materialising in everyday care situations. We pay attention to carers' views on public participation and care responsibilities, and on the choices they make in the emerging market of social care. Finally, in the conclusion we discuss how the whole idea of being active has changed in line with the discourse on active citizenship, and suggest what kinds of tensions this major shift in elderly care politics brings into being.

Public policy on elderly care in Finland

The developments of social care policies for the elderly as well as for children have followed slightly different routes of modernisation in different countries (Anttonen, Baldock & Sipilä 2003). In some countries it is the public sector that carries the main responsibility for care service provision, while in others the role of welfare organisations, the church or private service providers is more prominent. And there are also countries where the overall responsibility of care production lies even today in the hands of individuals and families. Yet, nearly everywhere an increasing proportion of social care functions are removed from the private domestic sphere of household towards the formal economy of the market, the voluntary and charitable sector and the state and local governments (ibid. 172).

Care, then, has 'gone public', in that it has become a major focus of public policy and policy discourse (see Hernes 1987: 39), producing care-related rights and benefits. Rights as such do not necessarily guarantee access to benefits because of targeting and professional assessment. Assessment of care-related public goods often includes (female) family members' willingness to give care without pay. And even if the work of informal carers is recognised in terms of care allowances or other kinds of support systems, these benefits tend to be of a low monetary value and are not always accompanied with basic social protection rights, such as pensions (Ungerson 2004; Ungerson & Yeandle 2007). In addition, in societies where public policy of care has become an acknowledged part of welfare policies, the status of social care tends to remain low compared with policy areas such as education and healthcare.

Finland represents the Nordic welfare model: a model characterised by high levels of social service provision and the principle of universalism (Anttonen 2002; Kautto et al. 1999; Kuhnle 2000). It has been argued that Nordic universalism has the grand idea of social citizenship and social rights as its backbone (Esping-Andersen 1990). But to understand the distinctive nature of the Nordic welfare model, it is also important to note the significance of the role of municipalities. Although the state sets the frames through its legislative power, responsibility for service provision rests with fairly independent and, to a large degree, financially self-sufficient local authorities (Kröger 1997). Municipalities are subsidised by central government grants, but the government does not control local activities in detail.

ANNELI ANTTONEN AND LIISA HÄIKIÖ

Today, municipalities carry the main responsibility for financing and providing social services. Following the severe economic recession of the early 1990s, the central government reduced state subsidies to municipalities. The introduction of greater legislative freedoms coupled with limited financial resources contributed to the development of new forms of governance in Finnish municipalities (Häikiö (2010); Haveri 2006). Local authorities have changed from that of producer of services to that of promoter, defining the local framework of activity. Municipalities have created structures based on the separation of purchasers and providers and enabled market or voluntary services to replace public services. The terminology of service provision now includes words like choice, customer orientation and contracts.

This reorganisation of social policy has challenged the idea of universal protection for the elderly through social rights. In the 1960s and 1970s, rehabilitation and prevention were set as important goals for elderly care, and local service centres and municipal home help were institutionalised. In the 1970s and 1980s, older people were included as potential users of social care services, even if they had only minor care needs. But times and policies have changed. During the latest wave of reform there has been a strong tendency to reduce the costs of institutional care and privilege care at home. The home help service has become much more tightly targeted to only those whose care needs are extensive (Anttonen 2009). Moreover, the service fees have gone up, and there are now more who use private services. Local government continues to occupy a key role in funding and planning care services, but voluntary organisations and family carers are now also involved as producers.

Commercial services were, up until the early 1990s, virtually non-existent, but their role and significance have since been steadily increasing. The state is now actively promoting the purchasing of private services, partly through taxation reforms. In 2001, the tax credit for domestic help became part of a tax reduction scheme whereby the householder pays remuneration to a formal private sector company for services such as cleaning or home repairs, or for care of an elderly person or a child in the home.

These developments in Finland are in line with those taking place in the other Nordic countries. Nordic scholars have pointed to the informalisation of care (Rostgaard 2004; Szebehely 2005), the privatisation of the management and provision of public care services (Szebehely 2004; Vabø 2006) and the marketisation of service provision (Trydegård 2000). The so-called 'old' politics of social care that was founded on strong centralised institutions, the universal treatment of 'clients' or 'patients' and professional needs interpretation has been replaced at least partly by the 'new' politics of social care. In the 'new' politics of elderly care, the figure of the client/patient has been replaced by the figure of the 'consumer' making 'free choices' on the emerging social care market (Clarke 2006: 425; Kremer 2006).

Active citizenship in official policy discourse

Finland is a 'latecomer' in the transition to market-related social policies, but within Finland the city of Tampere was among the first municipalities to adopt an extensive purchaser provider model (Häikiö 2010). As such, it offers an interesting landscape for us to analyse and evaluate official policy discourse on active citizenship in elder care policy. Our data comprises fourteen policy documents published between 2001 and 2008. Half are national ones, including government policy documents, white papers published by the Ministry of Social Affairs and Health and other relevant national documents. The other half comprises local policy documents produced by the city of Tampere, including strategy papers and elderly care policy documents. Our intention is not to present a detailed analysis of the policy documents but to focus on discourses around active citizenship and to examine changes in elderly care policy from the vantage point of active citizenship.

Active citizenship is a phrase that is not much used as such in the policy documents, though it is more common in national rather than local documents, and its use increases over our period of study (2001-2009). The policy documents published between 2001 and 2004 do identify a kind of general frame of active citizenship, while documents published after 2004 construct much more clearly the idea of active citizenship through such keywords as participation, responsibilisation and choice.

Most particularly, a rights-centred discourse has increasingly given way to a responsibility-centred discourse. The transition between the rights-centred discourse of social citizenship and the responsibility-centred discourse of active citizenship is clearly seen when looking back at the documents of early 2000, some of which refer to the constitution as the foundation of social citizenship and social security:

> Social protection is intended to support equal opportunities for all citizens. Section 19 of the new Constitution of Finland, which came into effect on March 1, 2000, guarantees the right to indispensable subsistence and care for those who cannot themselves obtain the means necessary for a life of dignity. The section develops this theme by guaranteeing the right to basic subsistence in the event of unemployment, illness, disability, old age, at the birth of a child or in the event of the loss of a provider. This is a general right to be provided in detail under separate legislation. The public authorities are also obliged to guarantee adequate social, health care and medical services for all and to promote the health of the population. (*Strategies for social protection 2010*, 2001)

This reference to the constitution implies that traditions of social citizenship define the relation between individuals and society. The rights-centred discourse underlines the notion that public authorities have the main responsibility to meet citizens' basic needs and that citizens have entitlements to care and many other things. Therefore, the relation between individuals and the state is a relation marked by individual social rights and public responsibilities of the state and municipalities.

However, the policy documents gradually construct a more active idea of citizenship, and there are fewer references to the constitution and citizens' rights after 2004. Instead, documents emphasise the need to increase the *participation* of older people and the need to create new channels for them to be active in the production and planning of social care services. In addition, the issue of *responsibility* becomes extensively debated, with the responsibilities of different actors coming under continuous discussion and redefinition. There is also reference to *partnership* and cooperation between different service providers and increasing *choice*-based talk. We go on to analyse a bit more closely active citizenship discourse in terms of these notions of participation, responsibilisation and choice.

Participation: an abstract idea

Citizen participation and public participation are generally important aims in public policies both locally and nationally in Finland (Bäcklund 2007). The most important legislative reforms during the last 15 years have established new possibilities for people as individuals and/or groups to express their opinions and have influence on policymaking and the determining of social services (Sutela 2001). Within the discourse on elderly care policy, citizen participation is viewed as a means of ensuring a high standard or quality of services. Old people are recognised as individual service users, community members and citizens:

> On the level of the individual we are concerned with making the principle visible in services for the elderly, in maintaining social functioning ability and in strengthening both the sense of social belonging in such a way that the individual, including the elderly individual, is a full member of his/her community. More comprehensively social participation signified people's opportunities to exert influence in the further development of their society and living environment. (*National quality recommendations for elder care and services 2008*)

Older people's participation refers to a number of activities, from taking an active user position in the service system to being active members of the community in which they live. The broadest definition relates to political participation and such things as having influence in a society. Most definitions in the documents are quite traditional, though some reference is made to new platforms designed for deliberative participation, such as senior councils (*vanhusneuvostot*) and local forums for residents (*asukasillat*). However, the means and modes of participation remain quite abstract in practice, as they are not defined in any concrete way either nationally or locally (Bäcklund 2007). The most concrete suggestion for advancing participation in elderly care is that of building up information and service centres (*Government Strategy Document 2007*), whose aim is to offer individual support and guidance for older people to manage their life and be socially active, rather than to nourish their overall political activity.

Responsibilisation: focus on individuals and social networks

Participation and responsibilisation frameworks are closely related to each other; however, responsibility and responsibilisation are more widely used terms than participation in the official policy discourse both nationally and locally. Attention is thereby directed to individuals and their responsibility for themselves and their relatives:

> Relatives, significant others and the rest of the immediate environment are important guarantors of the elderly person's welfare. Elderly people are first and foremost themselves responsible together with their close networks for their own well-being. They use largely the same services as other residents. It is the task of the service system to support, direct and motivate people to bear the responsibility for their own health and well-being. (*National quality recommendations for elder care and services 2008*)

Ageing at home for as long as possible is the most important policy goal in elderly care policy and strongly related to responsibilisation. Independent living at home, self-help and personal resources are key words attached to this policy goal, and these words connect responsibility to individuals instead of collectives. However, the importance of social networks is also made clear. There is a strong reliance on the idea that social networks and communities represent both new resources and create new modes of participation and responsibility. Social networks are thought to support individuals and informal carers while bearing a more wide responsibility for care and well-being.

The official policy discourse gives priority to such care arrangements, in which informal carers come to play a more central role. With the system of home care allowance (HCA), family members are expected to take the main responsibility for the care of older relatives and to participate actively in the assessment and planning processes. In practice, this happens by setting up a written document that serves as a contract between the municipality, the older person in need of care and the informal carer. In this document, the responsibilities of family members and relatives

ANNELI ANTTONEN AND LIISA HÄIKIÖ

as well as possible service providers are defined (Valokivi & Zechner 2009). The municipality thus carries its legal responsibility for elder care by delegating responsibility to informal carers and family members. This kind of shift, however, requires that relatives *voluntarily* assume responsibility for care:

> The legislation departs from the premise that an informal carer is not obliged to make a written contract on being an informal carer. If a person is in need of care and treatment and no informal carer is available, the municipality should make other arrangements. (*Support for informal care. Handbook for municipal decisionmakers*, 2005)

As public authorities, municipalities have the final (and legal) responsibility for caring for those who have objective care needs. Even though policy documents articulate individual citizen's responsibility fairly powerfully, it is evident that the fundamental responsibility (and power) remains in the hands of municipalities and public authorities at large. This responsibility is, however, redefined so that the responsibility of public authorities is to enable and create such conditions that make it possible for older people to be responsible for their own welfare – with the help of their family members and social networks.

A significant issue here is the relation between the purchaser and provider. The HCA system positions the municipality as the purchaser and the family member as provider of the care service. A written contract is made between the municipality, the person who needs care and the informal carer. Informal care becomes an objective of municipal and governmental policy and an alternative in particular to institutional care, and informal carers become service providers within the new welfare mix. This is analogous to the kind of division of responsibility between commercial service providers and public authorities. The reorganisation of the whole welfare production system from a local government centred one toward a network and market governance structure is identified as an important goal in both local and national documents. Various service providers are charged with the responsibility for the care of older people, with municipalities as the enablers of new modes of welfare governance, including the creation of markets.

Choice: creating market structures

Choice is the third framework through which the active role of citizens is emphasised and redefined. The move from a universalist and solidaristic rhetoric toward an individualist and consumerist one is very clearly evident in policy documents. The consumerist orientation first becomes visible in local policy documents, where 'communers' or local citizens are framed as clients with individual needs and expectations (Häikiö 2010). By the end of our time period, consumerism and choice have become central notions in the national discourse on elderly care as well as in local policy documents, with the notion of client becoming extended to incorporate the notion of consumer. An important aim is to increase users' choices and opportunities to express their preferences on public service providers, and to empower citizens to make individual choices in the social services market. Therefore, promoting partnerships (with 'third sector' organisations) and creating a social care market are the first priorities in reorganising the provision of social services. Policy documents recommend different methods of creating social care markets:

> Securing the provision of services calls for a sound financial basis and new ways of organising and producing services. The Government promotes partnerships between the public, private and third sector in the provision of services. The adoption of the purchaser provider model will be encouraged. The applicability of social service vouchers and the domestic help credit will be expanded which will contribute to the emergence of working service markets. (*The Government Programme*, Prime Minister Matti Vanhanen's second Cabinet, 2007)

Both national and local authorities seek to promote the emergence of a well-functioning social services market. Whether the aim is to create new markets for social services or to create market-like structures within public service provision, individuals are positioned as choice makers. Individual needs, demands and resources frame this type of position.

> The *Kotitori* ('homemarket') programme also makes it possible for old people to be both clients and patrons. As clients they use the services arranged by the city administration and as patrons they use services paid for with their own money. (*Home-market planning and decision documents*, 2 June 2008)

As this extract demonstrates, Tampere was, in 2009, starting up a *home-market* project, which promotes the idea of the citizen as a conscious consumer who needs help and support by care integrators (or care managers). This kind of conscious consumer is able, and also willing, to consume various public and private social services based on individual choices. The *home-market* care integrator, which is a private service provider, becomes responsible for setting up a package of services for each consumer according to their needs and personal financial resources. The care integrator also provides access to information covering all service provision within the municipality and beyond.

This is a major difference from the previous system in which municipal authorities were exclusively responsible for needs testing and assessment processes. Now, older people and informal carers are actively encouraged to organise care by using not only publicly funded services but also their own money. Vouchers are increasingly used for purchasing different kinds of services, whether from the municipal or private providers. However, the municipality retains legal responsibility for meeting the social care needs of its older citizens and informal carers as well as responsibility for quality control. All in all, the whole system has become very complex, with different parties having to negotiate with each other in order for care needs to be properly met.

Citizen carers: everyday life perspective on active citizenship

Policy analysis of the kind we have presented in the previous sections tells only part of the story. Here, we turn to the conceptions of active citizenship – participation, responsibility and choice – held by carers themselves. Our analysis draws on data from in-depth interviews with caregivers in the Tampere region in 2006. Out of 23 carers interviewed, fourteen were female and nine male, with ages varying between 41 and 83 years. Most of them were caring for a spouse. The data was analysed by asking what kinds of responsibilities, forms of participation and types of choices caregivers had; and how far they identified themselves as informal carers, care citizens or consumers of services. Those interviewed did not refer to active citizenship as such when they identified themselves as carers or described care practices and arrangements. The active citizenship discourse was, however, traceable in their depictions of everyday care practices and their opinions on care policy.

Three general points emerge from the data. First, the carers viewed public authorities as responsible for care services. As such, caregivers viewed themselves as serving society when they took care of their relative at home, and defined themselves both as service users and service providers. As service users, they most often took a rights-centred position and defined themselves as citizens entitled to care-related benefits according to their own or the care receiver's needs and social and legal rights. As service providers, they instead took a responsibility-centred position but simultaneously felt entitled to fair compensation for their services to society.

The second point is that for carers, participation, responsibility and choice were issues that arose in managing complex care situations. In organising services for themselves and for care receivers, carers could be divided into two different groups. One group saw themselves as operating in a new kind of governance structure in which they had to cooperate and negotiate with a number of service providers and to use the various opportunities offered to them. The other group did not recognise that the logic of governance had changed. Besides informal social networks (where these existed), carers in this group turned mainly to public authorities. They tended to think that care was to be managed in a welfare state context, in which public authorities acted on their behalf and treated them as clients.

The third point is that those interviewed presented a critical voice on the active citizenship and official policy discourses traced in the previous sections of this chapter. Our findings in Tampere are quite similar to those studies looking at the citizen-consumer in the UK (Clarke & Newman 2007; Clarke et al. 2007), with tensions arising between the policy discourse of citizen-consumer and peoples' identifications of healthcare practices. In both cases, the policy discourses did not recognise the everyday reality in which people live and consume services, and citizens did not identify themselves with positions that the policy discourses offered.

Having set out these general points, we now focus in more detail on informal carers' vantage point on issues of participation, responsibilities and choice.

Participation: social activity and individual influence

Citizen participation and public participation were not among the most important issues discussed in the interviews. In part, this reflects the formulation of the questions but it also derives from the actual circumstances in which carers live. On the basis of the interviews, it seems that carers had quite limited possibilities for participation. This corresponds to the findings of Burau and Kröger (2004). Based on their study of one Finnish city, they argued that local politicians, local administrators and some voluntary organisations – those with close links to politicians – had significant influence on local care policy. However, informal carers and service users were outsiders in relation to this power structure.

In our study, carers pointed out that voluntary organisations provided some possibilities for participation. In the following excerpt, one female carer describes her participation in one interest organisation. The excerpt gathers many of the aspects that the other interviewed carers associated with participation in the context of informal care:

> Regarding the informal carers around Tampere, (...) there is safeguarding of interests. In August I was (...) in rehabilitation for four days (...) you got it at half price. It included four sessions in the office there (...) pedicure or manicure and lunch and lectures and activities. (...) They were the ones who fixed the Parliament trip. (...) Minister Liisa Hyssälä was there talking to us. Then came the Tampere MPs, (...) They all said they were doing their best for the informal carers, (laughter). (...) I went there quite (...) since they enticed me. (Female carer, interview 2)

Participation was important for the informal carers because it gave them access to information, support and free-time activities. Interest organisations provided subsidised services at a low price or free of charge for their members. Family carers met with other informal carers to exchange experiences and share the care burden. Other types of participation were less significant but did exist. Only some of the carers had tried to influence national or local care policies. The female carer gives one of the few examples in the data about lobbying when a group of informal carers visited the national parliament and met MPs representing the Tampere region. She nevertheless identified herself as an external participant or service user without any wider assumptions about the possibility of influencing beyond her own case.

Participation in interest organisations, however, made it possible to construct a collective identity as an informal carer. Collective identities have many functions, but *sharing* was the key word for understanding the meaning of this kind of participation for carers:

> I went to it (activity for informal carers) because there was this men's group, peer group (...) There's been from five to ten blokes there with the same fate. (Male carer, interview 35)

Through these modes of participation in interest organisations, carers were able to maintain their social activity and capability as carers. But where they spoke about trying to exert influence of any kind, they only positioned themselves as individual citizens with rights in relation to administrative and political authorities. Individual positions have a strong cultural foundation in the traditions of the welfare state and particularly in the political culture of Tampere (Häikiö 2007). On the basis of the data, it seems that individual participation was an effective channel for influencing local authorities by challenging decisions over individual social benefits and services. The next example is a typical case of this kind of activity:

> The applications went to the informal carer support office. And back they came like a boomerang that there's no more money. (...) Then I sent great bunches of letters and questions to three city managers. I bombarded them until he (the city manager) took water in. (...) I have learned in six years. At first I waited, but nobody helped. Then it was time to start bawling and shouting, then things started to happen. (...) (The city manager) has called the informal carer support office to give them enough money that it would shut them up. (...) Then all of a sudden the money was found. (Male carer, interview 35)

The story here demonstrates how one man took an active position when he thought that he had been treated unfairly. Such citizens were able and willing to use their influence beyond the local administration to either the national or local political level. But even where they were able to influence policies, they were mostly able to achieve individual rather than collective benefits. The political structure appears to offer individualised opportunities rather than a collective influence on local care policy. It should also be noted that there are remarkable differences between caregivers' capacity to take this kind of active standing (Valokivi 2004). Some caregivers had a lot of resources for advocacy and for making demands, while others were in a very vulnerable position and just surviving in everyday life situations.

Responsibility: individual-public responsibility

According to our analysis, individual responsibility for taking care of old family members is a strong norm among carers. Yet many interviewees referred to the absence of any real alternatives when it came to the ways in which care could be organised and responsibilities defined. Typically, family members defined their individual responsibility as informal caregiver to be a kind of natural choice. One respondent explained that, even if she had siblings, she as the daughter of her mother had been given – and has also taken – the main care responsibility:

> But I thought that I just can't turn my back on an old person. I am now, I would say, I bear the main responsibility. (Female carer, interview 10)

Carers identified themselves as family or informal carers by using moral arguments such as 'one has to take into consideration other people's needs and well-being' or by simply noting that 'home is the best place for an old person to live and die'. It is interesting that most of these carers did not see themselves as having the same moral responsibility toward other relatives or close ones. In fact, few appeared to be sharing informal care responsibility with the primary carer. On the contrary, in our interview data it seemed that the role of wider social networks in care responsibility was very limited. Most carers had some networks of family, friends or peers. But even where family networks might, in some situations, have increased the 'care capital' among caregivers and care receivers (Anttonen & Sipilä 2007), the interview data confirms that care-related responsibilities and tasks were not shared widely within family networks:

> We have three children. (...) I use the boys when it suits them, so then they come to help. I try not to use them too much. (...) They have lives of their own, their own work and families, so I don't like to ask too much. (...) I've still tried to cope with everything alone. From time to time of course there's something to be done where I must ask for (help), but I try not to be a burden. (Female carer, interview 26)

Moral and highly individually defined responsibilities to care had not become extended to social networks, nor even to wider family networks. Even where family networks were regarded as very important, caregivers

ANNELI ANTTONEN AND LIISA HÄIKIÖ

mentioned them mainly as resources of *mental* rather than practical support. Apart from some trusted people, networks did not give support for care or help with actual caring in day-to-day situations. Carers did not refer to any practical situation in which friendship-based social networks would take responsibility for care. The only exceptions are some so-called trustworthy persons who took part in the everyday life care practices.

Carers interpreted that the boundary between public and private responsibility is an economic, as well as a moral, question. They were aware that home care is much cheaper than institutional care, which would be the only alternative for municipalities to replace the work of carers. This meant that carers felt that they had the right to ask for or demand support. In the following extract, a husband carer spoke of how the responsibility of the public authority to provide such support did not materialise:

> You get this feeling that those people responsible, even the political deci-
> sionmakers, they think that the informal carers will take care of their rela-
> tives in any case because they love them. Whether they get any support or
> not. (Male carer, interview 1)

From his perspective, municipalities did not fulfil their legal and moral obligations but 'misused' informal carers in the name of love. Informal carers were conscious of the fact that public authorities and professionals wanted to lean on the voluntary work of informal carers to save public money; in this way, authorities withdrew from their public responsibility. As in the context of participation, the boundaries between public and personal responsibility were negotiated case by case, individually. It seems that those who had resources to use their voice and act as active citizens were able to share care responsibilities with public authorities. In some cases, family members provided additional resources and played a very central role when the informal carer needed to negotiate with public authorities about the boundaries of their responsibilities (Valokivi & Zechner 2009).

Choice: within a public framework

On the basis of the interviews, carers' consumer power was limited because care governance structures and practices appeared unclear and fragmented. It was difficult for them to distinguish between private companies, civil society associations or public services and to see how these different agents were related to each other. From the carers' perspective, public authorities, however, formed the core of care governance, setting the framework in which they operated. This was in part because of their understanding that caring was a public activity and should be supported and financed by local authorities. But it was also due to the practices of needs assessment on the part of public authorities. This was a precondition for receiving a home care allowance or care services that were at least partly publicly financed. Even where civil society associations provided services, at the time public authorities nearly always decided who was entitled to those services by giving vouchers. The assessment seemed to be a matter of public authority and responsibility, and carers made their choices within this public framework.

Carers had two opposite ways of viewing the emerging customer and consumer position. A minority viewed consumerism as a good thing. Vouchers were seen to provide the possibility of making choices between alternative providers, freeing people from using public care and health services of poor quality and offering new opportunities to buy help in the home. But overall, consumerism was viewed as troublesome for carers. In the following, a daughter taking care of her mother explained why the aim of vouchers to provide alternatives did not function:

> I'm a bit sorry about this service voucher system. And this two-day holiday (refers to the legal right of informal carers to holiday). I wish that (...) I really could get a stand-in for two days at home that I could fix myself who it is. (...) The voucher is not enough for more than eight hours. That isn't even one 24-hour day. (Female carer, interview 8)

What she is actually criticising here is the fact that she could not choose: vouchers did not guarantee that she would be able to buy the services she wanted. She was not in the position to define her own or her mother's needs. If she chose to organise care during her legal *right to take holiday* by using vouchers, she would have to pay a large part from her own pocket because the market value of the voucher was so small that it did not cover the charge for the care service needed. The publicly recognised service providers are, however, the only ones that are able to accept vouchers in these types of situations.

Informal carers might receive vouchers either to purchase respite care or cleaning services. Despite this fact, caregivers perceived vouchers to be part of their salary as service providers. As 'wage earners', they would like to be able to use their salary as they wanted rather than to have to purchase regulated and targeted services:

> Now that was the last version when they replied that informal carers don't need money, only services. What service is it when they give you a coupon and that's to get services with. You don't get much at all with that. (...) (An external service) provider gets the money, not the informal carer. (Male carer, interview 36)

Informal carers often regarded themselves as being in an unequal position in relation to other service providers. They had to do most of the work and the others received the funding. The consequence of all these critical arguments was that caregivers did not want to, or were not able to, get engaged with social care services but turned away from care markets (exit) and provided all the care by themselves. And, since in some cases care arrangements cost more than those who needed help could afford, choice had not been a realistic option at any point.

For such reasons, most carers construed consumer practices as illusory and founded on misrecognition. For them, such practices did not create situations in which individual carers would become active citizens with an empowered position in the governance structure; they only created the illusion of doing so. Consumer practices did not provide alternatives or offer carers a real consumer position.

Conclusion

In this chapter we have analysed Finnish elderly care policy within an active citizenship framework. We have focused on participation, responsibility and choice as dimensions of active citizenship and traced the ways these dimensions are articulated in policy documents and in carers' everyday life. Our main conclusion is that the whole idea of being an active citizen has changed in the Finnish elderly care policy and care practices. Since the 1960s, older people have been defined as independent individuals who are active clients participating in service provision (Rintala 2003). It was thought that the growth of municipal services such as home help, transportation and meals-on-wheels would help to integrate older people into their community. Service centres represented the most advanced policy of activation and integration.

Against this background, the new discourse of active citizenship represents a different ideology of social care policy. Since the 1990s, activation has meant that families and social networks should play a more important role and that older people should use their personal resources, including their financial resources, to manage their lives at home.

This kind of change can be illustrated by paying attention to the verb *support* (*tukea* in Finnish) widely used in the documentary data. Support used to mean that the public sector promoted independent living for older people by providing them with a wide range of services. In the new discourse, support has a different meaning. It is the responsibility of the municipality to enable the older population to live independently by promoting solutions that make it possible for older people to stay at home as long as possible; for instance, by supporting social networks to take more responsibility for the care of older people and by promoting partnerships between different service providers. A rights-centred discourse thus becomes replaced by a responsibility-centred discourse so that the enabling role of the municipality is emphasised instead of its legal functions.

It can be argued that the discourse on active citizenship has replaced many of the ideas fundamental to social citizenship traditions. This new discourse, with its emphasis on participation, responsibility and choice, is now the dominant discourse in elderly care policy, and individual carers identify themselves as being positioned by this framework. Carers, however, continue to deploy a social citizenship discourse and to propound the ideal of universalism as the main norm for social services and benefits. They interpret their position in terms of social rights, whereas the policy discourse offers them individual activation and responsibilities. The shift from a rights-centred to a responsibility-centred relationship between individuals and society, and the privatisation of public responsibility, become sources of injustice as inequalities between citizens with different resources intensify.

Major tensions between the policy discourse and carers' interpretations and experiences relate to the fact that some elements of the active citizenship discourse do materialise in everyday life, but some elements do not. For example, emerging consumer practices and declining or withdrawn public responsibility become visible in care practices. Carers find it difficult to manage these complex situations and to meet care needs. For meeting these needs, policy discourses highlight the idea of social networks that bear and share care responsibilities. The existence of possible care networks, however, remains quite illusionary in actual care work. In everyday life, active citizens dealing with home care are quite tired and alone. The elderly care policy discourse constructs the ideal active citizen by marginalising difficulties that are present in the actual care work and by sidelining everyday life's cultural and moral norms.

References

Anttonen, A. (2002), 'Universalism and social policy: a Nordic-feminist revaluation', in *Nordic Journal of Women's Studies*, 10 (2): 71-80.
— (2009), 'Hoivan yhteiskunnallistuminen ja politisoituminen', in Anttonen, A., H. Valokivi and M. Zechner (eds.), *Hoiva – tutkimus, politiikka ja arki*, 54-98. Tampere.
—, J. Baldock and J. Sipilä (2003) (eds.), *The Young, the old and the state. Social care systems in five industrial nations*, Cheltenham.
—, J.Sipila (2007), 'Care Capital, Stress and Satisfaction', in Crompton, R. and C. Lyonette (eds.), *Women, Men, Work and Family in Europe*, 152-170. Houndmills.
—, M. Zechner and H. Valokivi (2009) (eds.), *Hoiva – tutkimus, politiikka ja arki*, Tampere.

ANNELI ANTTONEN AND LIISA HÄIKIÖ

Burau, V. and T. Kröger (2004), 'The Local and the National in Community Care: Exploring Policy and Politics in Finland and Britain', in *Social Policy & Administration*, 38 (7): 793-810.

Bäcklund, P. (2007), *Tietämisen politiikka. Kokemuksellinen tieto kunnan hallinnassa*, Helsinki.

Clarke, J. (2004), *Changing welfare, changing states: new directions in social policy*, London.

— (2006), 'Consumers, clients or citizens? Politics, policy and practice in the reform of social care', in *European Societies*, 8 (3): 423-442.

— and J. Newman (1997), *The managerial state: power, politics and ideology in the remaking of social welfare*, London.

— and J. Newman (2007), 'What's in a name? New Labour's citizen-consumer and the remaking of public services', in *Cultural Studies*, 21 (4-5): 738-757.

—, J. Newman, N. Smith, E. Vidler and L. Westmarland (2007), *Creating citizen consumers: changing relationships and identifications*, London: Sage.

Esping-Andersen, G. (1990), *The three worlds of welfare capitalism*, Cambridge.

Government Strategy Document (2007), *Hallituksen strategia-asiakirja 2007*. Prime Minister's Office, 2007. http://www.vnk.fi/julkaisut/listaus/julkaisu/fi.jsp?oid=225542. (accessed 15 July 2009)

Government Programme. Vanhanen's Cabinet 2003-2007. *Hallitusohjelma. Pääministeri Matti Vanhasen hallituksen ohjelma 2003-2007*. Finnish Government, 2003. http://www.valtioneuvosto.fi/tietoarkisto/aiemmat_hallitukset/vanhanen/hallitusohjelma/en.jsp. (accessed 15 July 2009)

Government Programme. Prime Minister Matti Vanhanen's second Cabinet *Hallitusohjelma. Pääministeri Matti Vanhasen II hallituksen ohjelma*. Finnish Government, 2007. http://www.valtioneuvosto.fi/hallitus/hallitusohjelma/en.jsp. (accessed 15 July 2009)

Haveri, A. (2006), 'Complexity in local government change. Limits to rational reforming', in *Public Management Review*, 8 (1): 31-46.

Hernes, H.M. (1987), *Welfare state and woman power: essays in state feminism*, Oslo.

Häikiö, L. (2007), 'Expertise, representation and the common good: grounds for legitimacy in the urban governance network', in *Urban Studies*, 44 (11): 2147-2162.

Häikiö, L. (2010), 'The diversity of citizenship and democracy in local public management reform', in *Public Management Review*, 12 (3): 363-384.

Homemarket planning and decision documents. Kotitori valmistelu- ja päätösasiakirjoja. *Tampere City Government*, 2 June 2008, 302.

Kautto, M., M. Heikkilä, B. Harvinden, S. Staffan and N. Ploug (1999) (eds.), *Nordic social policy: changing welfare states*, London.

Kelly, J. (2007), 'Reforming public services in the UK: Bringing in the Third Sector', in *Public Administration*, 85 (4): 1003-1022.

Kremer, M. (2006), 'Consumers in charge of care. The Dutch Personal Budget and its impact on the market, professionals and family', in *European Societies*, 8 (3): 385-401.

Kröger, T. (1996), 'Kunnat valtion valvonnassa', in J. Sipilä, O. Ketola, T. Kröger and P. L. Rauhala (eds.), *Sosiaalipalvelujen Suomi*, 23-85.

Kröger, T. (1997), *Hyvinvointikunnan aika. Kunta hyvinvointivaltion sosiaalipalvelujen rakentajana*, Acta Universitatis Tamperensis 561.

Kuhnle, S. (2000) (ed.), *Survival of the European Welfare State*, London.

Local strategy for elder care services. *Ihmiseltä ihmiselle.* City of Tampere, 2003. http://www.tampere.fi/tiedostot/4PiNtPsql/strate_vanh.pdf. (accessed 15 July 2009)

National quality recommendations for elder care and services 2001. *Ikäihmisten hoitoa ja palveluja koskeva laatusuositus.* Ministry of Social Affairs and Health & Association of Finnish Local and Regional Authorities, 2001. http://pre20031103.stm.fi/suomi/pao/julkaisut/paosisallys78.htm. (accessed 15 July 2009)

National quality recommendations for elder care and services 2008. *Ikäihmisten palvelujen laatusuositus.* Ministry of Social Affairs and Health, 2008. http://www.stm.fi/julkaisut/nayta/_julkaisu/1063089. (accessed 15 July 2009) *Strategies for social protection 2010 – towards a socially and economically sustainable society.* Ministry of Social Affairs and Health, 2001. http://pre20031103.stm.fi/english/tao/publicat/strategies2010/strategia2010eng.pdf (accessed 15 July 2009)

National social and health policy strategy 2015. *Sosiaali- ja terveyspolitiikan strategiat 2015.* Ministry of Social Affairs and Health, 2006. http://www.stm.fi/julkaisut/nayta/_julkaisu/1067373. (accessed 8 July 2009)

Roadmap for a good old age. Policy definitions for good care and services for older people 2015. *Tie hyvään vanhuuteen 2007. Vanhusten hoidon ja palvelujen linjat vuoteen 2015.* Ministry of Social Affairs and Health, 2007. http://www.stm.fi/julkaisut/nayta/_julkaisu/1058737. (accessed 14 July 2009)

Rauhala, P.L (1996), *Miten sosiaalipalvelut ovat tulleet osaksi suomalaista sosiaaliturvaa?*, Acta Universitatis Tamperensis ser A vol. 477.

Rintala, T. (2003), *Vanhuskuvat ja vanhustenhuollon muotoutuminen 1850-luvulta 1990-luvulle,* Helsinki.

Rostgaard, T. (2004), *With due care. Social care for the young and the old across Europe,* Copenhagen.

Sutela, M. (2001), 'Kuntalaisen roolin muutos: asukkaasta asiakkaaksi – tarkastelukohteena sosiaalihuollon asiakaslähtöisyys', in *Oikeus,* 304: 418-436.

Support for informal care. Handbook for municipal decisionmakers. National recommendation. *Omaishoidon tuki. Opas kuntien päättäjille.* Ministry of Social Affairs and Health, 2005. http://www.stm.fi/julkaisut/nayta/_julkaisu/1082656. (accessed 14 July 2009)

Szebehely, M. (2004), *Nya trender, gamla traditioner: svensk äldreomsorg i europeiskt perspektiv,* Stockholm.

— (2005), 'Care as employment and welfare provision. Child care and elder care in Sweden at the dawn of the 21st century', in H. M. Dahl and T. Rask Eriksen (eds.), *Dilemmas of care in the Nordic welfare state. Continuity and change,* Aldershot, 80-97.

Tampere's City Strategy 2001. *Kaikem paree Tampere 2001.*

Tampere's City Strategy 2005. *Kaikem paree Tampere 2005.* http://www.tampere.fi/tiedostot/58f5pF51f/kaupunkistrategia_2005-2016.pdf. (accessed 14 July 2009)

Trydegärd, G. (2000), *Tradition, change and variation: past and present trends in public old-age care,* Stockholm.

Ungerson, C. (2004), 'Whose empowerment and independence? A cross-national perspective on "cash for care" schemes', in *Ageing & Society,* 24 (2): 189-212.

— and S. Yeandle (2007), 'Conclusion. Dilemmas, contradictions and change', in C. Ungerson and S. Yeandle (eds.), *Cash for care in developed welfare states*, Houndmills, 187-206.

Vabø, M. (2006), 'Caring for people or caring for proxy consumers?' in *European societies*, 8 (3): 403-422.

Valokivi, H. (2004), 'Participation and Citizenship of Elderly Persons: User Experiences from Finland', in *Social Work in Health Care*, 39: 181-208.

— and M. Zechner (2009), 'Ristiriitainen omaishoiva – Läheisen auttamisesta kunnan palveluksi', in A. Anttonen, M. Zechner and H. Valokivi (eds.), *Hoiva – tutkimus, politiikka ja arki*, Tampere, 126-153.

5 Active citizenship in Norwegian elderly care

From activation to consumer activism

Mia Vabø

The term 'active citizenship', as it appears in European welfare policy, embraces a range of activities that people engage in to exercise influence and to act as co-producers alongside governments (see chapter 1). Even though the term has not been coined as a buzzword in Norway as it has in the UK and the Netherlands,[1] the idea that citizens should participate in and assume responsibility for the implementation of welfare programmes has been at the very centre of Norwegian welfare policy. The comprehensive welfare commitment characteristic of Scandinavian countries has not worked on the assumption that people are essentially passive or disengaged. Even though debates often tend to be dominated by a narrow rights-dominated (passive) version of socio-liberal citizenship (Johansson & Hvinden 2007), policymakers have regularly evoked notions of the active citizen in the hope that people will cooperate to realise ambitious welfare goals. According to the political scientist Bo Rothstein (1998: 35-37), Scandinavian social policy has been characterised by a communitarian/perfectionist principle that portrays the relation between the state and citizen as organic in character. In contrast to the liberal ideal stressing that the state should assume a neutral posture, that is, vis-à-vis an individual's choice of a life project, the communitarian/perfectionist ideal enjoins the state to take a stand in favour of certain collective moral principles and thus to hold out certain life projects as more desirable than others. In concrete actions, the state intervenes in civil society and tries to influence our values, for example by subsidising organisations that are assumed to work for commendable values and practices – whether these be temperance, solidarity with the Third World, participation in sports or healthy eating habits. However, more recent welfare discourses have been influenced by a liberal turn. Citizens are now increasingly viewed as autonomous rights holders and consumers acting with distant scepticism towards the service-providing state.

This chapter explores the underlying mechanisms behind these changing depictions of the state-citizen relation. Focusing on the Norwegian elderly care sector, an examination is made of how notions of citizenship have been reshaped through different eras of welfare reform. Based on the idea that politicians will seek support from the electorate, an exploration is also made into how citizens themselves have influenced reforms and accordingly contributed to shaping and sustaining images of state-citizen relations. The argument is that attempts by governments to influence people's self-awareness and the images they hold of themselves may succeed. However, citizens – especially truly active citizens – are not fully controllable. They may confront and speak against governments, or they may simply ignore or suppress public policies by focusing on policy agendas of their own. In fact, popular movements with a good command of mass media may be quite powerful in setting policy agendas (Semetko et al. 1991; Allern & Saglie 2009: 65-97). The Norwegian case explored here suggests that activist citizens may capture the policy agenda and act as a silencing power in public debate and in so doing, simultaneously suppress the interests of those people they claim to represent.

The Scandinavian trajectory of reform

Norway belongs to the family of generous Nordic welfare states characterised by a comprehensive infrastructure of tax-subsidised services offered to and used by all social groups. The legitimacy of the system is based on the assumption that even the discriminating tastes of the upper middle class should be satisfied (Vabø 2009: 346). The relatively strong welfare commitment between government and citizens has developed within a complex system of multi-level governance. The central government has exerted influence on local governments through judicial acts, funding, instructions, guidelines and so forth, but Nordic welfare societies have, to a greater extent than other Western countries, also used local authorities as agencies for implementing their welfare policies (Selle 1991; Albæk 1995: 241).

This is understood to be partly a consequence of long-standing historical traditions of local democracy, and partly because the size and complexity of the huge welfare commitment required considerable delegation and decentralisation of operational functions (Premfors 1998: 157). At the heart of the Scandinavian decentralisation trend was the intention of enhancing local democracy. As noted by Sehested (2002: 1524), this was 'concerned with the integration of citizens in the governing of public services and with the introduction of new governing structures based on dialogue and participation (like user boards, community councils, councils for the elderly, dialogue circles, etc)'.

Premfors (1998: 146) observed that decentralisation, corporatism and consensus make the Nordic trajectory of reform distinctive both from Anglo-Saxon and Continental welfare states. In the literature on public sector reforms, however, such major national reform trajectories are often ignored. It is taken for granted that all welfare states follow the same path, moving away from rule-bound welfare bureaucracies towards a business style of management and pluralised welfare markets – hereafter referred to as New Public Management (NPM). In these accounts, Anglo-Saxon countries figure as leaders whereas countries such as Norway figure as laggards (Christensen & Lægreid 2007), non-reformers or slow reformers (Sehested 2002: 1524). To redress the bias of these standardised narratives of public sector reforms, it may be more useful to think of the Nordic reform trajectory as characterised by an *alternative* succession of reforms. Whereas trust-based governance and horizontal collaboration is associated with a *post*-NPM era in Anglo-Saxon countries (Newman et al. 2004: 2), it is more convincing to associate this with the *pre*-NPM era in the Nordic countries.

The following account of the emergence of these different images of state-citizen relations is organised according to three different eras of institutional reforms, starting with the era of welfare expansion then moving through two different eras of stagnation – an era of radical decentralisation and collaboration followed by the era of NPM entangled with a shift towards re-centralisation.

The era of welfare expansion: care services become a citizen's moral right

The expansion of the modern welfare state in Norway is often described as a vigorous pull driven by a strong will on the part of the population to rebuild the country after World War II. Voluntary organisations and individual activists drew attention to unmet needs and pushed the state to assume responsibility for welfare programmes (Seip 1994: 289). In elderly care, voluntary associations of women played a 'push role', and their own care activities were gradually assimilated into public welfare programmes and turned into paid work. This represents a markedly different 'gender settlement' than that in Germany (discussed by Kuhlmann, this volume) and the UK (Barnes, this volume).

A core aim of the post-war elderly care policy was to avoid segregation among older people. They should be enabled to participate and take an active part in society in spite of infirmity and old age. A white paper (Sosialdepartementet 1966: 12) established that old age was no longer to be regarded as a passive phase of life; older people should be as active as possible both physically and mentally (see Newman in this volume, on parallels with early 21st century policy discourse in the UK). From this idea, a range of preventative actions were suggested to avoid the social exclusion and passivity of older people. These included improvements in the pension systems, better housing standards and a generous provision of home care. It was argued that home care was good for the elderly both because it would prevent and postpone institutionalisation, and because it would ensure older people maintained good contact with their own families and with the community as a whole. Hence, the 'ageing in place' policy was based on the idea that an active state would promote active (and happy) citizens who could live independent of their own children (Sosialdepartementet 1966: 13). In a later white paper (Sosialdepartementet 1981), it was determined that public home care was necessary because informal and unpaid care had been a burden on families and because the new occupation and family pattern made informal care even more difficult.

The development of municipal home care services brought about a new historical situation for the frail elderly who now could choose to stay in their own homes even with increasing care needs instead of being forced to move into either their children's homes or to a home for the elderly. Surveys carried out between the late 1960s and mid-1980s indicate that older people increasingly preferred public rather than family help, even when children were living close by. Informal help was preferred over public services only when there was a need for short-term assistance. Inter-generational solidarity was still strong, but less based on material necessity (Daatland 1990: 13). Lewinter (1999: 7) argued that publicly supplied and financed home care has the effect, among other things, of spreading the burden of gratitude the elderly feel due to their increasing dependence on assistance from others.

The rapid spread and popularity of public home care must be viewed in light of the informal, flexible and adaptable character of service provision. Research into the traditional home care service demonstrates that older people appreciated the sociability of stable relationships (continuity of staff) and the possibility of the staff acting flexibly to attend to their particular concrete and shifting needs (Wærness 1984: 199; Szebehely 1995: 281-288). The early home-helpers – mainly housewives paid by the hour to help a few clients in their neighbourhood – had free scope to make agreements with the elderly person concerning the essential service tasks. Services were not provided *for* individuals but to a large degree in cooperation *with* individuals.

Besides being welcomed by elderly themselves, the generous state sponsoring of social care in the 1960s and 1970s represented 'a freedom of choice' for middle-aged daughters who could now choose gainful employment despite an ailing parent (Szebehely 1998). In fact, public care provision facilitated women's gainful employment both through the provision of care to relieve their own care burden and as the employer of female labour (see also Leira 2006). Thus, not only older people but also their adult children had a stake in care services. This dual stakeholding is important to bear in mind in understanding how public care for the elderly came to be regarded as a social right and a taken-for-granted part of the social infrastructure. It should also be recognised that unlike in the UK, where carers of older people founded their own carer movement (see Barnes this volume), informal carers in Norway were not organised.

Hence only the older people themselves were recognised as stakeholders in the governmental discourse.

An era of radical decentralisation, high welfare ambitions and need for rationalisation

The 1960s and 1970s were decades of welfare expansion characterised by generous reimbursements by the central government and also by increasing government regulation of municipal care services. However, the mid-1980s marked the beginning of a new era of radical decentralisation.

According to the Norwegian historian Anne Lise Seip (1991: 40), the tension between centralisation and decentralisation may be viewed as a tug of war, not just between different principles of governance but also between different conceptions of equality. A social policy analysis commissioned by the Department of Social Affairs (Sosialdepartementet 1972) concluded that social policy should take a new step forward to realise the long-standing goal of equality and security. A new policy strategy was carved out which departed from the idea that equality meant an equal chance to realise one's own distinctive character. No one should be compelled to adapt to social systems; people should have the right to achieve their true potential (Seip 1994: 359). In order to achieve this new, ambitious welfare goal it was argued that the organisation and governance of care provision should be decentralised. Care services should preferably be provided by outside institutional settings, in close proximity to those in need. Ironically, however, these new ambitious policy aims were proclaimed at the same time that concerns about economy began to emerge (Seip 1991: 41).

As the decentralisation reform was implemented in 1986, legislative changes delegated the responsibility for a wide range of services to the municipalities with the aim of encouraging an integrated approach to the supply of care. Municipalities were assigned responsibility for primary healthcare and for various kinds of housing and care services. Medical treatment, rehabilitation and social care were supposed to be woven into a cohesive continuum of care. Buzzwords stressing awareness of local problems, flexibility, proximity and user participation flourished (Wærness 1984). But, as the previous reimbursement system was replaced by block grants, many municipalities experienced greater strain on their budgets and were now urged to bridge the gap between ambitious policy goals and scant resources. In care for the elderly, the number of beds in nursing homes was reduced and responsibility for those who were most frail was pushed 'down' to the home care sector. In order to improve the utilisation of caregiver staff resources, home care services (nursing care, personal care and domiciliary care) were integrated and organised in self-regulated service teams (Vabø 2006: 408).

As municipalities became increasingly focused on cost containment, several attempts were made to consider whether 'hidden' care resources could be mobilised (Daatland 1997). While social democrats had previously had a deeply rooted antagonism towards philanthropic welfare solutions, they now acknowledged the mutual dependence between public and civil welfare resources (Selle 1991). Steps were taken to enhance civic engagement, volunteerism and self-help. In 1991, for instance, the government launched an open-ended bottom-up programme in which the term *voluntary centre* was applied to encompass a multitude of local experiments. The idea was that experiments should be publicly funded but ideas and initiatives should be taken from below (Lorenzen & Dugstad 2008: 2). In the same era, various types of welfare hybrids (self-help groups, groups for unemployed, etc.) popped up, funded and structured by public authorities but still based on a principle of organisation borrowed from voluntary associations (Wollebæk et al. 2000). It was also possible to trace a greater valorisation of self-sustainability and family solidarity. While policy documents of the 1960s and 1970s stressed that good family relations should be free from a burden of gratitude, reports were now inclined to underline the value of mutual self-help and strong family ties. A green paper that was mandated to evaluate and discuss the further evolvement of public care provision (Sosialdepartementet 1992) made a number of suggestions for stimulating family care through payment for care, information, support and respite services, and proposed ways of reinforcing the ability of care recipients to look after themselves, for example by technical aids, practical housing, rehabilitation and welfare centres. A white paper (Sosial og helsedepartementet 1995: 18, 150) referred to research findings claiming that family care was 'commonplace' and 'normal'. On this basis it was proposed that public care services should only relieve needs beyond what was viewed as being 'natural' and within the capability of families to handle. The stress on self-sustainability and family care was reflected in the working principle of home care teams – help to self-help became the core working principle. Hence, even though home care services were provided on a universal basis – i.e., no applicants were excluded *a priori* on the basis that they should make their own provision – service staff were called upon to collaborate with and even to mobilise care resources from families. This working ideal certainly conflicted with the expectations of the most resourceful citizens who were able to mobilise their own coping resources (Vabø 2007: 172).

The Norwegian elderly revolt

Despite all the steps taken to join forces with citizens, the cutbacks following the decentralisation reform were met with protest. During the winter of 1990, the protests of activist (middle class) citizens turned into a nationwide people's movement, later known as the 'elderly revolt' (*eldreopprøret*). The movement was started by an ageing man, Per Hovda (82), whose wife was in need of care. Hovda became famous among Norwegians after he turned up in a popular current affairs programme and recounted his experiences in a local urban district ward of Oslo. Hovda felt that the care facilities offered by the city ward were insufficient. The tall, majestic old man, previously a professor in linguistics, pounded his fist on the table and spoke trembling with anger: '*Father, forgive them not, for they do know what they are doing!*' His authoritative presence and powerful words resonated among the general public. Newspapers and television kept the focus of attention on elderly care for days and weeks. A number of current affairs programmes invited well-educated and articulate senior citizens to discuss problems of elderly care with politicians. Senior debaters swept aside the politicians and proclaimed that people were tired of political nonsense – what was needed now was 'real solutions' and the allocation of money! The minister of health and social affairs was called to account on the front page of newspapers and was later pressed by opposition political parties to provide additional grants for care of the elderly.

The particular combination of a true story and authentic problem, recognised by the general population, and a media hype fronted by quick-witted people – a 'media protest' (Hole 1992: 160) – proved to have great impact. Two months after Hovda appeared on TV, one billion crowns was added to the state budget. The additional grant became known as the 'elderly billion' (*eldremilliarden*). But subsequent to the 'elderly revolt' and the 'elderly billion', questions were raised about whether the situation in elderly care really deserved to be labelled a crisis and whether the extra grant really was to be reserved for elderly care services (Hole 1992). However, Hovda and the elderly revolt came to symbolise a social consensus that public care provision was and should be a matter of public concern. The event had several spillover effects. Since the intensive debate during the winter of 1990, many smaller 'media protests' have occurred, often in local newspapers – always portraying an individual's grievance against local services and always with comments from various actors entering the role as champions speaking up for the elderly in need of care. The phrases 'elderly revolt' and 'elderly billion' became familiar idioms and continue to be expressed in debates on the shortcomings in the volume and quality of welfare.

The elderly revolt set a sharper tone for public debate and contributed to the creation of a 'crisis discourse' (Lingsom 1997: 56). It also prefigured the emergence of a more consumerist orientation paving the way for later market reforms (discussed below). This was a general trend in public debates of the early 1990s: there was a growing trend to focus attention on output and quality of services rather than political principles and also a growing tendency to value the well-informed and punitive behaviour of informed consumers. For instance, the Norwegian Consumer Council pushed municipalities to furnish people with information, contracts and better opportunities for redress and influence. It was argued that these measures were important as a substitute for consumer choice. Local administration services like homecare became increasingly viewed as prefixed goods, not as a relational service based on communication about needs, and individual users were neither portrayed as passive clients nor as collaborative partners but as consumers in a detached and critical role, ready to use their potential power. Even the national organisation for pensioners, traditionally a typical corporative and consensus-oriented association, was influenced by this punitive tone in their advertisements: '*Nice pensioners don't demand. Nice pensioners don't get. Be a devil! Support the Norwegian Pensioners Association!*'[2]

Above all, the elderly revolt put pressure on central authorities to demonstrate accountability in municipal elderly care. In response to the severe criticism, the government introduced new earmarked grants to the sector, adding to the general block grants to municipalities. During the massive turmoil in the media, the minister of social affairs asked the Board of Health Supervision to map the situation in the municipalities. However, realising that information on quality of care was missing – the local care apparatus was a black box – the ministry of social affairs initiated a project in the autumn of 1990 to develop a monitoring system (Gerix) to provide the national authorities with adequate information on the demand and supply of health and social services. The request made by the minister represented a quest for transparency. This was to form an essential part of a new track of reforms emerging in the late 1990s.

A new era of rationalisation, regulation and consumerism

In the late 1990s, Norwegian elderly care was caught in the global wave of NPM reforms. Business consultants entered the stage with a range of promising how-to prescriptions stressing efficiency, cost control, financial transparency, contracts, the creation of quasi-market mechanisms, free choice of provider, and the introduction of a business style of management. These new ideas were, however, not the only driver of change in that era (Vabø 2009: 346-359). Central government was already dealing with the problems occurring in the wake of the decentralisation reform and the elderly revolt and had taken several initiatives to control municipal service providers and to secure the enforceability of social rights. The new Social Service Act of 1991 stipulated that people had certain *procedural rights* in relation to local care providers: they had the right to an individual needs assessment, the right to make their views known, to receive a written and well-founded decision and the right to appeal to a higher court. Even though *substantive rights* to care were still limited, as allocation of care services always will be based on some kind of needs test, municipalities were now pushed by the state to put on paper what they regarded to be an adequate level of support. Municipalities were also required to be more accountable 'upwards' to central government. For instance, the Ministry of Health and the Board of Health Supervision mandated municipalities to implement systems for internal control and quality assessment. The call for accountability and transparency pushed the self-regulated care agencies to formalise work routines and performance.

The market discourse and the notion of consumers making choices between different care providers had great impact on the public debate. Elderly care became an increasingly important issue in electoral campaigns, and the right-wing parties – supported by the Confederation of Norwegian Enterprise – advocated that a larger share of grants for elderly care should be channelled directly to users in order to stimulate private provision and free choice (Bay 1998: 294). However, even though a number of municipal actors became enthused by promising ideas of competition and choice, Norwegian municipalities turned out to be comparatively reluctant about relying on private, for-profit providers for care services. With the exception of a handful of municipalities headed by a right-wing council, a majority ended up with less stringent NPM strategies, partly because they seemed to fit in well with the general quest for transparency by the central health authorities (Vabø 2009: 178-179). In home care, this NPM strategy was to implement some form of purchaser-provider model – even though the municipality did not have plans to tender services out to private-sector providers.

The separation of purchaser and provider functions was linked to multiple arguments: it was considered that this division would be more amenable to cost control and quality management. Local authorities were now in a better position to make quality demands and subsequently to control and manage quality at arm's length. The purchaser-provider split was also supposed to improve the capability of municipalities to deal with the new legal and formal aspects of service provision. It was believed that specialised care assessors would be apt to take a more detached view of care needs than would the hands-on care staff (Vabø 2006: 414). Paradoxically, while NPM textbooks argue that purchaser-provider organisation was essential to replace rule-based, process-driven routines with ex-post evaluation of results, the purchaser-provider model was implemented precisely because it was believed to enhance values such as predictability and due process (Blomberg 2004: 209; Vabø 2007: 265).

The modernised transparent care agencies promised predictability and enhanced consumer control. Citizens were to be provided with service specifications, citizen's charters, written agreements and improved mechanisms for redress. All of these measures signalled that citizens were expected to be empowered and activated in new ways – not as co-producers who collaborated on the 'inside' of welfare institutions but as consumers who act in a detached and discriminating role 'outside' welfare institutions. Like sovereign consumers in a service market, citizens were not expected to form trusting (collaborative) relationships with service providers but were supposed to act with scepticism and distrust towards service providers – always ready to take action if services failed, always looking for the best buy (Vabø 2006: 405).

The new organisational model suggested that both service providers and service receivers should enter their encounter with a new 'service script' telling them to be conscious of and attentive to the contract specified for the individual service receiver. Moreover, citizens were expected to be attentive and active in seeking information, making choices (where several service options were available) and taking action if services failed, thereby compelling service providers to amend their ways.

Contemporary public debates on elderly care

Since the elderly revolt of 1990, the right of frail elderly citizens to receive high-quality public care has remained high on the agenda. Media protests and efforts to mobilise a new elderly revolt occur regularly, although these now tend to be driven by special interest organisations. New associations and ad-hoc organisations have been added to the plethora of associations working for the elderly. Compared with the long-established 'collaborative' organisations, new activists are taking on a more offensive and confrontational role.

A telling example is 'Seniorsaken' (Senior Matters), an association launched in 2001 by the popular Norwegian comedian, Rolv Wesenlund, and supported by a range of celebrities and people from privileged positions in the media. Motivated by the slogan 'We are elderly, we are numerous and we are dangerous – wait and see!', this association works intensively to make the situation of older people visible in the news media and thereby to influence the standard of elderly care. 'Seniorsaken' offers a 24-hour SOS phone for people to report unacceptable conditions in elderly care. On some occasions, they have reported to the police the ways in which municipalities are breaching the law. In addition, the association offers its members consumer advice and discounts made possible through special agreements with banks, electricity and telephone companies, and travel agencies. Hence, the association also targets the interests of the still healthy and fit senior citizens. Using the term 'senior' instead of 'elderly', 'Seniorsaken' expresses a certain distance from the idea of ageing and powerlessness (Johannesen 2003: 78). On its website, 'senior citizens' appear as healthy and mentally fit – photographed as they are about to log on to the network to check stock market quotes, or dressed up in jeans holidaying in exotic locations. One of their recurring arguments is that older people should be treated with respect and dignity and as people who have been used to making choices in most situations in earlier life phases. They should not be deprived of the freedom to make choices the day they become old and dependent on care services.

Officially, 'Seniorsaken' does not have any particular political affiliation, but it shares some views with the populist Norwegian extreme right-wing party, the Party of Progress which, despite its neo-liberal profile, also campaigns for enforceable rights and generous public spending. A core argument of the Party of Progress is that, as one of the richest oil nations in the world, Norway should also provide the best elderly care in the world. Some of the traditional organisations working for older people have distanced themselves from the antagonistic approach of 'Seniorsaken', but the idea that high-quality elderly care should be an enforceable legal right and not just a moral right is a view widely shared among all activist organisations. In 2009 six organisations concerned with the welfare of older people joined forces to launch a campaign – the Elderly Care Campaign 2009 – working assiduously in the run-up to the September general election. The main issue they raised was that of improving the enforceability of citizen's rights, for instance by suggesting how prevailing quality regulations should be extended and made more concrete (see also Plant 1992).

The potential power of activists fighting for improvements in elderly care have obviously increased as elderly care has entered the political agenda. Until late 1990, elderly care policy was characterised by a general party-political consensus (Bay 1998: 292). There is still a consensus in favour of governments retaining the ultimate responsibility for elderly care, but care provision became increasingly politicised at the end of the 1990s as the NPM reforms entered the agenda. While right-wing politicians value competition and free choice of providers, left-wing politicians argue that care is too difficult to predefine, delimit or put a price upon. Today, Norwegian voters regard elderly care as one of the most decisive issues shaping their voting behaviour in elections (Karlsen 2009: 97-120).

Shortly before the 2005 election, the political dispute was fuelled when a former powerful Labour Party leader, Håkon Lie (98 years old at the time), complained on the front page of a tabloid newspaper about the strictly predefined time schedule of his own home helper. The old 'chieftain' accused the system of being Stalinist. His manoeuvre later became associated with the phrase 'stopwatch care' (*stoppeklokkeomsorg*) – a phrase he coined to draw attention to the constraining aspects of the free-choice model. Even though care recipients were free to choose among several care companies, the system did not provide freedom of choice for the service provider, and service receivers had to come to an agreement on what was needed there and then. In the election a few weeks later, the Labour Party followed their old 'chieftain' and argued that free choice was a sham and that older people wanted security, stability and enough help rather than the freedom to choose the logo of a home care company. Election surveys indicated that the Labour Party gained support upon taking this position.

The 'red/green' coalition government elected in 2005 opposed private, for-profit care and 'stopwatch care'. Nevertheless they also argued that purchaser-provider splits and quality assessments were crucial elements in their endeavours to secure the rights of citizens to high-quality care. It was emphasised that it is unacceptable for municipalities to refuse help or to transfer care responsibility to families on the grounds that family resources are available (Helse- og omsorgsdepartementet 2006). Political parties in general (both left and right-wing) tend to adopt elements from the entitlement discourse of activist citizens. As elderly care has become one of the core issues in election campaigns, politicians compete to enter the role as the champion of the elderly. They outdo each other with talk about quality, dignity and care, and in order to underline that this time they promise something more than lofty words, they often add words like 'assurance', 'binding agreements' and 'guarantees'. In order to ensure action by municipalities, a number of accountability arrangements have been set up such as statutory requirements, committees, ombudsmen and (above all) various forms of audits. In this way, politicians and officials from central authorities can assure the public that they hold a tight rein over municipalities.

To summarise, the current modernisation agenda draws on two discourses, a social-liberal discourse regarding the citizens as rights-holders on the one hand, and on the other a market discourse regarding people as discriminating and active consumers who enter contracts, make demands, forward complaints and exercise choice (Vabø 2006: 405). The two discourses are highly embroiled, as they both share a common language of entitlements and both discourses are based on the presumption that citizens are ready to make claims and to take action if services fail. In one respect, one could say that the government shares the language of the 'champions' fighting against the state. However, as the notion of active consumers is engineered through a managerial discourse, it tends to be used strategically to delimit public care responsibility (Vabø 2009: 188). In everyday service encounters, local care authorities tend to refer to 'entitlements' as formal decisions or restricted contracts: *'this is what you are entitled to – nothing more, nothing less!'* Senior activists for their part tend to talk about entitlements in a more open-ended moral sense: *'older people have the (moral) right to quality care'.*

Representing the elderly in need of care?

In the preceding sections I have demonstrated how notions of active citizenship have been evoked, shaped and reshaped in a dynamic interplay between citizens and policymakers. In a simplified account, the dynamic interaction may be viewed as a play in two acts: the first act deals with how governments supported and absorbed the collective spirit and civic engagement of voluntary organisations, and how they later turned it into a policy instrument and endeavoured to revitalise the same spirit in order to increase cost efficiency. The second act concerns the reprisals taken by middle class activists who felt indignant because governments abandoned their welfare commitment. A socio-liberal/consumerist discourse rich in emotive and moral appeal was mobilised 'from below' to reshape the public care service. Elderly people were then designated a more demanding role as rights-holders and powerful consumers.

The second act may be read as a triumph on the part of activist citizens: they succeeded in putting their own issues onto the political agenda and pushed the state to take steps to get a better grip on local service providers. If we take into consideration the accomplishment of the elderly revolt and the fact that elderly care has been an enduring theme in election campaigns, it is not unreasonable to draw the conclusion that the activism of senior citizens so far has been effective. Norwegian elderly care activists are not typical powerless grassroots activists. They are resourceful people from the 'talking middle class' in close contact with influential people in the mass media (Hole 1992). They have managed to capture the policy agenda. Still, it is questionable to what extent the policy measures resulting from their pressure really will bring about the results they want to see.

First, it must be acknowledged that processes of change are generally dynamic and contested rather than linear or evolutionary (Newman 2001: 26-39). Even if the activists win full acceptance of their desired policy reforms, it will have to be 'filtered' through an institutional level characterised by a complex mixture of external and internal pressures from a range of actors possessing different forms of power and knowledge (see Kuhlmann on the 'politics of mediation' in this volume). Apart from this, it is also questionable to what extent the voice of activists really represents the interests of older people in need of care. Senior citizen activists are energetic, passionate and committed, but can their strategies be considered as defending the interests of all elderly citizens? Was it really in the interest of people to replace the 'old' collaborative model with a consumerist model of home care?

To determine what is in the best interest of people in need of care is, of course, a highly political issue. On a political level, disagreements will occur due to the political preferences and ideological inclinations of different individuals and political parties. If we turn to the practical level of care, disagreements are likely to be influenced by the specific life context of individuals and their experiences with service providers. What is striking about individuals' experiences with public services in general is that they are distributed both socially and experientially, and that people themselves are neither stable nor unitary in their encounters with services (Clarke et al. 2007: 67).

In studying people's perceptions of service encounters in the Norwegian home care sector in the mid-1990s, I found that various baselines were brought into people's judgements depending very much on social, situational and individual circumstances (Vabø 1998). Evaluative statements – both praise and criticism – revealed that elements from the collaborative model of governance were valued and taken for granted. In line with a comprehensive body of Nordic care research (Szebehely 2005: 397), it was important for people both to *anticipate* (who the helper would be, when she would be coming and how long she would stay) and to *affect* the content of the help provided. People valued open-ended agreements and caregiver staff who were willing and able to adapt to unstable and changing situations. Their values fit well with 'the rationality of care' coined by Wærness (1984: 185-211) who stresses that the problems of the person being cared for cannot be completely pre-defined.[3] Accordingly, the orientation of care workers must not be limited to a specified sphere of competence but must be guided by a complex set of considerations that may differ from person to person, from day to day.

This general conception of 'good care' corresponds to the organic state-citizen relation as described by Rothstein (1998). Care services are generally expected to be concerned with people's well-being. One set of critiques levelled against the care agencies accused the service of not being *sufficiently* concerned. In particular, sons and daughters of the weakest among the elderly (those with ambiguous, unstable needs or insipient dementia) complained about the lack of time and attention taken by staff to interpret and understand the complex needs of service recipients. They called for caregiver staff to be more interventionist in making inquiries into the mental condition of their elderly parent(s). In their opinion, caregiver staff should not respond passively to the expressed '*Thank you, I'm fine*' response of their demented parents but be in a state of readiness to respond to needs not agreed upon (Vabø 1998). In fact, they called for the caregiver staff to recognise the incapacities of their parents and to act in a slightly more paternalist fashion. They felt a moral obligation to compensate for this lack of attention and were frustrated because their responsible attitude and active steps also meant that they allowed caregiver staff to abandon their responsibility.

A different set of critiques point in an opposite direction. Some interviewees had experienced service staff hinting that their lifestyle was not active enough, or not active in the right manner. This view was expressed by people who were mentally fit but physically impaired: for instance, a 'high and mighty' old woman who preferred to use her restricted energy on social and cultural events (not on housework) and an eccentric old artist who insisted on being served breakfast in bed and preferred to spend her days in a comfy chair with her water colour paintings. Both of them disliked the concerns expressed by caregiver staff about their lifestyles. In their opinion, elderly care was a self-evident right of citizens with legitimate needs, and services should be carried out according to clear entitlement criteria and incontrovertible agreements.

MIA VABØ

What is important to note here is that the home care service was pressured by two sets of critique which favoured different logics of governance (see also Vabø 2006). From the perspective of home care staff, the problems of meeting different user demands were attributed to lack of time and staff resources. Even though most people praised their work, it was frustrating to experience that they were unable to find sufficient time and pay satisfactory attention to the most frail. The frustration was amplified as they felt pressured to pay attention to the claims made by demanding people with moderate needs. The tension between conflicting user interests and different user demands was also evident in a case study from the home care service a few years later, after several reform steps had been taken to make services more transparent and in tune with modern elderly consumers (Vabø 2002). In this regime, caregiving staff were to concentrate on efficient service delivery, while the responsibility for making agreements and for rationing services were handed over to specialised purchaser units.

However, because of the presumption that all care recipients were consumers who would take advantage of prefixed agreements, the dilemma of balancing competing user interests was in practice passed down the hierarchy to frontline staff. Caregiver staff continuously experienced moral choices about when to deviate from contracts, whether to change the priority ranking of cases, and how to vary staff time allotments in order to meet the unforeseen needs of the most frail elderly (Vabø 2006: 414). Many of them explained that it was often easier to ignore the terms of the contract than to adhere to the acute needs of these persons. However, the opportunity to spontaneously meet unexpected needs was constrained, partly because their work time was increasingly used to adhere to new procedures associated with formal user agreements, quality records and control routines.

Caregiving staff saw few signs of active consumer behaviour among the elderly. On the contrary, agreements, information and questionnaires (provided for security and legal protection) even gave rise to anxiety for elderly people who often lack the energy and acumen to read them through (Vabø 2006: 414). Interviews with older care recipients undertaken in 2008 point to the same conclusion: interviewees did not pay regard to the written agreement made for them but revealed that they entrusted either their own adult children or their home helper to explain to them and to act as a proxy in relation to the purchaser authorities.[4]

There is not space here to elaborate further on the various consequences of the realignments made in home care. What is important to stress, however, is that the 'consumerist' way of organising state-citizen relations did not fulfil the objective of empowering the elderly. On the contrary, my study reveals that a system based on formal agreements and procedures may bring about new relations of dependency for older people, as they are now increasingly reliant on the competency and capacity of carers (staff or family) to navigate a formalised bureaucracy. More-over, as the latitude of caregiver staff to act flexibly and with spontaneity tends to be restricted, so too is the opportunity of older people to influ-ence the help they receive (see also Szebehely 1995).

Narratives from the everyday level of home care indicate that some of the interests of severely dependent old people do not emerge in the pub-lic debate. Even though activists frequently speak on behalf of the most frail elderly (who deserve the best quality of care), they tend to stick to the powerful language of consumerism rather than to the evasive and almost poetic language of care. They talk about 'real' measures like qual-ity control, contracts, entitlements criteria and free choice. All of these are measures that in practice entail some new ways of controlling and constraining the behaviour of those who deliver services. In line with the discussion above, they bear the potential to undermine what people often perceive as good care. Hence, the activists act like a silencing power. They disregard the perspectives often generated from carers' viewpoints – perspectives that stress how assisting another adult to lead a life of good quality can be very complex. Care is social and relational in character (see Barnes in this volume); it can be embarrassing and disem-powering, and it is usually provided in a context of risk in the sense that it is often preventive in the minds of those involved and therefore not valued in itself, but for what it wards off (Baldoc 1998: 179).

This chapter has highlighted some of the paradoxes of the consumerist turn in social care services for the elderly. A consumer orientation can, as I have shown, be deployed by activists seeking to bring about transfor-mations in elderly care services as they are generating new demands and look back to older rights-based discourses. However, where consumer-ism assumes a form of citizenship that is willing to, and capable of, mak-ing rational choices based on clear information and stable preferences, this may not be in the interests of many elderly service users. It also produces new dilemmas for care staff, as difficult moral and ethical choices are devolved to them.

The inclination to view older people as sovereign consumers and not as dependent elderly may reflect the fact that organised activists are pre-dominantly people in their 'third age' rather than the severely dependent elderly in need of care, or carers speaking on behalf of the most frail. Senior citizens speak from their own heart as resourceful citizens who have the 'gift of the gab': they do not speak out from the perspective of themselves as demented or worn out by ill health. This is understand-able, but it does not rule out the fact that they may one day be demented or worn out themselves, and thereby caught in their own trap.

Notes

1. The reason 'active citizenship' has not become a buzzword in Norway is probably because the English word 'citizenship' translates into two different concepts in the Norwegian language: *'statsborgerskap'*(state-citizenship), which is a narrow legal/political term referring to peoples' membership in a nation state, and *'medborgerskap'* (co-citizenship), which is a broader label referring to the social and cultural aspects of citizenship, i.e., the way people act in their role as members of a society/community. Strømsnes (2003: 16) links the two concepts to Kymlicka and Wayne's distinction (1995: 284) between 'citizenship-as-legal-status' (*statsborgerskap*) and 'citizenship-as-desirable-activity' (*medborgerskap*). A spirit of *'medborgerskap'* implies positive exhortations like good citizenship, public spirit, responsibility and participation. The term and its associated values have attracted increased attention over the past decades, partly in response to a general decline of party political participation and partly in response to challenges associated with multiculturalism.
2. The National Council for Senior Citizens (*Statens eldreråd*) was founded in 1970 based on the idea that all matters concerning elderly care were to be submitted for comment. Under pressure from the Norwegian Pensioners' Association, municipalities gradually copied the model and established local senior citizen councils (Daatland & Svorken 1996). In 1991 they were made obligatory. In some municipalities, local senior citizen councils are closely linked to the public administration – for instance by having delegated authority to allocate public funding for local senior associations.
3. Coining the concept 'rationality of caring', Wærness argues that unlike the 'scientific rationality' typical of medical treatment, for instance, and which is based on pre-defined means of 'caring', this concept is directed towards more comprehensive and elastic problems.
4. These interviews were made as part of an ongoing project, *Manoeuvring in hybrid health care organisation*, funded by the Norwegian Research Council.

References

Albæk, E. (1995), 'Reforming the Nordic welfare communes', *International Review of Administrative Science*, 61: 241-264.

Allern, H., and Saglie, J. (2009), 'Velferdens valgkamp: Arena for interesseorganisasjoner', in A. Bay, A. W. Pedersen and J. Saglie (eds.), *Når Velferd Blir Politikk. Partier, Organisasjoner og Opinion*, Oslo: Abstrakt.

Baldoc, J. (1998), 'Old age consumerism and the social care market', *Social Policy Review* 10: 165-198.

Bay, A. H. (1998), *Opinionen og Eldrepolitikken*, NOVA, Rapport 24.

Blomberg, S. (2004), *Specialiserad Biståndshandlägging inom ien Kommunala Äldreomsorgen. Genomförande av en Organisationsreform och dess Praktik*. Dissertations in Social Work 17. Lund.

Christensen, T., and P. Lægreid (2009), *Transcending New Public Management. The Transformation of Public Sector Reforms*, Surrey.

Clarke, J., N. Newman, N. Smith, E. Vidler and L. Westmarkland (2007), *Creating Citizen Consumers. Changing Publics and Changing Public Services*, London: Sage.

Daatland, S.O. (1990), 'What are families for', *Ageing and Society*, 10: 1-15.

— (1997), *Social Protection for the Elderly in Norway*, NOVA, Skriftserie 4. Oslo.

— and B. Svorken (1996), *Eldreråd og Elders Innflytelse – et forprosjekt*, Rapport 3, Norsk gerontologisk institutt, Oslo.

Eliasson-Lappalainen, R., and I. Nilsson Motevasel (1997), 'Ethics of care and social policy', *Scandinavian Journal of Social Welfare*, 6: 189-196.

Eikås, M., and P. Selle (2002), 'A contract culture even in Scandinavia', in U. Ascoli and C. Ranzi (eds.), *Dilemmas of the Welfare Mix. The New Structure of Welfare in an Era of Privatization*, New York.

Helse-og omsorgsdepartementet (2006), *Mestring, muligheter og mening. Framtidas omsorgsutfordringer*, St. meld Nr. 25 (2005-2006). Oslo.

Hole, T.R. (1992), *Eldremilliarden 1990 – Strakstiltak i Opprørsstorm*. Hovedfagsoppgave i Statsvitenskap, Oslo: Universitetet i Oslo.

Johansson, H., and B. Hvinden (2007), 'What do we mean by active citizenship?' in B. Hvinden and H. Johansson (eds.), *Citizenship in Nordic welfare States. Dynamics of choice, duties and participation in changing Europe*, London.

Karlsen, R (2009), 'På dagsorden', in A. Bay, A.W. Pedersen and J. Saglie (eds.), *Når velferd blir politikk. Partier, organisasjoner og opinion*, Oslo: Abstrakt.

Kymlicka, W., and N. Wayne (1995), 'Return of the citizen: A survey of recent work on citizenship theory', in R. Biner (ed.), *Theorizing citizenship*, Albany: State University of New York Press.

Leira, A. (2006), 'Parenthood change and policy reform in Scandinavia, 1970-2000', in A.L. Ellingsæter and A. Leira (eds.), *Politicising parenthood in Scandinavia*, Bristol: The Policy Press.

Lewinter, M. (1999), *Spreading the Burden of Gratitude – Elderly Between Family and State*, Ph.d. dissertation, Department of Sociology, University of Copenhagen.

Lingsom, S. (1997), *The Substitution Issue. Care Policies and their Consequences for Family Care*, NOVA, Rapport, No. 6. Oslo.

Lorenzen, H., and L. Dugstad (2008), 'The history and dilemmas of Volunteer Centres in Norway', paper delivered at conference 'Volunteering infrastructure and civil society'. Rotterdam. [http://www.cev.be/69-other_publications-EN.html]

Martin, B. (2007), 'Activism, social and political', in G. L. Anderson and K. G. Herr (eds.), *Encyclopaedia of Activism and Social Justice*, California.

Newman, J. (2001), *Modernizing Governance. New Labour, Policy and Society*, London: Sage.

Newman, J., M. Barnes, H. Sullivan and A. Knops (2004), 'Public participation and collaborative governance', *Journal of Social Policy*, 33: 203-223.

Johannesen, H. S. (2003), 'Ansiktene som mangler på TV', *Samtiden*, 3, Oslo.

Plant, R. (1992), 'Citizenship, Rights and Welfare', in A. Coote (ed.), *The welfare of citizens. Developing new social rights*, London.

Premfors, R. (1998), 'Reshaping the Democratic State: Swedish experiences in a comparative perspective', *Public Administration*, 76: 141-159.

Rothstein, B. (1998), *Just Institutions Matter. The Moral and Political Logic of the Universal Welfare State*, Cambridge.

Sehested, K. (2002), 'How New Public Management reforms challenge the roles of professionals', in *International Journal of Public Administration*, 25: 1513-1537.

Seip, A.L. (1991), 'Velferdskommunen og velferdstrekanten – et tilbakeblikk', in A.H. Nagel (ed.), *Velferdskommunen. Kommunenes rolle i utviklingen av velferdsstaten*, Bergen .

— (1994), *Veiene til velferdsstaten. Norsk sosialpolitikk 1920-75*, Oslo.

Selle, P. (1991), 'Desentralisering:Troll med minst to hovud', in A.H. Nagel (ed.), *Velferdskommunen. Kommunenes rolle i utviklingen av velferdsstaten*, Bergen.

Semetko, H.A., J.G. Blumler, M. Gurevitch, D.H. Weaver with S. Barkin and W. G. Cleveland (1991), *The Formation of Campaign Agendas: A comparative Analysis of Party and Media Roles in Recent American and British Elections*, New Jersey: Lawrence Erlbaum Associates.

Sosialdepartementet. *Om hjemmehjelp for eldre*. Innstillingskomitéen for eldreomsorgen, instilling avgitt 28. juni 1966.

Sosialdepartementet. Om hjelpeordningene for hjemmene, St.meld.nr 120 (1980-81). Oslo, 1981.

Sosialdepartementet. Sosiale tjenester, NOU 1972:30. Oslo 1972.

Sosialdepartementet, *Trygghet – verdighet – omsorg*, NOU 1992:1. Oslo, 1972.

Sosial- og helsedepartementet, *Velferdsmeldingen*. St.meld. Nr. 35 (1994-95). Oslo, 1995.

Strømsnes, K. (2003), *Folkets makt medborgerskap, demokrati og deltakelse*. Oslo: Gyldendal Akademisk.

Szebehely M. (1998), 'Changing Divisions of Carework. Caring for Children and Frail Elderly People in Sweden', in J. Lewis (ed.), *Gender, social care and welfare state restructuring in Europe*, Aldershot: Ashgate.

— (1995), *Vardagens organisering. Om vårdbiträden och gamla i hem¬tjänsten*. Lund.

— (2005) (ed.), *Nordisk äldreomsorgsforskning. En kunskapsöversikt*, Tema Nord 2005: 508, Copenhagen.

Vabø, M. (1998), *Where to Draw the Line*, (English summary) NOVA, Rapport 8/98. Oslo.

— (2002), Quality Management in Home Care – New Accountability Policy, New Challenges, (English summary) NOVA, Rapport 18/02. Oslo.

— (2006), 'Caring for people or caring for proxy consumers?' *European Societies*, 8: 403-22.

— (2007), Organisering for velferd. Hjemmetjenesten i en styringsideologisk brytningstid. Unipub, Oslo.

— (2009) 'Home care in transition: The complex dynamic of competing drivers of change in Norway', *Journal of Health Organisation and Management*, 23: 346-359.

Wærness, K. (1984), 'The Rationality of Caring', *Economic and Industrial democracy*, 5: 185-211.

Wollebæk, D., Selle, P., and Lorenzen, H. Frivillig innsats. (2000), *Sosial integrasjon, demokrati og økonomi*. Bergen: Fagbokforlaget.

6 Mobilising the active citizen in the UK

Tensions, silences and erasures

Janet Newman

Active citizens are everywhere the focus of government attention but are not the invention of governments. Citizenship has been the focus of many expansive and transformatory struggles (Newman & Clarke 2009): in 20th and 21st century Britain, such struggles have centred on claims for political inclusion and social rights, for access and voice in welfare provision, and for equality and justice in the face of economic retrenchment and securitisation. We are currently witnessing an expansion of popular mobilisations and protest, not only on 'local' issues or claims on the part of particular disenfranchised groups but also through participation in global anti-poverty and environmental movements. Not all such mobilisations are progressive, of course – protests linked to economic retrenchment following the crash of 2008 have targeted both migrants ('British jobs for British workers' was a common refrain) and the political classes (in the 2009 scandal around MPs' expenses), while 'Fathers for Justice' campaigns and the Countryside Alliance suggest a resurgence of anti-feminist and anti-cosmopolitan sensibilities.

Nevertheless, the prevalence of citizen mobilisations tends to undermine the idea that citizens have become passive, reliant on an overprotective state and on welfare services that produce dependence. What matters for governments is that citizens are active in ways that support, rather than challenge, their current political projects: it is not that citizens are not active, but that their activities need to be channeled to appropriate ends. As such, the last decades have seen a range of different political projects directed towards welfare service users, those living in run-down neighbourhoods, those without paid work and those considered to be irresponsible in the way they live their lives. Such projects have sought to dismantle the welfare settlements of the post-war years in Britain and to install new citizenship relationships and identifications. This does not necessarily mean the withdrawal of the state but a shift in its role towards the 'empowerment' of citizens in order that they might participate fully as partners in projects of modernisation and reform, and as self-steering consumers in the new economy of health and welfare services.

In this chapter I begin by tracing the contours of these political projects since 1979, then go on to analyse the forms of active citizenship mobilised in three sets of policy documents: those relating to the modernisation of the NHS, the transformation of social care services, and the renewal of 'community' and civil society. I then look across these different projects that summon up the active citizen, highlighting possible tensions between them and also suggesting ways in which the forms of active citizenship embraced by government may seek to silence or erase more activist formations. I do not suggest that these silencings and erasures are effective – activism is alive and well in Britain in the early 21st century, and citizens may well refuse or resist the new forms of identity and practice offered to them. They may, indeed, sidestep the forms of power opened up through 'empowerment' projects. But I do want to suggest that the policy discourses I analyse suggest the emergence of new governmentalities of citizenship tailored to post-welfare, globalising, consumerist formations of policy and politics.[1]

Active citizenship as political project

I begin my account by looking back to the premiership of Margaret Thatcher, which saw the emergence of significant challenges to the postwar political and economic settlements on which the welfare state had been based. Citizens were invited to become market actors, taking up share options in newly privatised public facilities and, for public housing tenants, to buy their own homes. But the New Right in this period also attempted to disrupt the welfare settlement which, they argued, had produced high levels of dependence on welfare institutions and little sense of obligation to others. The shift of responsibility from state to civil society, and to the 'private' domain of family and household, relied on citizens becoming more active, participating through voluntary work and charitable giving. These social dimensions of active citizenship were amplified in the post-Thatcher conservative governments in what Dean (2002) viewed as an 'antidote' to the excesses of Thatcherism and an attempt to return to traditional conservative values of philanthropy. But throughout the period of conservative government, forms of agency associated with trade unions, community activism and political protest were rendered less legitimate through a range of restrictive legislation – legislation, for example, that curtailed the power of trade unions following the miners' strikes of the 1980s, and that introduced new powers for the police and security forces in the aftermath of the racial tensions of the same period. The civic dimensions of citizenship – its boundaries, rights and freedoms – were being curtailed at the same time that the restructuring of the economy and cutbacks in public spending meant that the state was no longer to be viewed as a benevolent guarantor of security from poverty and illness for many citizens.

JANET NEWMAN

Under New Labour, the Conservative agendas of active citizenship were extended alongside further attempts to manage dissent and to control 'anti-social' forms of activity. But New Labour also introduced a set of welfare reform policies that sought to 'activate' those citizens not in paid employment, targeting young people, lone parents, disabled people and other groups as well as the long-term unemployed. As such, the dominant conception of activity under New Labour has been waged work, with the worker citizen at the centre of political strategies to reduce reliance on state welfare, to produce more 'flexible' labour markets and to build capacity for the global economy through programmes of self development and training. Access to and willingness to take up paid work was viewed as the basis of a thriving economy, able not only to meet the challenges of global competition but also to respond to the current financial downturn. Despite the implications of the credit crunch for the prospects of rising unemployment, in 2009 paid work remained the centrepiece of the Labour government's economic and social strategies – and indeed was being intensified through a range of new programmes. This focus on paid work was cast as a means of redressing long-standing structural inequalities, providing a means through which women, disabled people, the elderly and others could realise their potential for full participation – to gain the benefits of not only economic well-being but also the social and political benefits of full social citizenship. 'It is waged work that "inserts" people into the social; that attaches them to citizenship rights; that reduces public spending; that gives their lives a sense of value and purpose; that provides their children with role models, and, not least, ensures the happy congruence of the national and global economy' (Clarke & Newman 2004: 60).

This seemingly supports the idea that the UK is a prime example of a neo-liberal state, in which work and consumerism dominate current programmes of modernisation and welfare reform. But as I will argue, such a depiction tends to simplify what have been complex trajectories of change. While policy developments on activation through work and consumerism are certainly very significant, we can also trace a proliferation of other policy themes and discourses. In the next section I tease out some of the dominant themes in New Labour policy documents. I also look across these themes to suggest key lines of tension running through UK governance, and suggest how such tensions may be displaced – to professionals, communities and citizens themselves.

However, before going further I want to sound two notes of caution. First, although I write about the UK as a nation, the processes of devolution to countries within the UK have produced a complex pattern of governmental responsibilities and authority. I cannot hope to do justice to this complexity, so most of my focus in what follows is on policies relating specifically to England and Wales. Second, this chapter is being written in a period of profound political uncertainty, not only produced by the exhaustion of the New Labour government which produced the policy documents with which I am concerned, but also due to the extraordinary conjunction, in 2009, of profound financial and political crises. There can be no assumption, then, that the political projects of which I write will be maintained in their present form. Rather my arguments should be viewed as an attempt to capture the forces and programmes in a specific period: a period in which Britain, along with many other western European countries, was facing both 'modernising' pressures and the potential rupture of established political settlements.

Modernising projects and institutional mediations

The active citizen is a discursive construct, constituted through political and policy texts that draw on different forms of mobilising rhetoric. It is, however, not a singular subject position but summons up a range of possible identifications and forms of practice. To illustrate something of its multiplicity, this section takes extracts from policy documents produced by different government departments engaged in projects of modernisation and reform. The first are taken from documents on modernizing the National Health Service (NHS), a national institution covering England and Wales. The second batch comes from policy documents on the future of adult social care (part funded by government and with services commissioned by local authorities, with service providers coming from private companies, third-sector providers and a few residual 'in-house' providers). The third relate to the expanding role of local authorities in supporting and sustaining community and civil society. These represent different institutional mediations of the political projects of activating citizens.

Modernising the NHS

The National Health Service was the key symbolic marker of New Labour's project of reform: one that sought to respond to the demands of its middle class supporters while not abandoning less advantaged citizens. The aim was to retain the idea of a national health service free at the point of use while moving towards greater responsiveness and choice. At the centre of this project stood the citizen consumer, a modern conception of the citizen attributed with desires and expectations that could no longer be met by what elsewhere was deemed to be the 'old fashioned' health service dominated by 'producer interests':

> For fifty years, the structure of the NHS meant that governments – both Labour and Conservative – defended the interests of the NHS as a producer of services when they should have been focused on the interests of patients as the consumers of services. In today's world that will no longer do. People today expect services to respond to their needs. They want services they can

JANET NEWMAN

trust and which offer faster, higher quality care. Increasingly they want to make informed choices about how to be treated, where to be treated and by whom. (Milburn 2002)

This extract from a speech by the then Secretary of State for Health captures a dominant narrative – that citizens *had already* been transformed into consuming subjects. Although the figure of the citizen consumer had entered the policy lexicon in the early 1990s under the Conservatives, under New Labour it was presented as part of a political project to mark the historical distance from old welfarism to new consumerism (and as New Labour's name indicates, ideas of new and modern were of powerful symbolic value). Addressing people who use public services as consumers proved a potent organising device for thinking about the dynamics and direction of public services, allowing a rhetorical contrast between the dull, oppressive and unresponsive style of public service 'monopolies' and the vibrant, innovative and liberating experiences of consumer culture (and the market relations that underpinned them).

By 2006, the mechanism of choice had become embedded as the driver of modernisation of the NHS but, as the following extracts suggest, played different functions in the reform process and offered different engagements with notions of the active citizen:

> In the NHS, people now have more choice of the hospital they go to, with resources following their preferences. Patient choices have begun to play a role in developing the secondary care system, including driving down maximum waiting times (DH 2006, s3).

> For people who are clearly exhibiting signs of mild depression or anxiety, psychological ('talking') therapies offer a real alternative to medication. They can extend choice, reduce waiting times for treatment and help to keep people in work or support them to return to work (DH 2006, s 2.45)

> We will introduce a new NHS 'Life check' for people to assess their lifestyle risks and to take the right steps to make healthier choices (DH 2006, s 14).

Choice, we can see, was an instrument for improving the performance of providers, especially in terms of reducing waiting times, but also for opening up greater diversity (offering 'alternative' forms of provision). The citizen here is constituted as a 'demand-steering' actor. However, choice does not only relate to the consumption process: it also opens up greater personal responsibility for lifestyle decisions. As well as being offered choices in a new marketplace of health services, citizens were also encouraged to be *responsible* choice makers in their personal lives, supported by extensive (and expensive) programmes of public education – on obesity, smoking, exercise, parenting and, crucially, on the proper use of the health service itself with the figure of the 'expert patient'.

At the same time, a number of different programmes of patient and public involvement were launched; citizens were invited to serve on governing bodies of the new Foundation Hospitals and Primary Care Trusts; and to take part in numerous community health programmes. 'Self-help' groups played an ambiguous role, from one perspective acting as pressure groups seeking to influence policy, from another taking their place in the growing informal economy of services on which professionals and governments rely, and from yet another forming potential 'representatives' of particular interests in public participation initiatives. We can, then, trace multiple forms of active citizenship in the modernisation of health services: each of the three formations of active citizenship discussed in this volume (choice, responsibility and participation) are overlaid on each other in complex ways but with choice dominant.

Transforming social care

Some of the same dynamics were evident in government policies on social care. Here, service user movements have been key actors in the reshaping of national policy and also strongly influential in the reshaping of professional discourse. There are some parallels here with Norway (Vabø, this volume), where elder care movements resisted particular reforms and successfully mobilised to drive service improvement. However, in the UK the key role of service user movements has been that of elaborating critiques of paternalistic welfare policies and offering alternative paradigms. For physically disabled people, for example, medical models of disability were critiqued and social models put forward; for people with learning disabilities, policies that promoted their continued dependence were challenged and calls were made for more 'adult' models of citizenship. And for all groups, including older people, new models of well-being expanded the meanings of care. Such challenges were often supported by professionals who, as in the Netherlands (Tonkens, this volume), were often staunch critics of existing models; and some groups of professionals and leading advocates of change from service user movements became quite close to policymakers in the new 'partnership' ethos of policy development under New Labour.

As a result, independence and choice became central themes in the modernisation of adult social care in the UK. They were foregrounded in the 2005 white paper 'Independence Well Being and Choice', which argued that:

> Our society, quite rightly, values the independence that we all try to develop as adults: our own income, our own family and our own choices for leisure, meals and lifestyle. That is why, in future, social care should be about helping people maintain their independence, leaving them with control over their own lives, and giving them real choice over those lives, including the

JANET NEWMAN

services they use. Services must recognize the changing world, our changing attitudes and our ageing population. (Department of Health 2005: 6)

In setting out the vision for the future of social care, we find the theme of independence reiterated, here within a discourse of social inclusion:

> Our vision is one where the social inclusion of adults with needs for care or support is uprooted by... ensuring that, wherever possible, adults are treated as adults and that the provision of social care is not based upon the idea that a person's need for that care reduces them to total dependence. [other bullet points in this list omitted] (Department of Health 2005: 7)

This account is structured around two key discursive constructs of the social care service user. First is the discourse of adulthood: what is striking is the offer of 'adult' forms of citizenship, implicitly counterposed against the infantilising practices that produce dependence. This can be viewed as an extension of critiques of the welfare state and its tendencies to produce dependence, and the desired move to active, responsible citizenship as a response. However, it is important to note that the critiques here were not only from an anti-welfare politics of the right, but also from the politics of service user movements: particularly on the part of people with learning disabilities, who objected to the paternalistic and overprotective character of social care services. The rights of adult citizenship, for them, were highly desirable.

The second discursive construct is a discourse of personalisation, implying the co-production of services to meet the needs of individual persons. This clearly brings great benefits: gone (or nearly gone) are the days of universal services for an undifferentiated mass of claimants (see also De Leonardis's account of care services in the Friuli region in Italy, this volume). But the articulation of personalisation and independence, especially when conjoined with notions of choice, produce a tendency towards individualisation. The achievement of adult citizenship may, then, imply the erasure of the space in which collective claims-making practices on the part of service users take place. In addition, struggles around race or ethnicity, or against abuse or discrimination, become the focus of negotiations between services and persons: that is, wider claims-making processes are dissolved in the practice of tailoring services around individual choices, needs or ambitions.

The social care user thus condenses specific forms of active citizenship: those of becoming an active consumer, but also of taking responsibility for the matching of personal needs and delegated resources, responsibilities that had previously been carried by social care professionals involved in the commissioning and the management of resources. Service users were also invited to participate (as co-producers) in the assessment and management of their needs, as well as to become market actors, employing and managing personal assistants and seeking out appropriate services. As with the health service, we can see the inflection of independence and choice (as 'empowering' strategies) through a consumerist ethos that claimed to liberate service users from the 'dependency' cultures associated with professional/producer dominance in the past (Clarke, Smith & Vidler 2006).

However, paradoxically this is all taking place in a financial climate where eligibility for social care services is being limited to those with only the most acute needs: state-funded provision of social care is now highly conditional. Those left behind by the withdrawal of funding, people whose homes have to be sold to pay for care, and their children who face losing their expected inheritance, are now being appealed to as political parties jostle to seek the electoral support of the 'greying' population.

There are, then, striking absences and silences in the discursive framings of independence and choice. One is the social care workforce, who get only a brief paragraph in the 2005 white paper where they are recognised for 'the gift of caring' they bring to their work. A second is carers. Again, they get a brief mention in the sentence 'We want to support carers to care and individuals to live as independently as possible and for as long as possible' (DH 2005: 6). Carers, then, can care while the individuals they care for can live independently. Notions of active citizenship in relation to adult social care, this suggests, are very different in respect of service users and of carers (see Barnes, this volume). The discourse of independence, well-being and choice is partial and conditional: it applies only to some, and with independence and adulthood comes the conditionality of responsibility.

Producing 'community'

The third set of extracts I want to consider focus on the enhancement of the citizen's role in sustaining community and solidarity. This became a key responsibility of local government in the UK as its role shifted towards local *governance* through the 1990s (Stoker 1999, 2004). It is notable that in health and social care the dominant framings of active citizenship stress *independence*, while in local governance it is *interdependence* that is sought, though in both cases the goal is enhanced self-governance:

> Government has an interest in promoting active citizenship across the spectrum because:
> – it will help people and communities find *common solutions to shared problems*;
> – it can generate '*social capital*' – bridging and bonding;
> – it can stimulate *collective efficacy* – social pressures on groups of people to behave responsibly and look after each others' interests;

- it can achieve *'co-production'* – government working alongside the third sector to achieve shared outcomes in public services;
- there can be clear *progression routes* along the spectrum into forms of civic involvement which support democratic and public service infrastructure' (DCLG 2008: 15, emphasis in original).

While public participation and involvement are key themes running through the modernisation of mainstream services such as health and social care (see Barnes et al. 2007), in local governance notions of voluntary and civil activity and 'deliberative' participation come to the fore. Citizens are invited to take part in local planning exercises, civic forums, neighbourhood councils, area-based committees, residents' and tenants' groups; to become active partners in community safety initiatives, Sure Start and Children's Centre projects, youth programmes, school governance and many other developments. Local organisations, community projects and 'social entrepreneurs' are to be equipped with the skills and capacities to work in partnership with local government or to take over particular services, functions and sometimes the management of (previously public) resources. It is through local involvement and 'local partnership working' that problems of parenting, crime prevention, urban deprivation and social exclusion are to be addressed. Across these different policy framings of active citizenship run a set of deeper concerns about what has come to be termed the 'democratic deficit' – a deficit that has implications for the health of the polity and for the legitimacy of governments and Putnamesque concerns about the vitality of civil society.

However as with choice, we can see significant slippages in meaning here. A 'participative' discourse summons a quasi-democratic subject, viewing citizens as stakeholders in public service provision, participating in consultation exercises, deliberative forums or citizen panels, taking part in governance arrangements, contributing to evaluation exercises and so on. However, a 'responsible public' discourse assumes a self-disciplining subject or a self-governing community. This form of citizenship responsibility was encouraged by a range of governmental targets and strategies (for example to increase volunteering, to promote community 'ownership' of previously state owned assets and to foster civic involvement). Notions of responsible citizenship can also be traced in the rise of citizenship education in schools and programmes of induction for asylum seekers and new migrants.

The projects of capacity building and empowerment are linked to a new pedagogy of citizenship (Newman, 2010; Pykett, 2010), including new programmes designed to promote effective citizenship: for example the 'Active Learning for Active Citizenship' programme of the Home Office, and a guide for local authorities on 'Promoting Effective Citizenship and Community Empowerment' (Andrews, Cowell & Martin 2006). The latter notes that:

> Effective citizenship means, at its simplest, members of local communities being ready, willing and able to get involved in local issues. This is not simply about people having the opportunity to participate, but also about possessing the skills, knowledge and confidence they need to take part. (2006: 9)

This new pedagogy of citizenship seeks to shape active citizenship in ways that produce particular notions of effectivity: the capacity to make appropriate and informed choices, to take responsibility for one's own care and welfare, to participate in democratic and service-based forums and, above all, to participate through paid work.

Paid work is the shadow presence against which the discourses of choice, responsibility and participation I have traced throughout this section take their form. Work matters, we read, since

> Worklessness and a weak neighbourhood economy is personally damaging for the individuals involved, undermining personal confidence and their power to contribute to society, not just economically but through decision-making and community activities. It is also economically inefficient for society as a whole, and high levels of workless can:
> – undermine community cohesion
> – create the conditions for an increase in crime and anti-social behaviour, reducing the quality of life for all residents; and
> – reduce the possibility of private sector investment making it difficult for a neighbourhood to break the cycle of decline (Department for Communities and Local Government 2008: 18)

Paid work is not only associated with the benefits of active participation in the economy, then: it is also associated with benefits to local governance. Preliminary notice of a White Paper on Empowerment brought together different meanings of empowerment in an apparently seamless whole. The consultation document spelled out three themes: 1) 'encouraging active citizens/local democracy'; 2) 'improving public services'; and 3) 'work and enterprise for all'. What is important here is the overlaying of discourses of responsibility (to participate), consumerism (choice as the driver of public service improvement) and work. These are not separate activation strategies but are assembled together here. Work (or rather, paid work) is not just the route to economic inclusion for the individual, it has wide consequences.

Widening the focus of analysis to encompass activation through paid work brings into view the gendered character of contemporary governance transformations. Welfare to work policies draw more women into the labour market, while pressure on welfare states is intensifying the care needs of those whose access to state-funded services is becoming more conditional. At the same time, the pressures on 'civil society' – traditionally a gendered domain of informal labour and voluntary work (Howell 2007) – is intensifying. The idea of the self-governing subject –

JANET NEWMAN

whether an individual, a family or a community – appears gender neutral. But responsibility, in particular, is highly gendered, while women remain the dominant 'consumers' of both health and social care services, on behalf of their families as well as for themselves (Newman 2005). The elasticity of women's labour has to be further stretched to reconcile these responsibilities (to participate as carers, parents, families and members of the community) with the requirement to engage in paid work. Consumption appears as a potential resolution of the contradictions that result, with an expanding market of care and domestic services. But this in turn opens out new lines of inequality (bringing into view class-based and racialised divisions) and may intensify the division of labour within households. It also produces further exploitation of highly vulnerable groups of workers, many of whom are migrants. Active citizenship, then, can be viewed as the site of widening inequalities and new forms of gendered and racialised exploitation: themes we develop further in chapter 12.

Tensions, exclusions and erasures

Active citizenship, as I have argued, comprises multiple – and contradictory – discourses and practices. These contradictions flowed from New Labour's attempt to selectively engage with, and appropriate language, images and meanings from different political struggles. User and social movements struggling for 'empowerment' in the context of welfare policies and practices were accommodated through varieties of 'consuming' practices and identities. New Labour also drew on the mobilisation of concerns about the health of civil society and the polity, giving rise to notions of 'responsibility' for practical participation. As a result, multiple discourses of active citizenship swirl across the policy landscape, being combined – albeit uneasily – in different institutional mediations.

These political forces can be traced across the spectrum of left and right. At the time of writing, the Conservative party in waiting is promising to re-emphasise the moral responsibilities of citizenship to participate in the 'Big Society', while Labour is likely to continue its emphasis on the 'empowerment' of citizens and communities to take greater responsibility for their own welfare. However, it is not possible to draw clear lines between Labour and Conservative agendas: different philosophies of citizenship can be traced within each party, and both place primary emphasis on the significance of paid work as the route both to social inclusion and national renewal.

As in other chapters of this volume, we might trace an emerging hegemonic framing of citizenship that transforms it from a status, carrying rights and entitlements, to a set of responsibilities and duties. However, I want to suggest three issues that may complicate such a narrative. First, we need to examine not only the content of policy discourses but also to look at what is missing in or silenced by them. I pursue this in the section on exclusions and erasures, below. Second, I want to highlight the multiplicity of discourses and the tensions that this multiplicity produces – and the possibility that such tensions might fail to be resolved around a unified figure (see 'tensions' below). Third, I highlight some of the tendencies that arise in the processes of displacing tensions away from the state and polity and on to particular services, professions, communities, families and persons. Together these processes, I suggest, all complicate simple narratives of a shift from one form of citizenship to another: from rights to responsibilities, from passive to participative engagements, or from dependency to choice.

Erasures and silences

A focus on policy discourse can suggest not only the kinds of subject summoned by new governmentalities of citizenship, but also the discursive work of exclusion and the erasures of other forms of citizenship identity and citizenship practices. The summoning up of new forms of active citizenship, especially the individual citizen-consumer and individualised worker citizen, potentially erases more collective forms of identity and agency. This is an uneven process: we can trace the marginalisation of some identity-based claims (around, for example, gender and race/ethnicity) while others, especially those that can be articulated with modernising projects, are unevenly recognised: the current programme of social care modernisation could, for example, be viewed as the transformation of collective claims for recognition on the part of disabled people, those with learning disabilities and others, through individualising (choice based) and personalizing reform strategies. And while collective claims around racial discrimination and disadvantage have been successfully marginalised, 'faith'-based organisations – or at least those deemed to be 'responsible' – have been enabled to take their place as legitimate members of civil society and as actors in the growing marketplace of providers.

This last point suggests that arguments about the erasure of gender, race and other collective identities need to be made with care. We do need to examine the material and embodied ways in which active citizenship is experienced by women and men, and by different minorities. But we might also examine ways in which gender and ethnicity serve as symbolic resources around which the image of the active citizenship is constructed. The active citizen is apparently gender neutral and unracialised, and stripped of other identity-based characteristics and claims. Yet both women and some black and ethnic minority communities offer idealised images of citizenship: becoming social entrepreneurs, working hard, generating activity in the informal economy that creates wealth, maintaining social bonds of neighbourhood and community, being active in civil society organisations, performing multiple forms of paid and unpaid work without protest, being difficult to unionise, and, certainly in the case of women, being ideal consumers (McRobbie 2009). Gendered and racialised differences are, then, both present and absent.

Other erasures and exclusions appear more tangible, in particular those produced by the boundaries of nation and nationality. Citizens with marginal or ambiguous claims – migrant workers, 'sans papiers', asylum seekers – are not summoned as active citizens. But their claims to citizenship status relies on their successful accommodation (through intensive forms of pedagogy and subsequent testing) with a mythical assembly of British norms and values, including many of those promulgated by the policy documents examined in this chapter.

The discourse of work as the route to citizenship is based on its own exclusions and erasures. Some of these are based on the definition of paid work: unpaid labour (for example, informal care) is not included, though others (volunteering) are highly valued by governments. And the discourse of work as a route to social inclusion and the resolution of equality claims, especially of women but also of disabled people, people with learning disabilities, those with long-term sickness and others, erases the processes through which paid work might be the route to greater hardship.

The preceding analysis draws attention to the limited conceptualisation of power often inherent in discussions of active citizenship. Rather than viewing state-citizen as a binary in which power is distributed in a zero-sum game, I want here to consider the multiple forms of power and agency at stake in the mobilisations of active citizenship and the displacement of other forms of attachment and mobilisation. The desired economic settlement based on the worker citizen contributing in full to the attempt by 'UK plc' to position/reposition itself successfully in the global marketplace of both goods and labour contains within it the seeds of an unsettled social settlement. The contradictions between women's and disabled people's desired place in both the economy (as full worker citizens) and the greater pressures on community and civil society produced by a retreating welfare state may make a move to a new settlement extremely problematic.

As I have argued, the idea that work serves as the principal route to inclusion and equality does not take account of the intensifications of inequality produced by work itself. The consequences of deregulation, privatisation, contracting out to offshore providers, flexibilisation and other trends are likely to be profound and may further limit the power of trade unions to protect workers. The growth of marginal and peripheral workforces operating in the 'grey economy' maps uneasily onto existing patterns of marginal/peripheral citizenship (for example the use of 'illegal immigrants' in industries of exploitation, from cockle picking to prostitution). This reminds us that the attempt to form a new economic settlement for a global age based around the worker citizen and the citizen consumer rests on particular images of the nation and the maintenance of its borders.

One of the most noted characteristics of the 'Third Way' approach of New Labour was its attempt to address the fragmenting consequences of the Thatcher years and previous cycles of recession while also responding to new social claims (Newman 2001). Here, however, there is a paradox: in order to address the claims for equality and inclusion on the part of groups that had experienced failures of both redistribution and recognition, equality itself has to be reframed in terms of an individual, rather than collective, good. To understand this, we have to situate the turn to active citizenship under New Labour in its wider political project. The discourse of choice, discussed earlier in this chapter, enabled the party and government to appeal both to its traditional constituency, for whom notions of equality and justice were fundamental, and to its new middle class support base. It was a policy concept that enabled equality to be detached both from structural conditions (the causes of poverty, discrimination, etc.) and from notions of fair process within state bureaucracies and to be reinscribed in new discourses of choice:

> Extending choice – for the many, not the few – is a key aspect of opening up the system in the way we need. But choice for the many because it boosts equity. It does so for three reasons. First, universal choice gives poorer people the same choices available only to the middle-classes. It addresses the current inequity where the better off can switch from poor providers. But we also need pro-active choice (for example, patient care advisers in the NHS) who can explain the range of options available to each patient. Second, choice sustains social solidarity by keeping better off patients and parents within the NHS and public services... Third, choice puts pressure on low quality providers that poorer people currently rely on. It is choice with equity we are advancing. Choice and consumer power as the route to greater social justice not social division. (Blair 2003)

I have quoted this at length since it demonstrates something of the difficulties of ascribing consumerist forms of active citizenship to a straightforward shift to neo-liberal rule. In this extract we can see traces of social democratic concerns ('sustaining social solidarity' by defending public service provision) as well as responses to pressures from social movements ('enhancing social justice' for those in poverty). These are, however, uneasily aligned with neo-liberal conceptions of the market as the route to equality. In the end, despite increased investment in public services and some successes in programmes for their modernisation, choice has failed to serve as a form of attachment to either public services or to the wider polity. This is very evident in qualitative research among users of health and social care services in the UK, where citizens continued to prefer notions of 'membership' (members of a community, members of the public) to notions of consumption and choice (Clarke et al. 2007).

Alongside choice, as I have argued, we can see other attempted settlements based on citizen participation through deliberative practices and user involvement. One difficulty here is that participation too easily slides into consumerist logics and local community responsibility. Indeed, consumerism seems to serve as a *proxy* for democracy. The multiple inflections of choice noted earlier cannot be contained in acts of consumption and may spill over into claims for participation and voice (on the part of citizens) or into the drive towards responsibility (on the part of state actors/professionals as producers). The idealised figure of the participating citizen, renewing the polity and civil society through democratic and civic involvement, interacts uneasily with the ideal of responsible citizenship. On the one hand, we might view democratic participation (in its multiple forms) as a new kind of responsibility. But on the other, responsibility tends to direct attention to the familial, the local and the communal, all on the margins of what might be viewed as the public domain of political participation.

Displacements

The consequences of these attempts to disrupt earlier social settlements, and the images of the citizen on which they were inscribed, are difficult to assess. This is in part since the prime audience for many of the reforms traced here are public service and local government professionals/managers who are to take on new roles of empowerment, mobilisation, activation and pedagogy. We have traced elsewhere how such professionals and managers translate new discourses, aligning them to professional goals and organisational missions (Clarke et al. 2007; Newman & Vidler 2006; see also Wright 2006; Halvorsen et al. 2007 on how activation policies are translated by actors at the 'front line'). Such studies show how the tensions produced by the interaction of competing discourses are in part *displaced* to the organisational actors charged with delivering new policy agendas, actors who are of course themselves citizens (Barnes & Prior 2009).

Displacement takes place through a set of neutralising and depoliticising technologies: the social care assessment process, the rules and norms through which deliberative practices are managed, the 'contract' with the job seeker or anti-social tenant, or the systems that guide and manage the expression of consumer preferences. Displacement also arises as a result of the managerial imperatives confronting civil society, voluntary and community-based organisations as they become 'partners' with state agencies or take on devolved responsibilities. These processes of displacement are profoundly depoliticising, bracketing away potentially 'disruptive' forms of agency (as has been the case where civil society or third-sector groups become service delivers and so come to prioritise managerial imperatives imposed by the contract over value-based missions).

Active and activist citizens

The active citizen, then, is a flexible and resourceful worker, discharging her responsibilities in family and community and becoming a good consumer in the new marketplace of health and social care. Protests and forms of dissent that potentially destabilise the social order are not viewed as active citizenship. But this raises a paradox. Many of the current policy discourses of active citizenship attest to the success of social movements and other forms of activist engagement (see the Introduction to this volume), and such movements continue. As we argued in Barnes et al. (2007), new spaces in which citizens are invited to participate are not readily containable by governmental actors, but may produce new forms of social and political action. And governments themselves are attempting to expand the possibilities of new mobilisations, experimenting with web-based forms of activity, trying to catch up with Twitter and other mediums as well as creating new spaces and opportunities (the e-gov petition, for example) that can be more readily managed.

New discourses of active citizenship, then, however much they might be oriented to the production of responsible subjects and consensual processes of decision making, produce new sites of social agency. At the same time, active citizens are discursively constituted in ways that strip them of activist engagement and practices. But a binary separation of 'active' and 'activist' is perhaps unsatisfactory. There is no doubt that pressure from user groups and responses to participation exercises have produced changes in how services are delivered, albeit at the margins. The explosion of deliberative spaces creates new opportunities for citizen voice and agency, as well as bringing state actors into direct conversations with potentially challenging voices. There is also no doubt that the dispersal of power to community-based, not-for-profit and voluntary organisations carries with it the potential for new sites and spaces of agency that produce unpredictability and instability within the public policy system. And as we have seen, citizens can re-inflect dominant discourses, bringing their own meanings of citizenship to the strategies of mobilisation.

But while new forms of active participation are welcomed by governments seeking to enhance their legitimacy among particular publics, the boundaries between active and activist are carefully delineated and managed – though only visible, perhaps, when they are breached. As I write this chapter (August 2009), many people are heading to London to participate in a Climate Camp. Are these legitimate participating citizens, engaging in self-education workshops, learning new skills and attempting to mobilise support among a wider public, or are they activists, in-

JANET NEWMAN

fringing the law and seeking confrontation with the police? What notions of responsibility or welfare are they enacting (e.g. responsibility for the planet, the welfare of future generations) and how does this intersect with – or conflict with – the more localised senses of responsibility for one's own community or the welfare of one's family favoured by government? And what forms of choice are they offering? In foregrounding ethical and moral choices they are confronting market rationalities as the cause of problems rather than their solution. This may all seem a long way from a discussion of active citizenship and social welfare, but I include it since I think it throws into sharp relief the limited conceptions of both 'active citizenship' and 'welfare' in current policy frames and governmental programmes of reform.

Note

1. The coalition government elected in 2010 has many continuities with the New Labour strategies outlined here, though intensified market logics and extended citizen responsibility as part of the image of the 'Big Society'.

References

Andews, R., R. Cowell, J. Downe, S. Martin and D. Turner (2006), *Promoting Effective Citizenship and Community Empowerment*, London: Office of the Deputy Prime Minister.

Barnes, M., J. Newman, and H. Sullivan (2007), *Power, participation and political renewal: Case studies in public participation*, Bristol: Policy Press.

Barnes, M., and D. Prior (2009) (eds.), *Subversive citizens*, Bristol: Policy Press.

Blair, T. (2003), *Progress and Justice in the 21st Century*, The Inaugural Fabian Society Annual Lecture, 17 June 2003. http://politics.guardian.co.uk/speeches/story/0,11126,979507,00.html

Clarke, J. (2004), *Changing Welfare, Changing States*, London: Sage.

— (2005), 'New Labour's Citizens: Activated, Empowered, Responsibilised, Abandoned?' *Critical Social Policy*, 25 (4): 447-463.

— (2007), 'Unstable encounters: citizens, consumers and public services', *Journal of Consumer Culture*, 7 (2): 159-178.

— and J. Newman (1997), *The Managerial State: Power, politics and ideology in the remaking of social welfare*, London: Sage.

— and J. Newman (2004), 'Governing in the Modern World', in D. Steinberg and R. Johnson (eds.), *Blairism and the War of Persuasion: Labour's Passive revolution*, London: Lawrence and Wishart, 53-65.

—, J. Newman, N. Smith, E. Vidler and L. Westmarland (2007), *Creating citizen-consumers: changing relationships and identifications*, London: Sage.

—, J. Newman and L. Westmarland (2007), 'Creating Citizen-Consumers? Public Service Reform and (Un)willing selves', in S. Maasen and B. Sutter (eds.), *On Willing Selves: Neoliberal Politics Vis-à-vis the NeuroScientific Challenge*, Basingstoke: Palgrave Macmillan.

—, J. Newman and L. Westmarland (2008), 'The Antagonisms of Choice', *Social Policy and Society,* 7 (2): 245-253.

—, N. Smith and E. Vidler (2006), 'The Indeterminacy of Choice: political, policy and organisational instabilities', *Social Policy and Society,* 5 (3): 1-10.

Dean, H. (2002), *Welfare rights and social policy,* Harlow: Prentice Hall.

Department for Communities and Local Government (2008), *The Community Power Pack.* Communities and Local Government Publications (www.communities.gov.uk).

Department of Health (2005), *Independence, Wellbeing and Choice,* London: Department of Health.

Department of Health (2006), *Our Health, Our Care, Our Say,* London: DoH cmnd 6737.

Halvorsen, R., J. Nervik, J.A. Salone, T. Thoren and R. Ulmestig (2007), 'The challenge of decentralised delivery of services: the scope for active citizenship in Swedish and Norwegian activation policies', in B. Hvinden and H. Johanssen (eds.), *Citizenship in the Nordic Welfare State: Dynamics of choice, duties and participation in a changing Europe,* London: Routledge, 80-94.

Howell, J. (2007), 'Gender and civil society: time for cross-border dialogue', *Social Politics,* Winter: 415-36.

McRobbie, A. (2009), *The Aftermath of Feminism: Gender, culture and social change,* London: Sage.

Milburn, A. (2002), *Redefining the National Health Service,* New Health Network 14 January.

Ministers of State for Department of Health, Local and Regional Government, and School Standards (2004), *The Case for User Choice in Public Services.* A Joint Memorandum to the Public Administration Select Committee Inquiry into Choice, Voice and Public Services.

Needham, C. (2007), *The reform of public services under New Labour: Narratives of consumerism,* Basingstoke: Palgrave Macmillan.

Neveu, C. (2007) (ed.), *Cultures et Pratiques Participatives: Perspectives comparatives,* Paris: L'Harmattan.

Newman, J. (2001), *Modernising Governance: New Labour, Policy and Society,* London: Sage.

— (2004), 'Modernising the state: a new style of governance?' in J. Lewis and R. Surrender (eds.), *Welfare State Change: Towards Third Way?,* Oxford: Oxford University Press, 69-88.

— (2005), 'Regendering Governance', in J. Newman (ed.), *Remaking governance: peoples, politics and the public sphere,* Bristol: Policy Press.

— and J. Clarke (2009), *Publics, politics and power: Remaking the public in public services,* London: Sage.

—, C. Glendinning and M. Hughes (2008), 'Beyond modernisation? Social care and the transformations of welfare governance', *Journal of Social Policy,* 37 (4): 531-557.

— and E. Vidler (2006), 'Discriminating customers, responsible patients, empowered users: consumerism and the modernisation of health care', *Journal of Social Policy,* 35 (2): 193-209.

— (2010), 'Towards a pedagogical state? Summoning the "empowered" citizen', *Citizenship Studies,* 14, 6: 711-723.

Office of Public Service Reform (2002), *Reforming our Public Services,* London: OPSR.

Pykett, J. (2010), 'Introduction: the pedagogical state: education, citizenship and governing', *Citizenship Studies*, 14, 6: 617-620.

Scourfield, P. (2007), 'Social care and the modern citizen: client, consumer, service user, manager and entrepreneur', *British Journal of Social Work*, 37: 107-122.

Stoker, G. (1999) (ed.), *The New Management of British Local Governance*, Basingstoke: Palgrave Macmillan.

— (2004), *Transforming Local Governance: From Thatcher to New Labour*, Basingstoke: Palgrave Macmillan.

Wright, S. (2006), 'The administration of transformation: A case study of implementing welfare reform in the UK', in P. Henman and M. Fenger (eds.), *Administrating Welfare Reform: International transformations in welfare governance*, Bristol: Policy Press.

7 Dividing or combining citizens

The politics of active citizenship in Italy

Ota de Leonardis

Active citizenship: from politics to policy

During the 'trente glorieux' years following WWII, the Italian welfare system developed along two different lines. In the first, political cultures and practices imbued with particularist tendencies and even patronage produced a weak adherence to universalistic principles in social benefits and public service provision. As a consequence, families – particularly women – went on bearing the greater burden of caring for their members in need, so conferring on the Italian welfare system a familial nature. A central role was also played by private charities and church bodies, partly because of the cultural and political influence of the Catholic Church. These features of social service provision suggest that the Italian welfare system, categorised as 'corporatist' by Esping-Andersen, has in fact greater affinities with the 'Mediterranean' model (Ferrera 1996; Mingione 2001).

But a second, and equally important, line of development in the same period configured a welfare regime of rights consistent with the universalistic model. I refer here to normative innovations that were promoted by social claims and political mobilisations, as well as what would now be termed 'practices of active citizenship'. In that period, Italy was marked by a high level of politicisation, a strong communist party, trade unions playing an important role even in welfare issues, widespread and diverse social movements (not least women's liberation), the mobilisation of public service staff, and a myriad of local initiatives and bottom-up experiments.[1] Three building blocks of an universalist welfare were introduced: (i) the Workers' Statute (1971) that not only established rights linked to employment status but also allowed work to be recognised as a right in itself; (ii) new legislation on mental health (1978) that accomplished fifteen years of de-institutionalisation and the invention of new services, and abolished internment in psychiatric hospitals, and which led to a more general mood against total institutions and in favour of granting civil and social rights also for the disabled and children; and (iii) the health reform instituting the National Health Service (in 1980).

However, by the time the National Health Service was established the situation was already undergoing rapid change: the above-mentioned social forces were exhausted, and the 'crisis of the welfare state' was officially inaugurated. A phase of 'reforming reforms' began. Throughout the 1990s, the discourses and practices of welfare re-organisation were generally steered by criticisms against paternalism and welfare dependency and directed towards giving citizens an active role. 'Activation' – in its various meanings – became a key word in Italy as well as in other states, and underpinned the efforts of Italian governments during the 1990s to respond to the requirements for entering the European Union. These efforts produced an important cycle of administrative reform, inspired by the model of New Public Management that introduced principles of responsiveness of public administrations towards citizens. It also led to a national law on social welfare in 2000, providing devices for the 'activation' of recipients and for 'participation' in local policy governance.

A third set of reforms was heralded in the Italian Constitution of 2001, which introduced the principle of subsidiarity. Subsidiarity was both vertical, entrusting many social responsibilities to local levels of government, considered 'closer' to citizens; and horizontal, enhancing the self-organising potential of civil society. Public institutions, as the new Article 118 stated, were to have the task of 'favouring the autonomous initiative of citizens, single and associated, to perform activities of general interest, on the basis of the principle of subsidiarity.' These changes revealed a strong impulse to promote active citizenship in the relationships between citizens and institutions. Welfare policies constituted the main laboratory in which these principles were enacted, in both the governance and the organisation of services. It is here that active citizenship is most strongly developed and expressed. In the re-organisation of welfare, which in Italy is based on a model of a welfare mix between state, market and civil society, it is civil society, termed the 'third sector', that was to be the central actor in policy design and implementation.

These reforms mean that expressions of active citizenship are now very different from those expressed in the political mobilisation and bottom-up initiatives of the 1970s. In the present discourses, in the forms of organisation and in the practice of active citizenship, a shift can be easily identified in policy arenas from political participation to civic involvement.[2] Militant politics have been replaced by volunteering in service provision; taking part in citizen organisations is now less expressed through the repertoires of contentious politics (Tilly & Tarrow 2006), than through involvement in the local governance of welfare policies; initiatives aimed at constructing services from the bottom up have given way to 'social entrepreneurship'. An important question here is how far it is possible to recognise the success of past claims for broadening and strengthening political citizenship in these new forms of active citizenship; or whether instead they are the fruit of the incorporation and neutralisation of such claims within the 'new spirit of capitalism' as Boltanski and Chiappello maintain (Boltanski & Chiappello 1999; see also

OTA DE LEONARDIS

Tonkens, this volume) so that they are made consistent with the liberal idea of self-organisation of civil society. A clear and unequivocal answer to this question cannot be given since, as the research below illustrates, local contexts are different, policy arenas are shaped differently and different ways of becoming active citizens can be observed – with different repertoires of action and relative grammars of justification. Moreover, the ground for research looks somewhat like a laboratory, in which active citizenship continues to be in the making, processes are still open and at best research can only suggest tendencies.

The three types of active citizenship illustrated in the introduction to this volume can be easily recognised and they will recur in the course of this chapter: the citizen as consumer (service recipient) will appear, as will the citizen as entrepreneur ('social' entrepreneur as well as 'entrepreneur of him/herself'). Also appearing will be citizens as responsible individuals/families, or more precisely made 'responsible for the autonomous production of the required services' (and similar updated forms of familism). And in certain policy contexts, the active role of citizens – especially as service recipients – is expressed through voice and participation in the decisions on the services concerning them. This is the political version of active citizenship.

These different expressions of active citizenship are combined in different ways. The combinations remain unstable in Italy, but I will show how some are tending to crystallise in two regional welfare regimes. Attention will be focused on service recipients, their position in the policy arenas and the repertoires they have for exercising an active role. In particular, since we are observing the field of welfare, where the weakest voiceless citizens are most concentrated – 'silenced subjects', as they were once called – special attention will be paid to the position they assume in policy arenas where active citizenship is promoted. Does the spread of active citizenship involve the weakest citizens and empower them, and if so, how and when? Are the weakest recipients involved in choices or are they disciplined by subjugation? Do practices of active citizenship tend to generate and extend spaces for citizen participation politically (in forms both of conflict and co-operation), or do they silence political subjectivity?

From this exploration an important problem will emerge precisely at the junction between citizens as welfare recipients and their interlocutors as service providers – often themselves active citizens. What kind of relations is created *between* citizens, particularly between these two types of active citizens? I will argue that within practices of active citizenship, dynamics of expansion and inclusion (or conversely, of division and selection) take shape; I will also argue that processes of disciplining, silencing and subjugation take place between citizens, as do processes of collective support for the most disadvantaged in order to make their voice heard. But the position and action of public institutions are not extraneous to these two dynamics: rather, it is through the interface between public institutions and citizens that new formations of active citizenship are translated and enacted.

New welfare policies and active citizenship: a view from the recipient's perspective

Research on the re-organisation of welfare in Italy has highlighted significant differences between regions.[3] The introduction of vertical subsidiarity and the subsequent devolution of welfare policies to regional governments has brought about the emergence of different regional welfare models. These regional differences concern the levels and modes of recognising citizens' social rights as well as the means of promoting their agency. Regional differences, then, offer a fertile ground for comparative research into ways in which active citizenship is constructed.

The research I am drawing on investigated how citizens' activation has been interpreted by social/healthcare and social housing policies in several regions – both at the level of governance, in which citizens are involved in policymaking, and at the level of service provision, where citizens are supposed to be active service recipients and caretakers. I focus on the regions of Lombardy and Friuli-Venezia Giulia, where active citizenship takes on very different profiles. The analysis follows the approach based on policy instruments developed by Lascumes and Le Galès (2004, 2007). The choice of investigating 'governing through instruments' is appropriate for the analysis of governing 'at a distance', a form of governing that does not intervene authoritatively but rather makes (or lets) 'the actors do', involving them in the policy arena (see also Newman & Clarke 2009). This focuses attention on the ways in which citizens get moving and organise themselves, how they are embedded within policy arenas and what the organisational effects might be (Bifulco et al. 2007; see also Barnes, Newman, Sullivan 2007, especially chapter 4).

I focus on two types of activation instruments. The first – following a contract prototype typical of marketised welfare – confers on citizens the status of partners in their relations with institutions or other citizens. Here (section 3) we will see that the contract prototype is translated into diverse policy instruments and gives rise to diverse forms of citizen activation. The second type of activation we highlight concerns the activation of citizens as belonging to a territory (see also Neveu, this volume). In section 4 we will explore the 'space' of citizenship, its constituent anchorage that ties it to a territory. We will observe the process of territorialisation of welfare policies, at the intersection between 'place and people' (Donzelot 2006) and discover diverse configurations of citizens and territory.

OTA DE LEONARDIS

Contractualised welfare policies: active citizens as recipients or providers of services

The process of externalising services and creating welfare mixes – a key characteristic of the re-organisation of welfare in Italy – has been accompanied by the spread of contracts regulating both public/private partnerships at the level of governance, and the relations between citizen-users and services at the level of service provision. Such services, mostly provided by the so-called 'third sector', are supposedly the expression of an organised civil society. My focus here is on the level of service provision, where recipient-citizens and citizen providers meet, and therefore where the critical issues concerning active citizenship arise. The contractualisation of service relationships offers a fertile ground for tackling the question of how far active citizenship opens up dynamics of discipline and exclusion, or of developing support for the active exercise of citizens' rights. Does the definition of recipients and providers as partners in a contract change the asymmetry of power intrinsic to the service relationship?

To answer that question, we will examine two contractual arrangements introduced in Lombardy and Friuli respectively: the 'voucher' and the 'budget for care'. Both are core instruments in the welfare policies characterising the two regions, and they reveal some crucial differences between them. Both cases concern monetary transfers particularly designed for 'weak subjects' – the elderly, the disabled, users of mental health services – in order to support them to remain in their home environment and avoid institutionalisation. In both cases a contract is set up between the user and the third-sector organisation delegated to provide the service. However, the voucher and the budget for care are designed in different ways. They create two different kinds of service organisations and two different active beneficiary positions (Monteleone 2005, 2007; Bifulco & Vitale 2006; Giorgi & Polizzi 2007).

The voucher is a coupon for acquiring social and healthcare services given by the public authority to the citizen-user, who is free to choose one of the accredited private suppliers competing with each other. In the Lombardy welfare model – which in Italy represents the most extreme neo-liberal version of the re-organisation of welfare – it acts as a strategic lever for reducing public services to a residual role by externalising the supply of services to private officially non-profit organisations (and qualified as initiatives of the civil society). It is based on a market model of self-regulating processes of supply and demand, with active citizens being able to express on the one hand their freedom of choice as recipient-consumers, and on the other hand their freedom to generate new economic initiatives as providers. Last but not least, the Lombardy model promotes 'responsible citizenship'. The family – always written in the singular in normative texts! – is given a central role in the 'autonomous production of services'. In this scenario, the contract for using the voucher corresponds to the prototype of the buying-selling contract in the market. It is therefore of a private, rather than public, nature.

'Budget for care' is a typical policy instrument in the Friuli welfare regime. Friuli is noted for its strong culture of public service provision and for the 'territorialisation' of services in local communities. Always at a local level, it supports the third-sector organisations, but with a fairly restrictive form of regulation that encourages collaboration with public services in order to strengthen the social protection of individuals. The aim of citizen activation is geared to weaker citizens and is defined as 'creating opportunities' for the growth of 'possible autonomy'.

These traits of the Friuli welfare regime are most evident in the health sector, where a patrimony of technical and institutional innovations was realised and released during the course of de-institutionalisation in psychiatric services, with the closure of asylums and the creation of territorially based services to take their place. The Friuli region was the cradle of this transformation and of the social pressure that promoted it, and it is the region where the national law legalising it has been most fully implemented (De Leonardis 2006). The guiding principle behind these transformations – promoting asylum inmates as 'protagonists' – has left its mark in the focus on the weakest recipients and in the ways of understanding their agency and freedom.

Budget-for-care is an item in the public social and healthcare budget that citizen-users may use for the care project they choose to pursue. The contract stipulating use involves three partners: the citizen-user, the third-sector provider and the local public authority responsible for the citizen's well-being. The public authority partner plays a strategic role in the contract, supporting the citizen-user (i.e. the weaker contracting party) via the system of public services. The public authority attributes the budget to the third-sector provider and monitors the compliance of the contract. The involvement of this public authority thereby confers a public nature on the contract.[4]

Budget-for-care binds the contracting parties to a 'personalised project for care and re-habilitation' of the user. Such a project involves changes in the living conditions of the citizen-user relative to three 'axes': 'home, work and social life'. Through this contract, the public authority binds the third-sector provider to operate in the interests of all three. Therefore the provider is charged with pursuing the improvement of housing conditions ('the quality of social habitat') of the person involved; to increase his/her chances of work, or at least of conducting an active life; and to enrich his/her network of personal acquaintances. It follows that the subject matter of the contract is very different from the one underpinning the voucher system. In the voucher system, the contract concerns a package of social healthcare services at home, corresponding to a standard assignment record. The object of the transaction in the voucher system concerns the performance to be provided, while with the care

OTA DE LEONARDIS

budget it concerns changes in the three components of the individuals' well-being – what counts are the results obtained in all three.

Let us now take a look at how the two types of contract shape the service relations between recipients and providers. The focus in particular is on changes to the asymmetry of power between them, bearing in mind that the recipients in both cases are weak subjects, and that both partners are supposed to be active citizens. With the voucher, the agency of recipients is based on their freedom to choose a service provider and draw up a contract which equates them to market consumers with the 'negative freedom' of exit (Hirschman 1970): to change suppliers (of pre-packaged services) in a supposedly competitive market. It turns out that the exit option is seldom used, and then mostly by citizens with a stronger so-cio-economic background.

Are all the others then 'satisfied customers'? Probably not; it seems more likely that this formal freedom does not imply real contractual power for users. Neither does it represent any threat to the services, nor provide sufficient information for quality checks on services in a compe-titive market. Conversely, citizens' organisations providing services only have very soft obligations towards citizen-recipients: the contract does not bind them to respond to any needs for service changes that could arise, nor to listen to the voice of the person involved. Moreover, they can choose their clients and exclude the most burdensome and difficult cases. Beneficiaries who have more serious problems and/or less con-tractual power are more exposed to the risk of non-renewal of the con-tract by the provider. In the world of welfare, it is indeed easy to become an undesirable client. Criteria of performance in the market framework give the service organisations powerful incentives and constraints to be-have in this way.

All in all, the recipient, with little exit power and even less voice, is forced to 'choose' loyalty, or rather to adapt to a tie of dependence (Mon-teleone 2005; De Leonardis 2009). This gives the service the power to decide on modes of intervention, on what must be done for the custo-mer, and also what the customer must do: this contractual arrangement stresses the recipient's responsibilities more than his/her freedom, and this is supported through moral and moralising arguments.[5] Many as-pects of this arrangement recall the *contrat d'allégeance* (contract of sub-jugation) that Alain Supiot (2004, 2007) has observed in the world of work.

In the budget-for-care framework, on the contrary, the agency and free-dom of the recipient is exercised not in choosing a provider from which to acquire pre-packaged services, but in choosing the services to be pro-vided: that is, in participating in the definition of one's own personalised project, in everyday choices to put it into practice, and in the ongoing evaluation of its effects. Individuals express themselves not through 'exit' but rather through the 'voice' option. But as we are talking about really 'fragile' people, with limited autonomy and a restricted capacity for control over their lives, we must have a closer look at the way in which voice functions here.

The contractual power and agency of the weaker partner is not presupposed in the contract but is underscored as its objective. It is what all the partners are committed to cultivate. Consequently, the power asymmetry between services and users is taken into account as a problematic question to be dealt with in everyday service regarding practical issues in people's lives, such as where to live, how to run a home, deal with troublesome family ties, get around the neighbourhood, choose a context for gaining work experience, etc.

All these are food for discussion and decisions shared by interested parties and operators. Interviews and observations gathered in the field show that operators often highlighted questions of power intrinsic to their function – for example, regarding the 'tensions between supporting and controlling people', as they often put it. Operators tackle questions of power like these, since the choices at stake regard *real-life issues* – more than matters of professional performance – where the person whom it concerns has the right and the competence to make decisions and have a voice.

Furthermore, in the person's project several actors are involved, along with her and the operator. On the one hand, the three parties of the contract are engaged in an Evaluation Unit, and every three months they check the progress of the project and the changes under way in the user's life. On the other hand, as the project is about real-life matters, also relatives and friends as well as actors from other welfare services or citizens' organisations are involved.[6] There are discussions and exchanges of ideas on the issues to be dealt with leading to agreements on actions to be undertaken. The plurality of voices appears to be a key factor for enhancing the user's voice. It points to the presence of a plurality of forms of support that weak people can lean on when expressing their own voice. These multiple ties and relationships of interdependence can be contrasted with the voucher system, which is characterised by one-way dependence in a dual relationship between user and service.

To sum up, the option of voice is created by building the appropriate conditions for the weakest to acquire and enact their 'capability for voice' on their personalised projects (Sen 1994; see also Bonvin & Farvacque 2006; Bifulco et al. 2007).

A further element favouring the expression of voice by the most disadvantaged lies in the organisational effects of service relationships (De Leonardis 2009). In the voucher situation, the service relationship ends with performing the service. The voucher only organises the provider-customer exchange. Customers are only involved in a dual relationship with the main provider: they have no contact with other providers or managers from the service organisation. The service organisation operates in isolation: absorbed in a competitive market, it is organised like a company with a corporate structure chasing an increase in market share: networks with other service organisations are limited to enhancing their lobbying power. The operators who carry out their duties at the user's home also lack a voice and an organisational context in which to use it.

Let us now look at the organisational environments around the budget-for-care. Organisation – or rather, organising (Czarniawska 1997; Weick 1995) – is precisely what the service relationships around the budget-for-care tend to generate and cultivate. On the one hand, service organisations have open, fluid borders and a decisively hybrid nature. Recipients continuously move across these borders and into hybrid situations. On the other hand, such organisations are expected to promote and cultivate other organisations, projects and processes in a variety of real-life fields. In order to implement personalised projects, service organisations find themselves multiplying organisations.

From the point of view of the recipient, the differences between the organisational environments generated by the budget and the voucher systems are crystal clear. There is a marked organisational vacuum around the voucher user, in sharp contrast with the density of organisational texture around the budget user, with a variety of spaces where relationships of cooperation and support can arise, and where discussion and conflict and co-responsibility are formed. This goes far beyond a service relationship as usually understood.

This finding mirrors Robert Castel's description of the present re-organisation of welfare: the weakening of social protections, he says, is happening precisely through the weakening or dismantling of 'collectives' and the redefinition of citizens as 'collections of individuals' (Castel 2001). The voucher produces 'collections of individuals': isolated consumers in the market who are free but alone – 'individus par defaut' – while the budget generates real-life contexts dense with 'collectives' in which people participate, and get support and recognition.[7]

As for our question on the inclusion-exclusion cleavage, the voucher shows clear tendencies to select, exclude and discipline while the budget-for-care shows marked tendencies to include, backing the agency of weak citizens. These result from the different ways in which asymmetries of power and inequalities are faced.

Focusing on territory-making: territories as private or public spaces

The so-called 'localisation' of welfare policies – another driver in the processes of reorganising traced in several chapters of this volume – has taken place in Italy, too. As well as the devolution of welfare to regional administrations, we can also trace a territorialization of policies, especially of urban policies (housing, the regeneration of degraded areas, as well as urban safety) in which local governments make considerable investment. Altogether, we are witnessing the emergence of *territorial modes of governance* (Bricocoli, De Leonardis & Tosi 2008; Bricocoli & Savoldi 2009). The 'territory' is the object of much concern: it influences repertories of action, vocabularies of motives and the justifying grammars of citizens' initiatives and organisations. In a way, active citizenship becomes a matter of 'taking care of the territory'.

The territory is thus a crucial point of observation for a critical analysis of active citizenship, bringing into view the variable of space (so important for issues of citizenship; see Neveu, this volume). Do territorial practices generate selective and excluding dynamics and divisions between citizens, or are they directed towards widening citizenship and creating support for the inclusion and participation of the weakest citizens in discussions and choices relating to their collective interest? How are inclusion and exclusion inscribed in the organisation of space and the way active citizens construct their territory?

The territory to be cared for may be treated as an extension of a personal private space. Here citizens may mobilise through a rationale of appropriation seeking to enclose a territory in order to exclude or expel other citizens. The citizens (or denizens) suffering such exclusions are usually foreign migrants, but such a rationale also becomes evident in mobilisations against the construction of a mosque or a gypsy camp, or in favour of fencing off public areas. In a more benign variation, the territory is treated as a common good for which all citizens are responsible.

Here, citizen initiatives are developed to create self-run residential areas in which 'to live among ourselves'; the possible involvement of disadvantaged individuals or families denoting a social calling in the project. Catholic culture strongly pushes towards such a communitarian orientation. In other policy contexts, the territory is instead constructed as a public space: the space for taking part in discussions and decision making over issues of collective interest, starting from the fact that citizens have a direct knowledge of it, given that it is the context of their everyday lives (see Neveu, this volume, on the constitution of *les habitants* in the French context of participation).

Territorial governance and active citizenship are interdependent (if not mutually constitutive) and are formed together (Ostrom 2005). I want to put this interdependence under the microscope by discussing the results of a second comparative study about the two welfare regimes of Lombardy and Friuli regarding urban programmes in two cities, Milan and Trieste. In both cases they concern social housing programmes that combine in various forms 'people and place' (Donzelot 2006), meaning that they are supposed to integrate interventions on people (such as traditional social services and policies) with those on living spaces (like urban and residential policies).

OTA DE LEONARDIS

The research carried out into social housing policies in Milan registers the influence of a market frame, placing property prices, private property and more generally the appeal of the city in a competitive rationale. Indications of this include the presence of strong economic interests in the partnership bodies for managing those programmes; a selective orientation concerning the districts and social groups in question; and a tendency to exclude the most problematic ones (see also Ruppert 2006). In governing the territory, the municipality tends to emphasise issues of safety, introducing preventive and repressive programmes and actions against potentially dangerous social groups (such as Islamic immigrants and gypsies).

Where is active citizenship in this scenario? It is provided, perhaps, by citizens' associations, philanthropic agencies or bank foundations offering social housing through agreements with regional or municipal governments for public funding or the release of public land. Consider a social housing project launched by an influential Catholic-based bank foundation in agreement with the region and aimed at promoting the social integration of persons and families with social problems by improving their housing conditions – one example of many supposedly civil-society-originated projects. This programme is designed to create 'villages', a widespread definition for residential development in Milan. The foundation provides the construction of estates (entrusted to a real estate company with social aims). It governs the selection of recipients based on the idea of *mixité*, by combining 'normal' families (medium-low incomes and/or young couples) with 'problematic' families (including migrants). The programme also involves volunteer associations and non-profit companies providing social services. There is no involvement of the local system of public health/social services. Residents are expected to assume formal responsibility particularly for the management of common services and areas.

The selection of recipients is a crucial element of the analysis. The programme was created and operates independently of public regulation of social housing by the Regional Agency (ALER), even with regard to the selection of recipient citizens and the assignment of apartments. Selection is thus not subordinated to publicly determined procedures and criteria of entitlement. It is carried out with procedures and criteria that are established independently by programme promoters, and is thus not marked with forms of selective universalism based on positive discrimination or other public values. We therefore find ourselves faced with private decisions: the allocation of dwellings is no longer made on the basis of entitlement to a right – of which public authorities, criteria and procedures are guarantors – but looks more like a concession, or perhaps a co-optation, based on privatistic and particularistic norms. The contract signed by the tenants, based on the exercise of their freedom of choice (we are in Lombardy), again presents some similarities with 'adhesion contracts' – adhesion, in this case, to the programme and its rules, together with the rules of the community or 'village' it creates. The responsibility for supporting the situation of *mixité* also rests on their shoulders.

If we look at this from the perspective of the weakest citizens taking part in the programme – those problematic families whose inclusion legitimises the social vocation of the programme itself – inclusion comes to mean subjection, since such citizens are easily blackmailed and risk being blamed if anything goes wrong in the self-management of the village. Since the programme is not yet active, it is too soon to say whether these tensions and exclusions may be occurring within the villages, but on the basis of the literature, it is a reasonable hypothesis. Overall, we find ourselves faced with the initiative of an organisation with a social or civic vocation that is, however, private, endowed with the power to intervene on residential issues, which substitutes public powers and responsibilities for privatised actions (on the part of the agency) and personalised responsibilities (for the residents). The result is the creation of a social and residential space with its own rules of membership, a space that is privatised, unlike the city as a whole and its statute as a public space.

In the case of the Friuli region, I will focus on Trieste, the region's main city and very influential on welfare matters at the regional government level. Trieste has a high level of public welfare services and activities in deprived areas and an orientation to addressing, together with their recipients ('heavy users', they say), their social habitat and activating local resources and citizen organisations to improve it. The principal agencies influencing this orientation are the local agencies of the health service management, not least because of the legacy of the transformation of mental health provision mentioned earlier. Traces remain in both managerial and professional cultures of the lessons learnt from 'accompanying the mad back into town'.

This explains the apparent inconsistency of the programme (De Leonardis & Monteleone 2007; Bifulco, Bricocoli & Monteleone 2009). It is guided by the city's public health authority, but it is applied to difficult public housing estates, so that it deals with both people and their context, including the physical context of housing. The programme, called 'Micro-areas, Health and Community Development', was developed experimentally in 1988, put into effect at a local level in 2005 and then launched regionally in 2006. It implements the directive of the Friuli region for 'integration' between diverse policies both at a managerial and operational level, and is based on an agreement between the Health Authority, the Public Housing Agency and the municipality's welfare system. This agreement is intended firstly to bring together the staff operators of these different public services with the third sector in circumscribed areas of the city, and secondly to develop joint actions both on places and people, integrating social interventions, health care interventions and rehabilitation of housing and public spaces.

OTA DE LEONARDIS

Full accomplishment of social citizenship, in particular with respect to well-being and health rights, is considered an indispensable condition and vehicle for citizens acquiring and exercising an active role in the decisions that involve them and their life contexts. Activation is evident in transforming situations of deprivation by developing individual capabilities for action and for voice (in the same vein as the instrument of budget-for-care already examined), and also in involving citizens in choices concerning their life contexts, their neighbourhoods. The programme was developed in nine micro-areas (with approximately 17,000 residents out of a total of 245,000); each has a micro-area manager and an open centre, both aimed at linking citizens and institutions.

How have citizens of those areas been involved and activated, and how do they participate? The programme stresses the territorial vocation of health services and of the broad network of relationships between the public and the third sector, which are marked by a deep-rooted capacity for cooperation. The different health and social departments work on site throughout the territory, 'going down into the streets': 'We go where people live, we don't wait for them to come to the service.' They make themselves visible in a neighbourhood – for instance, by setting up a yellow beach umbrella in a square on a summer day, where public health service operators stand and wait for opportunities to practice active listening strategies. They listen to people talking about themselves, noting situations, providing assistance and participating in more or less organised citizen groups. In this sense, the programme enhances people's voices, their chances to speak, protest and make plans.

The territory is thus no longer the place sending single cases to the service, but the arena in which citizen demands, resources and initiatives are displayed. Micro-areas play the role of incubators for different kinds of self-organised initiatives. Groups of senior citizens take lessons from a physiotherapist and then organise soft gymnastics, take walks and go on excursions; another group of citizens creates an association with the task of transforming an abandoned, weed-ridden, rubbish dump of a lot into a garden and plant trees and flowers; another group organises itself to launch a project on the upgrading of a city square, and participates in meetings and discussions with the public housing authority, urban planners and experts from several universities.

Finally, the programme also intends to monitor improvements in citizen health (understood in a broad sense as well-being: we are in Friuli). Micro-areas are explored to find out what is not working in ordinary organisational practices and what needs to be reorganised to enhance well-being. This strategy also intends to expose institutions to a redefinition of their tasks and thus to the dynamics of institutional reflexivity. 'No possibility of choosing: everything enters the micro-area's base': citizens' voices – their demands, protests, proposals and initiatives – are intended to feed this institutional reflexivity, and thus become an integral part of the political process.

The cases of Milan and Trieste thus offer two different ways of understanding and valuing the active role of the citizens in a territory, and two corresponding territory-making processes. These differences recall the alternative 'I belong here, it belongs to me/us' that Newman and Tonkens mention (this volume). The social housing programme in Milan reveals an orientation that increases residential opportunities for disadvantaged people too but it gives the organising territory a privatistic character: both as a space for exercising decision making powers (in electing the participants and imposing the rules of the game) that displaces public authority and as a closed space, a separate social and residential area with respect to the city.

In the micro-areas programme in Trieste, however, territories become public spaces in which citizens – both as individuals and in association with each other – enter into a dialogue with the institutions responsible for their well-being. Issues of collective interest are discussed from different perspectives; decisions are granted public visibility and their consequences are submitted to criticism and judgment. Learning about the management of commons is nourished between institutions and citizens. Here, citizen involvement in the territory considered to be a public space acquires the features of political participation.

Conclusions

The analysis I have presented in this chapter has pointed to significant variations in how citizens are involved in welfare service provision. It has also traced not only the different positions of citizens as welfare users in different governance regimes, but also different ways in which citizens are involved in territorial processes of governance. Here I go on to consider how these might be related, and how different images of the active citizen are articulated. Recalling the images of the active citizen in Lombardy and Friuli, how do the images of citizens involved in voucher use, either as recipients or providers, converge with those of citizens bent on constructing their own 'village'? And how far do the images of citizens as budget users and as residents of micro-areas converge?

The two contexts of activation examined in each of the two regions offer similarities: they cohere around different regional 'political projects' (Newman & Clarke 2009) and different modes of governance, giving rise to different forms of citizenship. In the Lombardy regime we found significant traces of consumer citizenship, in line with the marketisation of services: recipient citizens as consumers, moral arguments responsibilising individuals and families, and citizen organisations that function like companies. Citizens are empowered – if at all – by enlarging their own private sphere. In Friuli we found a more political moulding of active citizenship, which recalls the social movements (especially women's) claims for 'politics of everyday life' but also the public institu-

OTA DE LEONARDIS

tions' strong activism in matters of welfare, corresponding to social protections established as rights.

How does the exercise of active citizenship feed the dynamics of selection and exclusion (or of expansion and inclusion)? Having taken the most disadvantaged recipients as sensors for detecting these dynamics, we found that these processes are generated and fostered precisely *in the relations between citizens*. Normative and institutional factors influence the forms that the relations between citizens take, including how active citizenship is positioned along the private/public axis.

The normative basis of the two types of contracts regulating relations between citizens as recipients and as providers (a voucher and a budget-for-care) is very different. The voucher is of a private nature corresponding to the original prototype of a market exchange between two formally equal subjects, endowed with an equal 'autonomy of will' (the traps of which are well known from Marx on with regard to contracts for the workforce). The contract for budget conversely brings in the public authority as a third partner and gives the signed agreement and the ties it establishes a public nature (whose ratio is well known from the history of collective work contracts). In the voucher, the contractual power of the recipient is presupposed, while in the budget-for-care it is finalised in the contract. Inequalities between the contractors remain private in the first case, while in the second they are a matter of public responsibility.

We also glimpsed at how the imputation of responsibility lurks behind the freedom of the voucher's contractors and how it justifies discipline and subjugation. In the exchanges between citizens, inequalities lie concealed: the normative framework furnishes no vocabulary through which inequalities might be recognised. The normative framework for the creation of 'villages' in Milan provides the acquisition of public ground by private citizens who are able to choose who else can live there. This selection is no longer a matter of public responsibility and choice – it is the prerogative of private actors, however well intentioned. This private and particularistic configuration gives private actors the corresponding grammars of justification to select, construct access thresholds, close off communities and resort to cream-skimming practices: in brief, to introduce dynamics of exclusion and discrimination. Conversely, the Friuli emphasis on public responsibility corresponds to a universalistic orientation, inclusive of the most disadvantaged citizens. The field of action in which citizens interact – both in personalised projects and living spaces – belongs to a public regime in which discussions and choices are publicly visible.

The analysis of institutional factors shows that service organisations in Lombardy correspond to the prototype of a market company, and as such relate to the citizen recipient as customer. The customer moves in an organisational vacuum, stripped of collective belongings and sources of support – of those 'supports to individuation' that Castel (2009) talks about. Conditions of isolation are created in this vacuum which expose recipients, especially if disadvantaged, to the risk of choices imposed by the service organisation and dictated more by corporate rationales than by the voices of the users. It is in this vacuum that selection dynamics take place and conditions of subjection are set up. In contrast in Friuli, both in the case of budget-for-care and in the micro-areas, 'multipliers' of organisations and networks are at work, feeding a variety of situations where people get involved and interact with one another and with public authorities. That is, participation is a shared, rather than individuated, experience.

I have already shown that the inclusiveness of this dense organisational texture is evident in relation to the weakest recipients and their capacity for voice. I will add that the density goes side by side with the variety of people involved, so that different citizens combine by enacting, say, de Tocqueville's 'art of associating together' (de Tocqueville 1988: Book II, Part II, chapter 5). Recalling his main argument on democracy is not without relevance here. It serves to underline the fact that in this organisational texture the relations that unequal and different citizens install between them are political, in the sense that they are mediated by a common belonging to a *political* community (Skocpol 2005; Urbinati 2006: chapter 4).

So it is by examining the interaction between citizens (including citizens as providers and as recipients) that dynamics of inclusion or exclusion are revealed. And it is in this interaction that selection and disciplining, discrimination and subjugation, are generated. Where these dynamics operate, not only inequality in treatment is set up, tending to reinforce social inequalities, but also power relationships between unequal citizens are established. These tend not to enter the public field of visibility: rather they remain unexpressed and opaque. This contrasts with contexts in which inequalities between citizens are named and faced. This only happens when relations among citizens are provided with political vocabularies for talking about power in a public regime of justification, and their participation nourishes the reflexivity of the institutions.

My analysis skirts a question that appears paradoxical, at least in Italy. Citizens liberated from impositions made by hierarchical authorities and left free to organise themselves are not able, even if they want to, to oppose the making of horizontal power inequalities and domination ties among citizens. Strong vertical ties and the active presence of public authority – as in Trieste – seem to be an essential condition for the public treatment of inequality among citizens. This confounds the widespread image of active citizens arrayed against the overweening power of public institutions.

Notes

1. Those years also saw the introduction of divorce and legalisation of abortion, both in the wake of strong social mobilisation.
2. This shift was also notably influenced by the crisis in the Italian political system following the 1992 so-called 'bribesville' scandal, which on the whole de-legitimised politics in general.
3. This research was carried out within the framework of the Research Centre *Sui Generis* on Sociology of Public Action at the University of Milano Bicocca. The most systematic part of the research focused on Lombardy and the regions of Friuli-Venezia Giulia and Campania. Some of the more limited research themes were also applied to local contexts in other regions. A follow-up on welfare and job insertion policies in these two regions is under way in the framework of the CAPRIGHT European Project.
4. Issues about privatisation or publicness of service governance and about what the notion of 'public' refers to were discussed in Bifulco et al. (2006). Also see Newman (2005), Newman & Clarke (2009), Cefai & Pasquier (2003) and Neveu (this volume).
5. On the relationship between responsibilisation and subjugation, see chapter 2. It is worth noting that in Lombardy some very influential Catholic organisations play a central role in giving moral justification to market behaviours and in promoting solidarity as intended as a matter of moral values more than of societal co-responsibilities.
6. It needs to be remembered here that the instrument of the budget-for-care answers another directive of the Friuli welfare regime, that of 'integration' between the policies and services of different sectors, which points to co-operation on shared projects both at a managerial and operational level. The regional law re-organising welfare is known as 'Integrated systems for social citizenship'.
7. It must, however, be emphasised that this relates to the way in which the policy instrument of the budget-for-care has been built up in Friuli, and is not intrinsic to the system of personal budgets per se (compare with Newman's account of individual budgets in the UK, this volume).

References

Barnes, M., J. Newman and H. Sullivan (2007), *Power, Participation and Political Renewal: Case Studies in Public Participation,* Bristol: Policy Press.

Bifulco, L., V. Borghi, O. De Leonardis and T. Vitale (2006) (eds.), 'Che cosa è pubblico?' *La Rivista delle Politiche Sociali,* 2: 201-217.

Bifulco, L., M. Bricocoli, and R. Monteleone (2008), 'Activation and Local Welfare in Italy. Trends, Issues, and a Case Study', *Social Policy and Administration,* 2.

Bifulco, L., O. De Leonardis, C. Mozzana and T. Vitale (2007), 'Policy Devices in Action. A Research Strategy for Analysing Normative Resources in a Capability Perspective', *CAPRIGHT Papers,* www. Capright.eu.

Bifulco, L., and T. Vitale (2006), 'Contracting for Welfare Services in Italy', *Journal of Social Policy,* 3: 495-513.

Bonvin, J., and N. Farvaque (2006), 'Promoting Capability for Work: The Role of Local Actors', in S. Deneulin et al. (eds.), *The Capability Approach, Towards Structural Transformations*, Dordrecht: Springer, 121-143.

Bricocoli, M., O. De Leonardis and A. Tosi (2008), 'Infléxions néo-libérales dans les politiques locales en Italie', in J. Donzelot, J. (ed.), *Ville violence et dependence sociale*, Paris: Editions du PUCA.

Castel, R. (2001), *L'insécurité sociale*, Paris: Seuil.

— (2009), *La montée des insécurités*, Paris: Seuil.

Cefaï, D., and D. Pasquier (2003) (eds.), *Le sens du public*, Paris: PUF.

Czarniawska, B. (1997), *Narrating the Organization. Dramas of Institutional Diversity*, Chicago: University of Chicago Press.

De Leonardis, O. (2006), 'Social Quality, Social Capital, and Health', *European Journal of Social Quality*, 3.

— (2009), 'Organization Matters. Contracting for Service Provision and Civicness', in T. Brandsen, P. Dekker and A. Evers (eds.), *Civicness in the Governance and Delivery of Social Services*, NOMOS, 2009.

De Tocqueville, A. (1988), *Democracy in America*, edited by J.P. Mayer. New York: Harper-Collins [1835-40].

Donzelot, J. (2006), *Quand la ville se défait*, Paris: Seuil.

Ferrera, M. (1996), 'The 'Southern Model' of Welfare in Social Europe', in *Journal of European Social Policy*, 6: 16-37.

Giorgi, A., and E. Polizzi (2007), 'Contrattualizzazione e mercato sociale: il caso dei voucher', in Monteleone (ed.): 105-122.

Hirschman, A. (1970), *Exit, Voice, Loyalty: Responses to the Decline in Firms, Organizations, and States*, Cambridge, MA: Harvard University Press.

Lascumes, P., and P. Le Galès (2004), *Gouverner par les instruments*, Paris: Presses de Sciences-Po.

— (2007), 'Understanding Public Policy through its Instrumentation', *Governance: An International Journal of Policy, Administration and Institutions*, 20 (1): 1-21.

Mingione, E. (2001), 'The Southern European Welfare Model and the Fight against Poverty and Social Exclusion', in M. K. Dolba (ed.), *Our Fragile World. Challenges and Opportunities for Sustainable Development*, EOLSS Publishers.

Monteleone, R. (2005), 'La contrattualizzazione delle politiche sociali: il caso dei voucher e dei budget di cura', in L. Bifulco (ed.), *Le politiche sociali. Temi e prospettive emergenti*, Roma: Carocc.

— (2007) (ed.), *La contrattualizzazione delle politiche sociali: forme ed effetti*, Roma: Officina.

Newman, J. (2005) (ed.), *Remaking Governance. People, Politics and the Public Sphere*, Bristol: Policy Press.

—, and J. Clarke (2009), *Publics, Politics and Power: Remaking the Public in Public Services*, London: Sage.

Ostrom, E. (2005), *Understanding Institutional Diversity*, Princeton, NJ: Princeton University Press.

Ruppert, E. (2006), *The Moral Economy of Cities: Shaping good citizens*, Toronto: University of Toronto Press.

Sen, A. (1994), *Inequality Reexamined*, Oxford: Clarendon Press.

Skocpol, T. (2003), *Diminished Democracy: From Membership to Management in American Civic Life*, Norman: University of Oklahoma.

Supiot, A. (2005), *Homo Juridicus*, Paris: Seuil.

— (2007), 'Les deux visages de la contractualisation: déconstruction du droit et renaissance féodale', in S. Chassagnard-Pinet and D. Hiez, *Approche critique de la contractualisation*, Paris: LGDJ, 19-44.

Tilly, C., and S. Tarrow (2006), *Contentious Politics*, Boulder, CO: Paradigm Press.

Urbinati, N. (2006), *Representative Democracy: Principles and genealogy*, Chicago: University of Chicago Press.

Weick, K. (1995), *Sensemaking in Organizations*, Thousand Oaks, CA: Sage.

8 Just being an 'active citizen'?

Categorisation processes and meanings of citizenship in France

Catherine Neveu

While the reference to 'active citizenship' has come to occupy a central place in recent transformations of public policies in many European countries, it has not been a highlight in the French case. A recent internet search for the term *'citoyenneté active'* showed results that referred either to campaigns for voting (being an active citizen means using one's right to vote) or to youth training programmes launched by the European Union. Such results tend to confirm that the notion is directly translated from 'European English' into French. And although the notion of 'choice' is currently high on the government agenda (when, for instance, official political discourses stress the need to give employees the choice of whether or not to work longer hours, or to work on Sundays, or to retire at a later age), it is not related to issues of citizenship.

It could be argued, then, that in the French context, the very notion of 'active citizenship' would be seen as pleonastic, with the dominant political culture viewing the citizen as being already active. But while the term as such has not been used in launching campaigns and framing policies, some citizens have been called upon to be more active in particular ways. In contrast to other chapters of this volume, in which the participation of service users in service design or policy development is addressed, my focus is on the mobilisation of citizens to participate in local decision making.

In France, the 'activation' of the citizen became a central policy theme in the late 1970s when inhabitants of derelict popular neighbourhoods were summoned to actively engage in their renewal. 'Poor people' had to show their ability to be actual citizens (Madec & Murard 1995) by participating in neighbourhood councils and all the other devices created within the framework of the *politique de la ville*, a set of urban public policies launched in the 1970s with the general aim of enhancing urban renewal and redeveloping social links in derelict neighbourhoods. Reconstructing social cohesion was seen as a requirement to revive these neighbourhoods, whose inhabitants were depicted only through their lack of all kinds of resources. As far as their citizenship was concerned, these inhabitants were – in that period and still are in a large measure – perceived as immature individuals unable to act as responsible citizens (Carrel 2004) and who needed to be 'taught' good citizenship practices.

'Activating' citizenship in such policies mainly aimed at young, poor or migrant people, and generally conceived of citizenship in terms of capacities rather than as a set of rights.

More recently, the field in which the activation of citizens has been a central theme is that of public participation. While in the 1960s and 1970s the reference to 'participation' was mostly linked to social movements involved in urban struggles, and was clearly thought of as a means of questioning the political system, in the 1990s it became the slogan of a series of top-down public policy initiatives (for more details, see Blondiaux 2008). Thus the law on 'propinquity democracy' passed in 2002 required all cities with more than 80,000 inhabitants to create 'neighbourhood councils' through which residents could contribute to urban management and decision making processes. While the law only made it compulsory for 50 cities, many other local authorities opted to create them voluntarily, not least because of the more general political climate during the French presidential elections of 2007 when the issue of 'participatory democracy' was presented as a policy priority by the socialist candidate.

Indeed the 'participatory imperative' (Blondiaux & Sintomer 2002) is today high in French politics and policymaking, and while recent years have seen cases of participative technologies (consensus conferences or citizens' juries) being used on general topics such as medically assisted procreation or genetically modified organisms, this imperative seems to be essentially translated into practices at the local level (see Barnes et al. 2007 for similar remarks on the British situation). This, then, is the focus of this chapter.

The field of public participation has largely been analysed in French political science. Research has explored how local neighbourhood councils are composed and organised, their working processes and the changes their creation implies in terms of policymaking and political relationships at the local level. Other studies have sought to understand more precisely the aims given to such practices: managerial (modernising management and enhancing managerial efficiency in public services); social (reinvigorating social links and cohesion); or political (transforming the relationships between elected representatives and citizens) (see Bacqué et al. 2005). Yet other studies have set out to understand, at a more general level, the extent to which these developments reflect deeper transformations in the very art of governing.[1]

This chapter will propose an exploration of a much less analysed dimension, that of the types of 'audiences' called upon to participate: 'users', 'consumers', 'citizens', 'residents', 'actors' or 'the public' are some of the many notions being used to refer to those agents that are called upon to become actively involved in democratic participation. Following Williams (1988), I will consider these categories as 'keywords':

Of course the issues could not all be understood simply by analysis of the words... Yet many of these issues, I found, could not really be thought through, and some of them, I believe, cannot even be focused unless we are conscious of the words as elements of the problems. (Williams, 1988: 15-16)

Taking words to be 'part of the problem' – studying how they appear, and are used differently in different situations – provides revealing insights into political projects, understood as 'those sets of beliefs, interests, conceptions of the world, and representations of what life in society should be... they (political projects) cannot be reduced to strategies for political action in the strict sense but... they express, convey and produce meanings that come to integrate broader cultural matrixes' (Dagnino 2007: 357).

My aim is thus to try to capture the variety of roles assigned to agents, and the diversity of their implied competences and positions, by analysing some of the categories used in a series of participation schemes. Indeed inviting people to participate as 'users', 'experts', or 'ordinary citizens', for instance, carries more or less explicit conceptions of them and of their role: as individuals or as organised representative collectives; as political actors to be listened to or to be trained and informed; as members of a territorially defined community or of an abstract (national) political community; as detached individual citizens or 'contextualised' agents. They are inscribed in regimes of government that 'elicit, promote, facilitate, foster and attribute various capacities, qualities and statuses to particular agents' (Dean 1999).

My analysis will draw on a series of recent research projects, both by the author and other social and political scientists, in a diversity of settings. Processes of categorisation in public policies, their political backgrounds and effects, have attracted the attention of social scientists analysing the large variety of participatory devices, both in Europe and beyond (see inter alia Neveu 2007; Barnes et al. 2003). The political and cultural French context has long privileged an abstract conception of the citizen as a 'detached' individual. But this sits in tension with other categories constituted in different participation initiatives (e.g. national commission for the public debate, neighbourhood councils, ad hoc bodies dealing with environmental issues or planning projects).

One line of enquiry, then, is the extent to which the different 'audiences' thus built can be clearly linked to the objectives, promoters, topics at stake or to the specific segments of the population supposed to become involved. A rather different line of enquiry concerns the political projects at play, since defining members of the public as individuals or as members of a collective, stressing the need to rely on their local experience or to support their capacity to be detached individuals, draw very different representations of what it means to be an active citizen. Indeed, contemporary public participation schemes in France are now inscribed with a significant genealogy.

While the above mentioned shift – from a 'bottom-up' process by which urban social movements contested urban renewal policies to a 'top-down' requirement government agencies address to (mainly) poor people – is important, it is too simple to attribute this to either the success of urban social movements, whose claims for 'more power to the inhabitants' would have been heard, or to the capacity of public policies to adapt to the new requirements of capitalism. Bacqué considers these participatory schemes to be built precisely 'through a tension between neoliberal ideology and democratic claims, both of which can converge in the criticism of too bureaucratic, too centralised, a public action' (Bacqué 2005: 82). Exploring the categories used in such a policy and in others thus constitutes a distinctive point of entry to understand the political projects at stake.

Defining publics

In a critical evaluation of public participation in France, Blondiaux underlines how the 'publics' of such practices are called upon:

> sometimes as users to whom services are delivered; sometimes as inhabitants whose advices are looked for but who are assigned to a territory and whose discussions are maintained within the neighbourhood's boundaries; much more rarely as citizens to whom the possibility would be given to express themselves on the discussed projects' relevance itself, to give discussions a more general turn, to simply do politics. (Blondiaux 2002: 9)

Indeed 'inhabitants' (*les habitants*) is the most frequently found category in public participation schemes in France; it refers to residents of a given territory, generally a neighbourhood. Their legitimacy to participate flows from the mere fact they inhabit this territory, and are thus considered to have '*une expertise d'usage*'. This means that their daily and routine uses of the urban space and services endow them with specific knowledge of their limits and of the ways to modify them positively. It is thus as 'users' they are called upon, but not as passive ones asked only to formulate their criticisms. Their routine knowledge puts them in a position to actively contribute to the improvement of services and arrangements; such a knowledge is mainly called upon on issues of routine urban planning (mobility and transports, local public services opening hours, etc.); in some cases reforming the functioning of local administrations (post office or housing services) was also discussed with users (see for instance Lorcerie 1995; Carrel & Rosenberg 2002). It is indeed because they are clearly rooted in a specific place, because of their attachment, that their potential contribution as 'expert users' is valorised and looked for by institutions: 'they (inhabitants) possess a specific knowledge linked to their belonging to a daily experienced propinquitous environment, through the use they put it to and the familiarity that flows from it' (Lafaye 2000: 25).

'Inhabitant' is indeed a complex category also because of its history. I will not explore in detail here the many meanings it has acquired and carried through decades of urban mobilisation and participation. Let it just be mentioned here that in the 1960s and 1970s mobilisations on housing and urban planning issues, *'l'habitant'* was the urban equivalent of the working class in factories, before *'les habitants'* came to designate the 'living forces' involved in modernising urban management, and later the socially and economically marginalised fractions of the population (Neveu 1999a, 1999b). Nowadays apart from being 'expert users', they are generally called upon as individuals (a kind of localised 'general public'), representing both the diversity of social conditions, interests and opinions and nobody/nothing else than themselves (Bertheleu & Neveu 2005), and sometimes, but rarely, explicitly contrasted to 'citizens': '(*l'habitant*) is the territorialized urban figure of a citizenship conceived of in terms of stakeholders and not of representation'.[2] Thus in certain public participation devices, 'inhabitants' are contrasted with associations and collective organisations. They can then be called upon so as to bypass or at least counterbalance these collective structures considered as not being representative of the local population in its diversity. The category of inhabitants can also be used to distinguish representative democracy (inhabited by citizens) and propinquity democracy. It thus becomes a very handy way of entering into a complex game of de/legitimation since inhabitants represent nobody but themselves and/or their localised knowledge. Citizens, in contrast are expected to express themselves by electing representatives and being 'detached', rather than through these exercises of propinquity.

There are many implications of how such categorisations are used to designate publics and call upon them to participate, but a central issue is how different categories are contrasted to each other, and how they create the 'stages' on which publics will act: as Barnes et al. note, 'It is through discourse that particular conceptions of the public realm are enacted and through which the public – in its many forms – is constituted as a governable entity' (2007: 67). In a very stimulating paper, Jobert (2009) explores the tensions at work in debates organised by the Commission Nationale du Débat Public (CNDP).[3] He highlights the co-existence of two conceptions concerning the aims of such public debate. In one, participation is an aim in itself (to create a public enlightened by discussion); in this case it aims to engage as large as possible a 'public', and participation is seen as 'unconcerned' and 'detached', and thus able to contribute to defining the 'general interest'.

The other conception stresses participation as a means to build decisions; in that case it is 'stakeholders' ('*acteurs*') that are engaged with, i.e., a limited number of people having specialised knowledge and defending specific interests; participation is thus 'expert', 'limited' and 'concerned'.

Most of the debates organised by the CNDP are thus, according to Jobert, structured by these tensions: there are always 'too many stakeholders and not enough public', and while the CNDP tends to give a large place for stakeholders to express themselves, it always at the same time tries to 'republicise' the debates. Strategies are then developed so as to organise actual 'stages' that have 'different aims but all aim at organising the relationship between the public (always to be created) and stakeholders (always to be identified, selected, validated)' (Jobert 2009: 62).

In her research on public participation in social housing neighbourhoods, Carrel points to similar processes through which conceptions of democracy and of citizenship are translated into different types of procedures relying on different expected qualities of their publics. Connecting two conceptions of democracy at work among institutions in charge of this participation[4] with two conceptions of how to organise 'poor' people's participation[5], she highlights four 'positions' on public participation. Within the egalitarian conception (no need to distinguish between individuals), she discerns two positions.

First, the idea that there is no need to organise participation as citizens already enjoy many means to make their voices heard through representative democracy. The second she names 'citizen participation', according to which participation is required, but it is institutions that are responsible for organising a different share of power between themselves and citizens. For those holding the view that poor people have less access to the public sphere and should benefit through specific schemes, one position is an injunction for these populations to participate: inhabitants should be properly trained so as to become 'good citizens'. Participation is thus more a social than a political issue. The other position (again following the idea that poor people have less access) pleads for a 'built participation', i.e., sees participation as a collective political construction requiring some kind of participatory engineering (Carrel 2007).

When calling upon citizens to participate actively, institutions thus translate, through the procedures and stages they build and in the names they use, the representations they have of different publics (i.e., of the qualities and competences they endow them with and on which they are expected to act), and also the conceptions held by their agents of democracy and citizenship. Institutions can thus be thought to have a more or less clear idea of how they want these publics to act. However, such expectations can be at odds with what actually happens. In the next section I now want to take this a step further by highlighting the tension between 'detached' and 'attached' conceptions of citizenship. But first I want to suggest that the issue of participation and public debate is structured by a diversity of agents, including social scientists. Institutions launching 'participatory' procedures are indeed 'consuming' social sciences in large quantities, and social scientists are often called upon not only to evaluate but indeed to create procedures and publics (see Blondiaux 2008; Carrel 2007).

Deconstructing institutional categorisation processes thus requires being aware of their high permeability to social sciences debate and categories. And these are far from immune to a series of 'blind spots', among which the same (mechanical) attribution of predetermined qualities to given categories. Blondiaux's quotation mentioned at the beginning of this chapter is interesting in that it highlights the close links between 'names' and processes (users/services provided; inhabitants/advice giving; citizens/politics – see also Clarke et al. 2007). But it does not question such associations, neither from the social scientist's point of view, nor from the public's/citizen's/inhabitant's point of view. It is to these issues I will now turn.

Does being an active citizen require attachment or detachment?

As I suggested in the previous section, issues of attachment and detachment are mobilised when publics are constituted: 'the public' of the CNDP is conceived as a to-be-enlightened detached public that would be in a position to define the 'general interest' precisely because it would not be directly concerned with the issues at stake, or at least only in an abstract, general manner. In contrast, 'inhabitants' are called upon, and their contributions legitimated, because they are viewed as possessing particular, situated knowledge flowing from their locations, while it is the defence of specific interests and the mobilisation of expertise that legitimates 'stakeholders'. Paradoxically, though, the same qualities are differently valued in other contexts and procedures; thus during 'public interest inquiries', commissioners[6] tend to exclude comments made by '*riverains*' (close-by residents) because they would be too directly concerned with the effects of the project, and thus blinded by particular and selfish private interests; interestingly enough, comments made by 'the general public' also tend to be excluded since they are not directly concerned by the project (Blatrix 1999).

Expectations about the (supposed) detachment/attachment of individuals and groups are thus always at play when the legitimacy of their presence and contributions is evaluated, or their competences judged. In France, the dominant model is the one Boullier calls 'citizenly purification', 'that only takes into account citizens, on the basis of a voluntaristic gamble, and pretends to cut off all beings who wish to speak from their attachments to the soil, so as to make politically pure beings out of them' (Boullier 2009: 22). Such a model implies that people engage in public (s) as 'pure', abstract and detached individuals; it also implies that 'politics' can be defined as a distinct sphere that can be detached from (infra-national) feelings of belonging and personal motivations.

A number of public participation schemes indeed aim to transform 'inhabitants' into 'citizens' by progressively teaching them to become detached from their immediate positions and feelings so as to attain a satisfying level of generality (see among others Lafaye 2000). More than a 'pedagogy of citizenship' aiming at the acquisition of technical and managing competences useful to contribute to decision making, creating 'good' citizens here means teaching people to become detached.

However, many analysts interested in understanding what actually motivates people's active involvement notice a reverse process: people engage publicly on the basis of strong attachments. Thus Boullier says about 'the un-heards' (les inouïs) that

> they are characterised [by institutions and elected representatives] as beings that are too much attached, unable to climb up in generality... Yet it is precisely that which makes them concerned, put them on the move, makes them speak: they are indeed attached, to a territory, their house, their children, their convictions, their soil... (Boullier 2009: 28)

Indeed, many public participation schemes rely precisely on strategies that aim to transform such 'attached residents' (concerned by very local issues and/or expressing themselves according to feelings and emotions, or lived experience) into detached 'citizens'. A slightly different version aims to design procedures that would allow such attachments to be voiced and heard, what Boullier, after Anselme (2000) calls passing 'from noise to speech'. But it has to be noted here that these attempts to either educate people or to design adapted procedures refer in most cases to a more or less implicit social distinction; those whose noise or silence should be turned into speech are the 'unheards', the poor, the socially disadvantaged or excluded, the 'sans-droits'. While there are significant differences between more 'evolutionist' approaches (educating people) and those that question the very boundaries of the political community (modifying them so as to include the excluded), both tend to maintain as if essential the 'purified' quality of citizenship.

This demonstrates the extent to which categorisations rely on fundamental oppositions embedded in 'political culture'. But it might be tempting to put the question differently, and wonder about the relevance of a (notion of the) citizen for which attachment and citizenship are viewed as antinomic. What Boullier calls 'territorial focalisation' (a focus on territory) can be a fruitful point of entry here; according to him, 'local residents' (les riverains) who mobilise against a project constitute a temporary public characterised to a certain degree by the existence of previous networks and relatedness flowing from a shared territory (Boullier 2009). More generally, Boullier argues, a focus on territory might be necessary to produce visibility:

CATHERINE NEVEU

To focus on undocumented immigrants without having St Bernard Church[7] is to lose an easy grasp on opinion. To debate about GMOs without showing a field and attacking it is to stay in experts' abstractions towards which one can feel indifference or powerlessness. (Boullier 2009: 33)

This connection between (attachment to) a territory, or (relation to) a material place on the one hand and the public('s) engagement on the other has been underlined by many authors so as to try and bypass the above-mentioned dichotomy of residents/'particular interests' (Nimbyism) *versus* citizens/'the general interest': 'it is thus in the name of their belonging to the territory [of the project] that residents claim the direct exercise of their citizenship' (Tapie-Grime 1997); or as Jobert underlines:

> When one would intend, according to the administrative logic of cutting out individuals, to cut out the citizen from the resident, the latter will on the contrary plea in the name of his/her experience of the territory. He/she will thus question the classical representation of citizenship, where the Nation constitutes the only territorial space of belonging. (Jobert 1998)

All of these authors therefore plea for a more dialogic relation between on the one hand (localised) practical experience and belonging and on the other, citizenship. It brings us back to Poche (1992), who stresses that 'place-sharing' is an essential dimension of citizenship, or to Massey when she evokes 'the politics of propinquity' (Massey 2004). In the same manner as transnational networks and practices have deeply modified the role played by the national scale (Appadurai 1996; Gupta & Ferguson 1997), so local (or more precisely localised) practices challenge the hegemonic position of national citizenship as compared with other levels of citizenship practices (see also Balibar 2001; Neveu 2005).

Such discussions stress the necessity of fully taking into account and carefully analysing how and when politics (and therefore citizenship and publicness) 'takes place' (*les lieux du politique*), including in the very physical and practical dimension of these place-taking/making processes. These physical and practical dimensions tend to be largely underestimated. Equally important, however, are careful analyses of situations and cases where territorial dimensions are *not* central, and where attachments and involvements are grounded in something other than territoriality (see for instance Sencébé 2004; or for different arguments Massey 2004). In their study of 'citizen-consumers', Clarke et al. stress that

> the other popular terms amongst people who use services were ones that invoked a sense of 'membership' – relationships of belonging in which people are part of something, and feel that being a member is a condition of entitlement or access to services. Larger collective imaginaries – the public and the local community – carry this sense of belonging and attachment. Ideas of belonging carry double meanings. Belonging can both locate an

identity and express a relationship of ownership: I belong here; this belongs to me/us. (Clarke et al. 2007: 128)

Taking into account people's own representations and identifications could thus allow for a more sophisticated understanding of the diverse registers of membership they activate when they become actively engaged (see Barnes et al. 2007). Not only can they be seen to overlap and be used simultaneously (Clarke et al. 2007) but they might draw a different 'portrait of the citizen' than as abstract and detached, as a 'wo/man without qualities'. By better understanding what and how people consider they 'belong to', by analysing the extent to which the analysis of 'citizenly practice requires to take into account membership, sociability and emotional involvement' (Carrel 2009: 99), a much more complex picture of what motivates their engagement can emerge; one that would contribute to an informed and critical questioning of institutions' and social sciences' categorisations of 'the public'.

Active citizens: individuals or collectives?

All this points to a last dimension I will touch on briefly here, that of the collective and/or individual dimension of citizenship processes. If one comes back to the term 'inhabitants' analysed earlier on, its evolutions through time clearly expose this tension. This term has designated very different 'publics' through the last four decades: the people or working class; organised social forces and movements; the poor and the excluded; individuals endowed with specific competences as users. Such a nominal continuity masks profound changes in the 'implications of significations' (Williams 1988) and thus in the social and political processes designated or aimed at.

The terms 'inhabitants' for instance changed from a notion referring to collective mobilisations to one referring to individuals; or it changed from a logic in which social movements and 'the State' were opposing each other to one of exchanges and collaboration between 'civil society' and institutions (Dagnino 2007). It is indeed the 'collective imaginaries' called upon to envision one's citizenship that should be explored in greater depth. Analysing citizens' relationships to public services, and their reluctance to endorse a 'consumer' attitude, Clarke stresses that 'this conception of citizenship is also debated because of the way it aims at decollectivising the public and its relations to public services, preferring to treat citizens as individual agents pursuing selfish interests' (Clarke 2010).

Bertheleu and myself made similar observations in our analysis of a local public participation scheme in Tours (Bertheleu & Neveu 2005). During our observation of the Conseils de la Vie Locale's (CVL) proceedings, we quickly noticed a strong feeling of discomfort among inhabitants as to the position assigned to them by local representatives. According to local elected councillors, inhabitants sat in CVLs only on their own behalf and on the basis of their 'expert knowledge', on a purely individual basis, representing nothing other than themselves or the diversity of the local population. Even though they often mistrusted voluntary groups sitting alongside them in CVLs, considering they were defending 'semi-collective self concerns', most of these inhabitants were uncomfortable with such an individualised call on their personal experience.

Some of them thus tried to organise in order to speak as a collective, formulating proposals that were collectively discussed during specific meetings. In the process, they also discovered that having a 'room of one's own' as inhabitants – a 'partial public space' (Neveu 2005) in which they were not under the gaze of institutions – was a precious and useful move. In meeting in this way, they seemed to express a nostalgic longing for more collective forms of discussions and social life in general:[8]

> at the level of lived experience and of the feeling of individual and social achievement, one cannot compare participating in a public space as voicing an advice, approving or disapproving discussed options, with participating as discussing the possible options raised by a specific question, or even as identifying new social issues. (Rudolf 2003: 112)

In other words, analysing what it means to be an 'active citizen' in contemporary public participation schemes in France, in terms of required qualities and competences, opens up the need to question the regimes of citizenship at work, and more particularly the new balance between conceptions that stress the individual dimension of citizenship and those that imply that in order to act as citizens, individuals need to rely on some kind of collective belonging or imaginary.

Notes

1. Blondiaux (2008) thus points to six sets of arguments referred to, to justify the necessity of participation: the growing complexity of contemporary societies, their more divided character, their growing reflexivity, unruliness or mistrust, or indeed the fact they would have become ungovernable.
2. *Note d'étape sur la création d'un Conseil Economique, Culturel et Social roubaisien*, Mairie de Roubaix, September 1997.
3. CNDP, National Commission for Public Debate, established in 1995 and enlarged in 2002. Its mission is to 'organise public's participation to the elaboration of planning projects'.
4. According to the first one, citizens' participation is not required since representative democracy (through elections) is the best guarantee for efficient decision making, while the second conception stresses that decisions are only legitimate if taken after deliberation with and among as many citizens as possible.

5. An egalitarian conception of citizenship pleading for an undifferentiated approach and one that stresses the need to take into account of inequalities among inhabitants and particularly the 'distance' between poor and disadvantaged groups (migrants, youth, etc.) and institutions.
6. These are compulsory procedures organised for certain types of planning, such as classified industrial plants (potentially dangerous for the surrounding population) or large equipments such as railways or motorways. The commissioners are in charge of receiving members of the public looking for information, and of rendering an advice (that has no constraining weight) once consultation is over; for more details on such procedures and their limitations, see Blatrix 1999.
7. The cause of undocumented migrants claiming residence permits in 1996 was largely publicised in the media when the police broke St Bernard church's doors open with axes so as to expel them.
8. When comparing urban renewal policies in France and the United States, Bacqué underlines the extent to which in France the *politique de la ville* was '(i)mplemented at a time when traditional forms of organisation of the working class and of popular neighbourhoods were weakening. (It) constituted, according to a high ranking civil servant who managed it, "a way to accompany the disappearance of the working class"' (Bacqué 2005: 88).

References

Bacqué, M. (2005), 'Dispositifs participatifs dans les quartiers populaires. Héritage des mouvements sociaux ou néolibéralisme? Empowerment zones aux Etats-Unis et politique de la ville en France', in M. Bacqué, R. Henri and Y. Sintomer (2005) (eds.), *Gestion de proximité et démocratie participative. Une perspective comparative*, Paris: La Découverte, Collection Recherches, 81-99.

—, R. Rey and Y. Sintomer (2005) (eds.), *Gestion de proximité et démocratie participative. Une perspective comparative*, Paris: La Découverte, Collection Recherches.

Barnes, M., J. Newman, H. Sullivan and A. Knops (2003), 'Constituting the public in public participation', *Public Administration*, 81 (2): 379-99.

—, J. Newman and H. Sullivan (2007), *Power, participation and political renewal*, Bristol: Policy Press.

Bertheleu, H., and C. Neveu (2005), 'De "petits lieux du politique"? Individus et collectifs dans des instances de "débat public"', *Espaces et Sociétés*, 123: 37-51.

Blatrix , C. (1999), 'Le maire, le commissaire-enquêteur et leur "public". La pratique politique de l'enquête publique', in Curapp-Craps (eds.), *La démocratie locale. Représentation, participation et espace public*, Paris: PUF, 161-176.

Blondiaux, L. (2002), 'Où en est la démocratie participative locale en France? Le risque du vide', in *Les Cahiers du DSU*, 35: 9-10.

— (2008), *Le nouvel esprit de la démocratie. Actualité de la démocratie participative*, Paris: Seuil, La Républi que des Idées.

— and Y. Sintomer (2002), 'L'impératif délibératif', in *Politix*, 57 (20): 17-35.

Boullier, D. (2009), 'Choses du public et choses du politique: pour une anthropologie des inouïs', in M. Carrel, C. Neveu and J. Ion (eds.), *Les intermittences de la démocratie. Formes d'action et visibilités citoyennes dans la ville*, Paris: L'Harmattan, Collection Logiques Politiques, 21-37.

Carrel, M. (2004), *Faire participer les habitants? La politique de la ville à l'épreuve du public*, Thèse de sociologie, Université Paris 5.

— (2007), 'Pauvreté, citoyenneté et participation. Quatre positions dans le débat sur la "participation des habitants"', in C. Neveu (ed.), *Cultures et pratiques participatives. Perspectives comparatives*, Paris: L'Harmattan, Collection Logiques Politiques, 95-112.

—, and S. Rosenberg (2002), *Face à l'insécurité sociale, désamorcer les conflits entre usagers et agents des services publics*, Paris: La Découverte-Syros.

Clarke, J. (2010), 'Parler de citoyenneté. Discours gouvernementaux et vernaculaires' *Anthropologie et sociétés*, 33 (2), forthcoming.

—, J. Newman, N. Smith, E. Vidler and L. Westmarland (2007), *Creating citizen-consumers. Changing Publics and changing public services*, London: Sage.

Dagnino, E. (2007), 'Participation, citizenship and democracy. Perverse confluence and displacement of meanings', in C. Neveu (ed.), *Cultures et pratiques participatives. Perspectives comparatives*, Paris: L'Harmattan, Collection Logiques Politiques: 353-370.

Dean, M. (1999), *Governmentality: Power and rule in modern society*, London: Sage.

Jobert, A. (2009), 'Dans les salles, trop d'acteurs, jamais assez de public', in M. Carrel, C. Neveu and J. Ion (eds.), *Les intermittences de la démocratie. Formes d'action et visibilités citoyennes dans la ville*, Paris: L'Harmattan, Collection Logiques Politiques: 49-63.

Lafaye, C. (2000), 'La figure de l'habitant et du citoyen dans les dispositifs de participation du Dunkerquois', in Plan Urbanisme Construction Architecture et al. (eds.) *Séminaire Dynamiques associatives et cadre de vie*. Compte-rendu, 1 (Jan-Nov): 22-34.

Lorcerie, F. (1995), 'L'Université du citoyen à Marseille', in *Les Annales de la Recherche Urbaine*, (68-69): 123-134.

Madec, A., and N. Murard (1995), *Citoyenneté et politiques sociales*, Paris: Flammarion, Collection Dominos.

Massey, D. (2004), 'Geographies of responsibility', *Geografiska Annaler*, 86 B (1): 5-18.

Neveu, C. (1999), 'L'anthropologue, le citoyen et l'habitant. Le rapport au politique dans une ville du Nord', *Ethnologie Française*, 29 (4): 559-567.

— (1999), 'Quel(s) espace(s) public(s) pour "les habitants"? Réflexions autour de l'expérience de Comités de quartier à Roubaix', in CRAPS-CURAPP, *La démocratie locale. Représentation, participation et espace public*, Paris: PUF, 347-366.

— (2005), *Anthropologie de la citoyenneté*, Habilitation à Diriger des Recherches, Aix-en-Provence: Université de Provence.

— (2007) (ed.), *Cultures et pratiques participatives. Perspectives comparatives*, Paris: L'Harmattan. Collection Logiques politiques.

Poche, B. (1992), 'Citoyenneté et représentation de l'appartenance', in *Espaces et Sociétés*, 68 (1): 15-35.

Rudolf, F. (2003), 'La participation au piège de l'enrôlement', *Espaces et Sociétés*, (112).

Sencébé, Y. (2004), 'Être ici, être d'ici. Formes d'appartenance dans le Diois (Drôme)', *Ethnologie Française*, 24 (1): 23-29.

Tapie-Grime, M. (1997), 'Le Nimby, une ressource de démocratisation', *Ecologie Politique*, (21).

Williams, R. (1976 edition), *Keywords. A vocabulary of culture and society*, London: Fontana Press.

9 Caring responsibilities

The making of citizen carers

Marian Barnes

In many parts of the world, citizenship remains a status and an identity to be claimed and struggled over. Such struggles amongst those excluded from citizenship reveal important understandings of what citizenship consists of: adherence to some notion of justice; recognition; self-determination and solidarity (Kabeer 2005). In the UK the emergence of service user and carer movements during the final decades of the 20th century highlighted tensions between strategies based on claims for citizenship and those based around the emerging identity of the 'welfare consumer' (e.g. Barnes 1997a, 1999). The power of the consumerist rhetoric is evident in the centrality of 'choice' within contemporary health and social care policy and its embodiment in the adoption of individual budgets as the mechanism through which a wide range of users of social care services will access support. Yet as Clarke et al. (2007) show, the identity of the 'consumer' remains problematic and the objectives of user and carer movements cannot adequately be understood by reference to consumerist discourse (Barnes 2009).

In this chapter I consider both official discourses relating to carers and carers' own constructions of their identities by reference to notions of citizenship. I do this by considering the emergence of the carers' movement in England, by drawing on interviews with carers about their experiences of caregiving, and by analysis of a recent government policy document setting out a strategy for carers (HM Government 2008a). The participation of service users in governance processes and in autonomous collective action has had an important impact on policymaking in England since the late 1980s. However, rather less attention has been given to collective action by those who provide care as family members or friends of disabled or older people than has been given to movements of disabled people, or users/survivors of mental health services.

Indeed, the emergence of collective action amongst different groups and the assertion of rights claims by both carers and disabled people have led to tension between these groups. The concept of 'care' has been rejected by some disabled activists (Wood 1991; Shakespeare 2000) and whilst there has recently been a recognition that disabled people and lay carers share interests in campaigning for good quality support services, there remains a reluctance amongst some within the disability movement to accept the language of care as the basis on which such help should be enabled (Beresford 2008).

The carers' movement evidences similar understandings of citizenship to those articulated by Kabeer (2005). It has also made a real impact in terms of achieving recognition that the private world of care is a public policy issue. To do this, it has demanded to be heard in public debates and demanded that individual carers should be able to exercise choice and autonomy in their everyday lives (see the introduction to this volume).

This does not mean that all dilemmas about the identity of citizen carers have been resolved, nor does it mean that the place of care itself as a social, political as well as personal value is no longer disputed. But it has created a space within which such questions can be more publicly debated.

In this chapter I examine both official discourses of care and carers, and what may (or may not) be counter discourses evident amongst carers themselves. I draw on different notions of 'responsibility' within government discourses of active citizenship and conceptualisations developed by feminist political philosophers in relation to an ethic of care in order to interrogate the way in which discourses of active citizenship may be mobilised and contested in relation to lay care in England.

The evolution of a new movement

The emergence of the identity of 'carer' in England predates its adoption elsewhere in Europe and beyond. Indeed, the English word 'carer' has been adopted in some other European states (Italy, for example) because there has been a much less clearly defined distinction between what are primarily familial relationships and relationships that are defined by reference to a particular role. Thus, in Italy, parents of children with learning disabilities or mental health problems are identified primarily as 'family members' rather than carers. In the UK, one political objective of the carers' movement has been to encourage family members (or friends or neighbours) who take on significant roles supporting disabled children, adult sons or daughters with a mental health diagnosis, or parents whose old age is accompanied by illness or frailty, to identify as 'carers'. Achieving official recognition for this identity and securing legislative and financial rights associated with it has been a fundamental achievement. Associated with this has been recognition for what carers have to contribute to policymaking and service development and a carers' presence in both local and national policymaking forums. Thus the English carers' movement reflects what the introduction to this volume suggests are the 'crowning achievements' of new social movements. Arguably, the carers' movement also demonstrates some of the more ambivalent aspects of active citizenship that this volume is exploring and that Janet

Newman examines in her chapter on active citizenship in the UK more generally.

The socio-demographic context for the evolution of the carers' movement in the UK was the increase in life expectancy in the second part of the 20th century, which meant a larger number of people living into old age. Unmarried women who were 'available' to care for their elderly parents because they did not have other family responsibilities found themselves juggling the need to earn a living with the task of looking after elderly parents. Following the Second World War, a high percentage of women over or at 40 years of age were unmarried.

One such woman, Mary Webster, was the first to identify her situation as a social problem, to seek to organise to secure recognition for this and to obtain a response from government. The National Council for the Single Woman and her Dependants (NCSWD, established in 1963) named the focus of concern quite precisely in a particular type of relationship, and the energies of the new organisation were directed primarily towards securing the financial and other support needed by single women whose ability to earn an income was constrained by their additional caring roles. Thus, the introduction of the Invalid Care Allowance in 1976 – the first financial benefit paid directly to carers – was only available to unmarried women. The assumption was that married women caring for elderly parents would be supported financially by their husband's income. It was not until ten years later, following an appeal to the European Court of Justice, that this allowance became available to married women carers.

The naming of the relationships involved as that of care for dependants emerged following the expansion of NCSWD into the National Council for Carers and their Elderly Dependants (NCCED). This maintained the focus on older people as recipients of care. When in 1981 the Association of Carers (AOC) was formed to represent all carers, some members of NCCED were unhappy about this and retained a separate organisation until 1988 when the two organisations merged to become the Carers National Association. This emphasis on care for older people probably accounts for the emergence of the carers' movement in a country that has been one of the earliest to experience the demographic changes associated with an ageing population.

In contrast, in a country like New Zealand where the population is still 'young', the emergence of the 'Carers Alliance' took place in the 2000s and has been led by those NGOs working with and for people with chronic illness or impairment (Leota, interview). Whilst the issue of 'caring' is considered to provide a common theme across diverse, 'condition'-based groups, there is little evidence of a carer-led movement and little indication that a broad-based concern about intergenerational relationships and gendered assumptions about the natural role of women as carers has underpinned this. Anttonen and Häikiö (this volume, chapter 4) identify little evidence of carer participation in the governance of care in Finland, and it is interesting to speculate whether the more 'family friendly' welfare policies of the Nordic states may have lessened the motivation for collective action to promote carers' identities and concerns in this context.

A key claim made at the time of the establishment of the AOC was that 'if you broke the experience of caring down into the emotional issues, the physical issues, the environmental issues, the financial issues, then all carers were really experiencing the same kind of stresses and suffering the same kind of problems' (Kohner 1993: 8). Politically, this position helped the high profile campaigning that has been pursued since the late 1980s. It reflects a similar stance within the disability movement that prioritised the common experiences of disablement as a political strategy to challenge the medical model of disability rather than reflecting on the diversity of subjective experiences associated with either different impairments or related to gender, sexuality or age. It established the identity of the carer and by naming this as an identifiable (if contested) social group, provided a basis on which policy and service development directed towards carers themselves, rather than those they support, could be developed. It also created an overarching organisation that was an easily accessible source of commentary, advice and collaborative input to the process of policymaking. Hence the advice of Carers UK to those new to caring starts with the following:

> 'Step one: Remember you're a carer! Recognising yourself as a carer is the very first step to getting the support you need. Many of us do not see ourselves as carers straight away: we are mums and dads, husbands, wives, partners, brothers, sisters, friends and neighbours. We are simply doing what anyone would, caring unpaid for a loved one or friend, helping them through when they are unable to do things for themselves. The fact is that you are also a carer, and there are things that you need to know. No one likes to be labelled, but recognising yourself as a carer can be the gateway to getting a range of help and support. (http://www.carersuk.org/Information/Newtocaring; accessed 3 March 2009)

The success of this strategy is evident in a number of policy developments that can be attributed, in part or entirely, to lobbying from the AOC and its subsequent incarnations, the Carers National Association and Carers UK. These include legislation that provides for carers' needs to be assessed separately from those they care for – the 1986 Disabled Persons Act and the 1995 Carers (Recognition and Services) Act – and eventually that such assessment should be followed by the provision of services (the 2000 Carers and Disabled Children's Act); continuing recognition of the financial impact of caring, most recently through provisions in the forthcoming pensions act that introduces a new carer's credit; the recognition of carers as a group that needs to be protected from discrimination and exclusion from work and study (2004 Carers Equal

MARIAN BARNES

Opportunities Act); and the publication by central government of two overarching carer's strategies – one in 1999 and the second in 2008.

There are also innumerable examples of carers' organisations at the local and national levels influencing thinking and practice relating to carer support. I was involved in research which included a review of an early such initiative developed in the context of the Birmingham Community Care Special Action Project (CCSAP, see Barnes 1997a: chapter 4). In the late 1980s and early 1990s, CCSAP was unusual in being a strategic initiative to give voice to service users and carers in the development of community care services. In the 2000s, opportunities for carers to provide input on service planning and inspection, as well as training for social workers and other health and social care staff, are common. The movement has also generated carers' NGOs – third-sector organisations (such as the Princess Royal Trust for Carers that has a network of locally run Carers Centres) that are not necessarily run by carers but which have developed to offer support, advocacy and in some cases to campaign on behalf of carers. Thus one aspect of the carers' movement focuses on self-help, respite, information and advice directed at carers.

None of this implies that carers are entirely satisfied with what has been achieved (see also Kuhlmann in this volume on 'patchy and uneven development'). For example, one group of carers organised a nationwide day of protest on 22 April 2009 against the continuing poverty experienced by carers:

> Tony: The protest is about carer poverty and the ridiculously low level of Carers Allowance. Carers need to be paid a non-means-tested benefit for the work we do.
> Christine: We also want to highlight the lack of affordable, reliable and appropriate respite that is currently patchy due to government cutbacks.
> Interviewer: What do you want to achieve?
> Christine: Hopefully both of the above will be increased to acceptable levels! But we also want to raise public awareness of how much we save them, as tax payers, what we have to go through in our daily lives and the fact that we are not scroungers.
> Tony: We are trying to rebuild the carer movement as a force to be recognised. We want the public and media to see how anybody could become a carer in a matter of seconds, and how we are abused by the government, and left to live in poverty. A fair wage for a fair day's work.
> (http://www.carersuk.org/Getinvolved/Carersinaction/1229098284; accessed 3 March 2009)

This exchange illustrates a number of perspectives on carers – that they are workers who should be paid the going rate for the job; that they are contributors to the national economy through saving the state expenditure on support services, and that, through their participation in the carers' movement, they are campaigners and activists. Thus it emphasises the *publicness* of care and the role of lay caregivers within this (see also Vabø, Anttonen, Häikiö, this volume). It also reinforces a message that appears frequently in relation to the promotion of both the contributions and needs of carers – that anyone can find themselves in this situation, a role that may not be (perhaps is usually not) chosen, but which should be distinguished from the relationship that preceded it – as daughter, mother, spouse, etc. Whilst the language of citizenship is not used explicitly here, this expression implies contributions that may be considered to constitute aspects of that identity.

From this brief analysis of the way in which the carers' movement has developed in the UK, its significance can be summarised in the following way:

- It has built an identity and constituency amongst carers in diverse situations.
- It has gained recognition for the value of the experiential knowledge that comes from caregiving.
- It has secured support for carers in their own right.
- It has promoted the value of care as well as rights for people in conditions of vulnerability.
- It has secured a place for carers in processes of service planning and delivery.

How then have official discourses of lay care giving come to be expressed?

The heart of families and communities

In order to explore official discourses of care and citizenship in England, I am here offering an analysis of the 2008 Carers' Strategy 'Carers at the heart of twenty first century families and communities' (HM Government 2008a). What is very evident within this text are the themes identified in the introduction to this volume; participation in an extended polity; extended responsibility for formerly public issues and 'choice' in the marketplace. But it also embodies other conceptions of 'carers' that are highly relevant to a consideration of the relationship between care and citizenship in contemporary social policy discourse in England.

As its title implies, the document emphasises the centrality of caregiving to the sustainability of everyday life – and also to ensuring social justice: 'our ambition to create a fairer Britain' as Prime Minister Gordon Brown states in his introduction. Thus a key role for carers is to enable 'the person they support to be a full and equal citizen'. They, too, can expect to benefit from co-ordinated support services in order to live as 'full and active citizens'. Yet a powerful message from this document is that, in spite of what might be considered a highly significant contribution not only to individual well-being but also to social justice, caring

MARIAN BARNES

is not enough. 'A life beyond caring' and how that might be achieved is a central theme. And that is primarily understood to mean the opportunity and capacity to take on paid work as well as undertake the unpaid work of care. The document justifies this by reference to carers' expressed wishes.

It could be argued that this goes right back to the origins of the carers' movement in Mary Webster's concerns that unmarried women's capacity to earn their living was compromised by the necessity also to care for elderly parents. Certainly a continuing theme in the campaigns of Carers UK and its predecessors has been the difficulties for carers in relation to sustaining paid work. But it is hard to ignore the fact that this fits very nicely with the dominance of the work ethic within New Labour social policy (see Newman, this volume) – that some have argued is promoted at the expense of an ethic of care (Williams 2004). Carers, who are still predominantly women (the figure of 70% is given in the forward to the document) may be undertaking important work for society, work that may be enough to secure for them the identity of 'citizens' in spite of a continuing reticence about identifying the private sphere as a locus for citizenship activity, but this does not mean that this attracts an income. From the government's perspective, the welfare benefits system should be seen as a safety net in terms of ensuring financial support for caring, and the argument that care is work that should be recompensed with a 'fair wage' is not reflected in government policy. It is better, it is claimed, if carers combine the role of caring with paid work. This is based on evidence that 40% of carers of working age who are not in paid work say they want to work 'now or in the future' – thus 60% do not, and an unknown percentage do not want to *combine* care with paid work. It also does not reflect the fact that most extended caring, i.e., for 50 hours a week or more, is carried out by those who are close to or past retirement age.

One identity for carers that the document explores is that of 'expert care partners.' Both notions – that of expertise and of partnership – demand closer examination in the context of conceptions of carers as active citizens. Once again, claims for recognition of the experiential knowledge of carers have been important for both individuals and the movement as a whole (e.g. Barnes 1997b). Recognition is fundamental to social justice (Fraser 1997), and the recognition of 'their unique knowledge and expertise' that the Carers' Strategy offers to carers reflects the success of the movement in not only achieving recognition for the distinct identity of carer, but also what might be considered higher level recognition of the significance of the value of their experiential knowledge (Barnes, Gell & Thomas 2010).

However, such recognition is tempered by two factors. Firstly, referencing 'Putting People First' (HM Government 2008b), a document that defines the principle of personalisation as a basis for the 'transformation' of adult social care services, the Carers' Strategy suggests limitations on carers being seen as 'partners in care' in circumstances where their views and aspirations are at odds with the service user. And secondly, whilst carers are experts they also need to be trained by, presumably, other experts who are 'professionals' in order to be effective partners with those who are paid to support disabled and older people. Carers may have unique knowledge but they also need to be tutored to be as effective as possible.

It is not new for carers to be seen to need information, advice and training from professionals (e.g. Ramsey et al. 2001). And, once again, such support has been sought by carers individually and collectively. The introduction of a 'Caring with Confidence' training programme (http://www.caringwithconfidence.net) which encompasses not only training in the practical tasks of caring and how to deal with the emotional impact of caring, but also how to effectively advocate for the person they care for and how to 'empower' carers in their dealings with professionals, may be welcomed by those who feel overwhelmed, isolated and lacking in confidence about caregiving and all that this entails, including the importance of being able to negotiate both the welfare system and claim a presence within 'caring partnerships'. But this can also be seen as part of a broader pedagogic process through which the state, claiming an objective of 'empowerment', seeks to train its citizens to become more effective in delivering official objectives (Cruickshank 1999).

Does this suggest that there will come to be a *duty* on carers to take part in such training programmes? Will the identity of 'caring partners' be restricted to those who have successfully undertaken prescribed training and can demonstrate not only their capacity to carry out their tasks effectively, but also to adopt the 'right' stance in relation both to the person they support and to paid care workers? This can be seen to reflect the introduction of parenting classes for parents of young children in what have been called 'chaotic families'. As the state seeks to support relationships within people's private lives, it also introduces normative expectations about how those relationships should be conducted and performed. If carers are to be recognised as partners with statutory service providers, they cannot assert a different view from that of the person they care for and they may also need to recognise their possible limitations and take the responsible action of receiving training in order to avoid struggling with the role. It is not impossible to imagine a situation in which they become expected to give account of their caring performance.

The appeal to partnership is one aspect of the New Labour discourse that has had a profound effect in attempts to transform the relationship between the state and citizens. The illusion of equality that the concept of partnership embodies has been seductive and in this context it appears to promote the 'citizen carer' identity with lay caregiving seen as equivalent to professional care (though some carers would argue the superiority of lay care). It can be seen as the contemporary equivalent of the carer as 'co-worker' model, one of three models Twigg identified in the way in which social care agencies conceptualised their relationship with carers (Twigg 1989). In discussing Twigg's analysis in an earlier publication (Barnes 1997a), I suggested that 'the co-worker model implies that informal and paid carers are colleagues and the "client" is left occupying a powerless position in relation to an alliance of carers' (ibid. 125). In contemporary discourse, where the responsibility of carers is to enable the citizenship of those they care for, they cannot be accepted as partners if they have different aspirations for the person they care for, or 'they are seeking to deny a family member the chance to experience maximum choice and control over their own life' (ibid. 117).

This reference to choice flags the other dominant discourse within contemporary social policy. As I noted in the beginning, consumerist discourses have long competed with those relating to citizenship in the social care arena. For both service users and carers making claims for rights and recognition, and for many undertaking analyses of the emergence and development of these discourses, there is a blurring as well as distinction to be drawn between the identities of the citizen and the consumer of services (e.g. Clarke et al. 2007). The adoption of 'choice and control' as the basis on which the transformation of adult social care in England is being pursued (HM Government 2008b) prioritises the capacity of individuals to determine how their own support needs will be met as the means to achieve the 'right of self determination' and enable people to 'participate as active and equal citizens' (ibid. 2). In line with this, the carers' strategy invokes notions of both responsible citizens and consumers, but within a firm commitment that better information to enable people to make better choices is empowering – i.e., that becoming an active consumer is the route to becoming an active citizen.

However, the 'caring' context provides a particular demonstration of the inadequacy of consumerism as a route to active citizenship. A key dilemma in the development of policies and services consequent on the identification of carers as a distinct social group with their own needs for recognition and support has been what has often been conceptualised as the competing needs and interests of carers and those they care for. A criticism of the previous carers' strategy (from 1999) was an absence of recognition of the relational nature of caring (e.g. Lloyd 2000). The 2008 strategy goes some way towards rectifying that absence, citing examples of mutual care such as the relationship between a woman with learning disabilities and her mother as they both grow older and the 'direction' of care shifts from the daughter to the mother. The report notes that 'carers and their caring role are inextricably linked to the people they care for. If the support and services are not right for the person being supported then both the individual and the family are affected'.

But the discourse remains that of 'individuals and families' rather than caring relationships. The first of the 'Common Core Principles to Support Self Care' set out in the Carers' Strategy is to 'ensure individuals are able to make informed choices to manage their care needs'. Six out of the seven principles refer explicitly to 'individuals' – assessing their own needs, developing skills in self-care, accessing support networks or technology to assist in self-care.

From a citizenship perspective, this reinforces a sense that carers may have to subjugate their own aspirations if these are not consistent with those of the person they care for. Because of the dominance of the 'citizen as consumer' discourse, a relational notion of caring citizenship does not really emerge. Ultimately, and in spite of assertions of the value of *carers, care itself* remains underexamined and inadequately valued. Whilst the carers' movement and struggles within feminist movements have achieved recognition of the significance of care as labour, care as a social, political and moral practice, and hence its significance as an expression of citizenship *per se,* has not been adequately recognised (Sevenhuijsen 1998). The strategy gives little acknowledgement of what 'choosing to care' rather than seeking to balance care with 'life' or 'paid work' might mean, nor does it touch upon how different aspirations within caring relationships might be explored and achieved.

The dominant concept of the individual within the personalisation discourse within which the carers' strategy is located is one that:

> ... implies a high level of self knowledge and reflexivity; substantial predictability in relation to needs and the circumstances in which they might be met, and a willingness to take on responsibility for constantly reviewing whether the support and help being given is enabling the achievement of objectives. (Barnes 2008a: 156-7)

This enables little accommodation for the 'messy moral dilemmas' associated with caregiving that in practice constitute both the context for and means through which carers and those they care for might struggle to assert their citizenship (see below). The notion of 'responsibility' in active citizenship is evident in the elision of 'caring' and 'responsibilities' in the foreword of the report. The theme of responsibility permeates the report:

> Our vision is that by 2018, carers will be universally recognised and valued as being fundamental to strong families and stable communities. Support will be tailored to meet individuals' needs, enabling carers to maintain a balance between their caring responsibilities and a life outside caring, while enabling the person they support to be a full and equal citizen. (HM Government 2008a)

As well as responsibilities relating to the exercise of choice, becoming effective partners and improving their care practices through training, this suggests that the responsibility of caring relates to the public objectives of creating strong families and stable communities, and to enabling those cared for to realise their citizenship. In order to sustain their caring role, one of the responsibilities that carers have is to ensure that they look after their own health. Carers aged 45-60 should take advantage of new 'Mid Life LifeChecks' introduced by the NHS that enable them to make an online assessment and develop a 'personalised plan to improve their health and well-being'. One proposal is to extend this to offer annual health checks for carers, thus detecting health problems at an early stage and enabling 'them to care for longer periods while remaining in good health'.

In recognition of the demands that fulfilling this responsibility makes, carers will receive demonstrations (both from government and from 'wider society') of the way in which that contribution is valued. They will also be supported to sustain some kind of 'care life balance.' This is expanded on in an acknowledgement that the state has responsibilities, but there are limitations to these and therefore 'any realistic solution to the challenge of improving carers' lives must recognise that the individual, family and state must work in partnership.'

The above analysis illustrates the way in which the claims of social movements and the official discourses of active citizenship can exist in a sometimes uneasy relationship with each other. Many of the claims made by the carers' movement have achieved a response in the government's strategy. In their response to the strategy document, Carers UK wrote:

> The Strategy contains a bold vision which the report says is a shared vision and responsibility between central and local government, the NHS, third sector, families and communities. Delivering this vision would mean genuine equality and recognition for carers, and it echoes our own call for a new 'social contract' which makes it clear what the state, employers, and others will provide and what individuals have to contribute. (http://www.carersuk. org/Policyandpractice/NationalCarersStrategy/PolicyBriefing/Policybriefing-NationalStrategyforCarers.pdf)

However, the major disappointment for Carers UK was the absence of any commitment to introduce carers' benefits.

Talking about care

If we are to understand how the public discourse of active citizenship may or may not reflect the meaning that caregiving has for carers in their everyday lives, we need to consider how carers talk about care in relation to their lives and relationships with those they care for (see also Anttonen & Häikiö, this volume). The following analysis is based on narrative life history interviews conducted with 12 carers, all but two of whom were active in carers' organisations and thus had publicly as well as privately identified themselves as carers. The references to named individuals (not real names) are extracts from carers' stories that are told in Barnes (2006).

What might be considered the 'normality of care' is evident in personal narratives that evidence both the number of caring roles that people may have throughout their lives and the way in which experiences of caregiving are interwoven with other narratives of life, death, love and work. Life histories demonstrate that caregivers may also be care receivers – at different stages of their life, or at the same time – and that the categorical distinction between carer and 'dependant' may not stand up. This applies in situations where people with learning disabilities become parents (Booth & Booth 1994), when spouses care for each other, when a disabled mother gives birth to a disabled child or when elderly parents provide as well as receive care from adult children. The 'taken for granted' nature of caregiving within carers' discourse is evident in phrases such as 'it's in-bred in you from a young age' and 'that's what life is about' (Barnes 2006: 109).

Carers (by and large) do not resist the notion that they have responsibilities to care for those close to them. Such responsibilities are based in 'pre-existing relationships, promises made, expectations about motherhood or cultural assumptions about care and reciprocity in family life.' (ibid. 148), rather than an obligation imposed on them by the state. The evidence here supports that of Fiona Williams and her colleagues in the Care Values and Future of Welfare (CAVA) programme with respect to parenting and partnering: 'Far from the dystopian vision of self-seeking individualism and moral decline which fills public debate... [people] are seeking to create new moral frameworks in which "fairness" and "respect" for others are key aspirations' (Williams 2004: 41).

Fulfilling those responsibilities requires negotiating a range of practical, emotional and moral dilemmas within the context of particular relationships. These complicate the notion that the responsibility of the carer is always to 'maximise choice and control' on the part of the person they care for. Stories told by carers included accounts of crises resulting from personal and interpersonal responses to illness, impairment and the frustrations of inadequate services. They demonstrate the dilemmas carers face in determining the 'right thing to do' in difficult circumstances and how attentiveness to the needs of those they care for also needs to be accompanied by attentiveness to their own needs. As Sevenhuijsen puts it, 'the moral subject in the discourse of care always already lives in a network of relationships in which s/he has to find balances between different forms of responsibility (for the self, for others and for the relationships between them)' (2000: 10).

An understanding of care as a moral practice as well as labour (not always of love) was evident in my interviews with carers and has been demonstrated by others (e.g. Brechin et al. 2003). The choices that are associated with caregiving are often moral choices that, if good care is to be offered, demand high degrees of ethical sensibility. Should Nell have refused to allow her disabled son James to continue to live with her after he set her house on fire? How should Alan have responded when his mother, who had had a drink problem for much of her life and whose other children wanted to have no more to do with her, reconstructed herself as a 'good mother' in her final years whilst he was caring for her? The decisions that carers make in these circumstances have important implications for their own and others' quality of life and are important in understanding care as a practice of citizenship. But official discourses give little if any attention to such dilemmas.

This emphasis on a relational notion of responsibility in the context of care suggests that the construction of responsibility as becoming better informed to make better choices is inadequate to a conceptualisation of what caring citizenship might entail. And the notion that providing self-assessment health checks and encouraging carers to develop healthier lifestyles in order to be able to continue to care fulfils the state's side of the 'contract' in supporting carers' health needs rings hollow in the face of accounts such as Emily's. Emily was admitted to hospital in crisis at the age of 79 after not being able to secure nighttime help in the care of her husband who had dementia – because she was getting up three times a night to tend him and sleep-in help was only available if the carer had to get up four times a night (Barnes 2006: 96-7). Whilst carers may not reject a concept of 'caring responsibilities' as central to a notion of active citizenship, their personal accounts suggest a rather different way of conceptualising what that means than is contained within official policy.

One aspect of this is the continuing claim by carers for financial and other support to become entitlements. Alongside claims for voice in individual decision making and at the collective level of policymaking, social citizenship as a status that confers rights becomes enmeshed with the more recent rediscovery of Athenian notions of citizenship as participation – the civic republican tradition of citizenship. But what carers' own accounts indicate is that it is hard if not impossible to understand these rights claims in terms of a binary opposition between those of carers and those they support. Thus Emily's anger and distress at not receiving the help she needed for herself was intimately connected to the consequences of this for her husband. He was admitted to a nursing home whilst she was in hospital. He died there and was not able to realise his wish to die at home.

This also connects to demands for recognition of knowledge based on the intimate and particular relationships that develop between carers and those they support. Some of the stories told by carers recounted battles with service providers for such recognition. These could have been interpreted as carers asserting their own needs rather than those of the person they cared for. Pauline's story of the battles she fought following the adoption of a disabled son could be seen in this way. She expressed no confidence in any of the various services and individual workers with whom she had contact, and it is easy to see how she might have prompted a reputation as a 'difficult' carer who was pursuing her own ideas rather than maximising the choice and control that could be exercised by her son Simon. Certainly there was no sense in her narrative of the emergence of a 'caring partnership' between her and the various doctors, social workers, residential care workers and others who were involved in Simon's life from childhood to young adulthood. The origins of this were in the difficulties Pauline and her husband had in trying to adopt in the first instance, were compounded by the response of their GP when they first took Simon to see him ('Why did you adopt that?') and further reinforced by experiences of rejection when they were looking for a school for him. In these circumstances, Pauline had no confidence in professional knowledge (although was constantly hoping to find someone who really understood and could help) and relied on her own experience of how to both support and challenge him until she met other carers who had similar experiences and shared their knowledge with her.

Whilst Pauline's narrative was the most explicit in containing a strong sense of the need to fight for justice for both herself and for Simon, most of the carers I spoke to experienced the need to battle for themselves and for those they cared for as a key aspect of what caring means in practice. For Rose, a key subtext in her story was a concern that, left to themselves, doctors would fail to resuscitate her severely disabled daughter if she became very ill. Lise's struggles to get the support that both she and her husband Eric needed following his stroke led to her becoming active in a local carers' organisation, and a similar trajectory was evident in Susan's story of sharing the care for her father with her mother after an accident left him with brain damage. This experience led Susan to change course in her career and to start to work for a carers' organisation. For these and many other carers, personal experiences of asserting their own needs and those of the people they cared for led to more public action in support of carers generally. Thus their 'active citizenship' can be understood at two levels, both of which encompass challenge and opposition to statutory services as well as asserting the interwoven nature of their own rights and of those cared for.

These political and moral questions that permeate carers' own discourses of care indicate that a feminist focus on care and citizenship in terms of the work involved in caregiving and the need for this to be appropriately acknowledged and recompensed is incomplete. The majority of this work has focused on child care rather than the care of adults and has examined different practices in different European states in relation to an analysis of welfare regimes (e.g. Lister et al. 2007: chapter 4). The work on a feminist ethic of care that emerges from political philosophy (Sevenhuijsen 1998; Tronto 1993) offers an important additional perspective that, combined with analysis of personal accounts of caregiving, can enable a much more nuanced understanding of caring and citizenship. Such an analysis confirms that the language of citizenship is not evident in carers' own accounts, but that these accounts do reflect an understanding of care as both a political and moral practice that has profound implications for the citizenship of both carer and cared for. As Kittay's work (1999) also emphasises, this is of particular significance in terms of developing a concept of social justice in conditions of vulnerability and dependency (see also Barnes & Brannelly 2008). To the extent that the achievement of social justice and the achievement of citizenship are linked, then this offers a deeper sense of the importance of citizenship claims from the carers' movement.

Conclusion

The key tension or dilemma associated with gender and citizenship has been seen to be the 'either-or' question: do women claim citizenship on the same basis as men, i.e., as citizen workers, or do they assert the equal but different legitimacy of caregiving as a basis for their citizenship? Many feminist scholars (e.g. Lister 1997) have eschewed such a binary analysis as a basis for policy prescriptions that challenge gendered assumptions about caring responsibilities. They have argued for policies that do not start from assumptions that women care and men work but which both encourage and support a more equal distribution of caregiving and work across genders.

One reading of the previous New Labour government's carers' strategy is that the 'either-or' binary has been resolved in favour of 'both-and': both women and men carers should be supported to fulfil unpaid caring responsibilities *and* be supported to continue or take up paid work. What Lister refers to as 'careful citizenship' – the right to time to care for both women and men – is acknowledged in policies such as rights to flexible working for carers and by an increase in the amount that carers can earn before this affects carers' allowances (a move intended to help those carers who want to work part-time).

But the contemporary context demands a more nuanced and multidimensional understanding of the nature of the dilemmas associated with care and citizenship. Whilst responsibilities in relation to paid work constitute a core dimension of the active citizenship discourse in the UK, there is much more to it than that. As I have sought to show in this chapter, the axes along which claims and counter claims may be made also include: the nature of the recognition given to carers' experiential knowledge vis-à-vis their need for information, support and advice; the moral dilemmas embedded in caring relationships vis-à-vis the prioritisation of individual choice and empowerment; and the expectation that officially defined public policy objectives will be delivered via complex negotiated relationships between paid workers, unpaid carers and those they support. These issues cannot be understood as binary oppositions between different principles held by government and carers themselves. Underpinning this is the significance of responsibility as a central concept in active citizenship and the necessity of distinguishing this from obligation (Tronto 1993). The responsibility for care felt by friends, lovers and family members is evident in their stories of their lives together and of the challenges they face. But the absence of an explicitly relational perspective on care within official discourse suggests very different understandings of what the responsibilities of care consist of: to undergo training to become more effective; to look after your health so that you can continue to care; not to assert your own views in opposition to those of the person you care for; and so on.

I suggest this analysis also has implications for the practice of citizenship within the public sphere of participative or deliberative governance that has opened up, in part as a consequence of action by carers and other users of social care services. What I have referred to as 'deliberating with care' (Barnes 2008b, 2008c) can also be understood by reference to ethics of care principles of attentiveness, responsibility, competence, responsiveness and trust. The practice of participation based on these principles maximises the possibility that transformative outcomes can be achieved through the participation of those previously excluded from such public forums – not least because they not only bring debate about the private realm of care into public arenas but also because they unsettle the distinction between supposedly private values of care and public values of citizenship.

References

Barnes, M. (1997a), *Care, Communities and Citizens*, Harlow, Addison Wesley Longman.

— (1997b) 'Families and Empowerment', in P. Ramcharan et al. (eds.), *Empowerment in Everyday Life: Learning Disability*, London: Jessica Kingsley.

— (1999), 'Users as Citizens: Collective Action and the Local Governance of Welfare', *Social Policy and Administration*, 33 (1): 73-90.

— (2006), *Caring and Social Justice*, Basingstoke: Palgrave Macmillan.

— (2008a), 'Is the personal no longer political?' *Soundings*, 39: 152-159.

— (2008b), 'Deliberating with Care: ethics and knowledge in the making of social policies', Inaugural lecture delivered at the University of Brighton, April. http://www.brighton.ac.uk/sass/contact/details.php?uid=mb129

— (2008c), 'Passionate Participation: emotional experiences and expressions in deliberative forums', *Critical Social Policy*, 28(4): 461-481.

— (2009), 'Authoritative consumers or experts by experience? User groups in health and social care', in R. Simmons, M. Powell and I. Greener (eds.), *The Consumer in Public Services*, Bristol: Policy Press.

— and T. Brannelly (2008), 'Achieving Care and Social Justice for People with Dementia', *Nursing Ethics*, 15 (3): 384-395.

— with C. Gell and P. Thomas (2010), 'Participation and Social Justice', in I. Greener, C. Holden and M. Kilkey (eds.), *Social Policy Review*, 22 Bristol: Policy Press.

Beresford, P. (2008), *What Future for Care?*, Joseph Rowntree Foundation. www. jrf.org.uk.

Booth, T., and W. Booth (1994), *Parenting Under Pressure. Mothers and fathers with learning difficulties*, Buckingham: Open University Press.

Brechin, A., R. Barton and J. Stein (2003), 'Getting to grips with poor care', in K. Stalker (ed.), *Reconceptualising Work with Carers, New Directions for Policy and Practice*, London: Jessica Kingsley.

Clarke, J., J. Newman, N. Smith, E. Vidler and L. Westmarland (2007), *Creating Citizen-Consumers. Changing Publics and Changing Services*, London: Sage.

Cruikshank, B. (1999), *The Will to Empower*, Ithaca and London: Cornell University Press.

Department of Health (1999), *Caring about Carers*, London: the Stationery Office.

Fraser, N. (1997), *'Justice Interruptus' Critical Reflections on the Post Socialist Condition*, London: Routledge.

HM Government (2008a), *Carers at the heart of 21st-century families and communities. 'A caring system on your side. A life of your own'*, London: Department of Health.

— (2008b), *Putting People First. A shared vision and commitment to the transformation of Adult Social Care*.

Kabeer. N. (2005) (ed.), *Inclusive Citizenship. Meanings and Expressions*, London and New York: Zed Books.

Kittay, E. F. (1999), *Love's Labor. Essays on Women, Equality and Dependency*. New York and London: Routledge.

Lister, R. (1997), *Citizenship: Feminist Perspectives*, Basingstoke: Palgrave Macmillan.

—, F. Williams, A. Anttonen, J. Bussemaker, U. Gerhard, J. Heinen, S. Johansson, A. Leira, B. Slim and C. Tobio with A. Gavana (2007), *Gendering Citizenship in Western Europe*, Bristol: Policy Press.

Lloyd, L. (2000), 'Caring about carers: only half the picture?', *Critical Social Policy*, 20(1): 36-57.

Ramsey, G., C. Gerada, S. Mars and G. Szmukler (2001) (eds.) *Mental Illness, A Handbook for Carers*, London: Jessica Kingsley.

Shakespeare, T. (2000), *Help*, Birmingham: Venture Press.

Sevenhuijsen, S. (1998), *Citizenship and the Ethics of Care: Feminist Considerations of Justice, Morality and Politics*, New York and London: Routledge.

— (2000), 'Caring in the Third Way: the relation between obligation, responsibility and care in *Third Way* discourse', *Critical Social Policy*, 20(1): 5-37.

Tronto, J. (1993), *Moral Boundaries. A Political Argument for an Ethic of Care*, New York and London: Routledge.

Williams, F. (2004), *Rethinking Families*, London: Calouste Gulbenkian Foundation.

Wood, R. (1991), 'Care of disabled people', in G. Dalley (ed.), *Disability and Social Policy*, London: Policy Studies Institute.

10 Active citizenship

Responsibility, choice and participation

Janet Newman and Evelien Tonkens

In order to give this rather free floating concept of active citizenship analytical power, we have in this volume focused on three of its constituent concepts – those of responsibility, participation and choice. These three concepts have been elaborated in the country-based chapters in this volume, both through analyses of policy texts and through studies of citizen perspectives. Our aim here is to draw out common themes and their implications for the remaking of citizenship. In doing so, we note how each concept is already intrinsically gendered, and how the reworking of participation, responsibility and choice might shift their gendering.

In the sections that follow, we highlight the contested meanings of the concepts; review the main findings on how the concepts have been selectively elaborated and reworked in the evolution of policies; and how they are understood and experienced by citizens themselves. The conclusion explores some of the ways in which the concepts are articulated with each other in specific sites, producing what De Leonardis terms emergent crystallisations, and suggest what the consequences might be, not least in terms of the erasure or displacement of struggles around access to and transformation of citizenship itself. From these conclusions, two themes arise that deserve further exploration for a future agenda on active citizenship: the changing power-knowledge relations between citizens and professionals and the gender dimension of active citizenship. These form the topic of the two future-oriented chapters that follow.

Responsibility

Responsibility, Isin (2008) argues, cannot simply be viewed as something added to citizenship by reforming welfare states; it is already inscribed in liberal conceptions of citizenship. We might extend this argument, pointing to the complex notions of responsibility embedded in the formation of welfare states. Such notions of responsibility are tied to generational, social and gender contracts. For example in the British case, women (as 'housewives and mothers') were charged with the familial and reproductive responsibilities necessary for the 'continuance of the British race and British ideals in the world' (Beveridge Report 1942: 52), while the responsibility of the state was carefully circumscribed to exclude certain categories of the population. In Germany, Kuhlmann argues that the Bismarckian model of citizenship already embodied strong notions of public responsibility, linked to communitarian values and the expectation that families would subsidise care services. Public responsibility was invested not only in the state but also delegated to stakeholder bodies such as employers and social insurance agencies. Responsibility later formed the focus of demands from user movements protesting against paternalism and a liberation from dependency cultures, as members of these movements demanded the right to take responsibility for their own lives, not hampered by paternalist do-gooders.

Notions of responsibility also flow across national boundaries in emerging concepts of global or transnational citizenship whereby citizens take some responsibility for those in other nations facing disasters, displacements or crises, whether through voluntary aid or public protest. And global or transnational citizenship has personal as well as public/political dimensions: workers may be part of 'global care chains' in which they have to balance their responsibility for those they care for as migrant workers against their responsibility to children or parents 'left behind' in the care of others. This has not only economic costs (with a high proportion of personal income being remitted, producing poverty and potential exclusion within their 'host' country) but also emotional costs, with the moral and ethical choices surrounding care being intensified.

Processes of responsibilisation in public policy are not restricted to health and social care: they also play a crucial role in policies for the improvement of poor neighbourhoods. In France, the reconstruction of social cohesion is seen as a requirement for revival of such neighbourhoods, with citizens learning to act as responsible citizens. This is particularly targeted towards young, poor and migrant people. Newman's analysis of the focus on community in UK policy texts shows how the mobilisation of active citizens within local communities is deemed to serve multiple goals, from civic renewal to economic regeneration through local entrepreneurship. Such moves are producing a new pedagogy of citizenship, linked to both national belonging and identity and to local participation. In both France and the UK, new pedagogies of citizenship and a focus on capacity building are particularly applied to new and migrant citizens.

We cannot simply view responsibility as something devolved from the state onto citizens: citizens are already responsible, and are tied into complex relationships of mutual responsibility, dependence and care. However, across the contributions to this volume we can trace how the rise of the ideal of active citizenship comes with processes of responsibilisation. This volume explores the expansion of citizen responsibilities in the various countries involved. These may include:

- *Economic responsibilities*: citizens expected to be prudent savers or to take out insurance against future care costs (under discussion in the

UK); citizens being asked for 'co-payments' of services formerly supplied free; or citizens taking on financial responsibility for their own care as access criteria to publicly funded care services are tightened.

- *Democratic responsibilities*: citizens asked to be responsible for the renewal of poor neighbourhoods (France), for the good governance of institutions (Germany) or more generally for the creation of social and community cohesion (Netherlands, UK).
- *Developmental responsibilities*: citizens being invited to take responsibility for their own development needs – whether as carers (e.g. training for carers in the UK), as service users (developing forms of expertise that enable them to manage their own illnesses, e.g. as 'expert patients' in Germany and the UK), or as democratic citizens (learning how to participate effectively, as in France).
- *Care responsibilities*: a common theme across most of the chapters, with citizens being asked to take greater responsibility both for the management of their own care (for example through personal budgets or vouchers in the Netherlands or Italy) and for the care of others in both the family and community.
- *Consumer responsibilities*: Kuhlmann offers a broad view of responsibility in which citizens are expected to take on greater responsibility as 'government's little helpers' in driving through the process of reform, not least through the exercise of choice and voice. Similar tendencies are evident in the UK where the exercise of choice is viewed as a means of curtailing entrenched 'provider power' and thus smoothing the modernisation process.
- *Creating a responsible society*: This is a strong theme in the reform initiatives in the UK (Newman) and the Netherlands (Tonkens). In the UK, David Cameron declared at the Conservative party conference in October 2009 that his party was committed to reducing the size and reach of the state; instead the emphasis would be on the creation of a stronger society that nourishes personal responsibility, strong families and community (*Guardian* 9 Oct 2009). We can see here responsibility taking on both narrow and more general meanings. The imperatives of choice and participation, considered below, might be viewed as new responsibilities through which citizens are asked to engage in the management or delivery of specific services. But more generally all citizens – whether service users or not – are being invited to consider themselves part of, and to help constitute, a responsible society.

Each of these forms of responsibility is gendered, classed and racialised. The 'feminisation of poverty' means that many women will struggle to meet the costs of care where these are devolved to individuals, either completely (where they do not meet tightening eligibility criteria) or in the form of co-payments. Democratic responsibilities are, as Neveu notes, often oriented towards participation in local communities, and women may well form the primary sources of local social cohesion and community participation. In some nations, community-based participation is often mediated by, or displaced onto, civil society bodies, with churches and 'faith' groups playing a significant role. In 'multicultural' contexts, faith-based opportunity structures are strongly marked by 'race' or ethnicity. Care responsibilities remain highly gendered. Finally, the creation of a 'responsible society' draws on images of family and community that are highly gendered and racialised. They also promulgate a conservative moral order that is antithetical to many of the accomplishments of women, gay and other activists of previous generations.

To sum up, with the rise of the ideal of active citizenship, women's traditional responsibilities for care and for sustaining civil society and community are thus not challenged but strengthened, despite women's increased responsibility to participate in the labour market. And since women are traditionally the primary users and providers of social welfare services, the modernisation processes underpinned by consumerist logics are, implicitly at least, highly gendered. Gender, ethnicity and sexuality are implicated in the turn to active citizenship, not only in terms of who is advantaged and disadvantaged, but also in terms of the imageries of citizenship that it promotes.

Responsibility as a relational concept

The articles in this volume did not, however, stop at the conclusion outlined above. We also wanted to find out how people react to these new demands of responsible citizenship. As our contributors show, citizens do not reject the idea of personal responsibility, though they tend to couple this with an affirmation of the need for state responsibility. Anttonen and Häikiö show that caring is a strongly felt responsibility, even if only within immediate families; however, they also emphasise the responsibility of the state towards them, sustaining a discourse of entitlement and rights. Similarly, Barnes shows that carers in England do not deny their responsibilities; however, they want to be recognised as actors and subjects in their own right, not just as those enabling the care of others. She argues that responsibility should be distinguished from obligation; carers do feel responsibilities but they are wary of obligations placed on them by the government. In Germany, Kuhlmann suggests that in the case of healthcare, patients are willing to take the idea of self-responsibility seriously and are also wiling to contribute their expertise to the governance of healthcare institutions. But they may form alliances with professionals to resist drives towards reform, especially where such reforms seek to reduce freedom of choice or to neglect individual needs and wants.

In most cases, responsibilities are not simply devolved by the state onto citizens, but state actors, municipalities and professionals also take on new responsibilities of empowerment and capacity building. 'Support' and 'empowerment' are key policy ideas, but their meaning has evolved: for example in Finland the role of government has shifted from supporting older people by providing a wide range of services to support-ing social networks so that they might take more responsibility for the care of older people. 'Rights-centred discourse thus becomes replaced by responsibility-centred discourse so the enabling role of the municipality is emphasised instead of its legal functions'. Carers in England are of-fered multiple sources of development and training (Barnes) or 'support' (the Netherlands). English patients are encouraged to develop their capa-cities to become more responsible for their own health and well-being (Newman).

Elsewhere, however, the stress on collaborative relationships between professionals and users or carers is diminishing. For example in Nor-way, even though staff may still be encouraged to collaborate in some municipalities, the tradition of collaboration that was strong in the 1980s and early 1990s is diminishing as greater stress has been placed on predictability (though the specification of standards and entitle-ments), leading to a more clear-cut division of responsibilities.

The contours and limits of responsibility are also often subject to ne-gotiation. In Tampere (Finland), the responsibility of family members and carers, and of service providers, are now spelled out in the form of a contract between the municipality, older person and informal carer. And in many countries, citizens retain the view that the state remains the responsible body, whether for the quality of care or for the financing of services. Responsibilisation strategies may be undermined by citizens as service users, carers and professionals, as in the elderly revolt in Norway or through the formation of new alliances between professionals and consumers in Germany.

In the Netherlands, Tonkens links the expansion of responsibility to a communitarian model of citizenship that stands in sharp contrast to the success of patients' movements in promoting both liberal and republi-can models of citizenship in the second half of the 20th century. The shift, she suggests, can be set in the context of a wider process of welfare state reform in which cost containment became a priority, leading to the development of strategies of government withdrawal from its responsi-bility for social welfare provision. This, as Tonkens clearly demonstrates, was backed up by new ideologies of active citizenship promulgated both by the political right and left: 'The welfare state had granted liberal rights to services, but these were now considered to have a dark side: they created passive, calculating citizens rather than active, responsible citizens'.

Features of communitarian policies are also evident in other coun-tries, where networks and communities are viewed as offering new re-sources and new modes of participation and responsibility. Anttonen and Häikiö show how this works for Finland, in the case of the home care allowance. Even in Norway, a country often associated with generous state-led care services, Vabø shows how tighter budgets in the 1980s gave rise to a stress on voluntarism and self-help, family solidarity and self-sustainability. In health and social care, we witness the construction of the care citizen in all the countries we studied. Care provided by family members is now a much stronger norm, though this is contested: Anttonen and Häikiö show how the responsibility of different actors is under continuous discussion and redefinition.

Yet to put all moves towards responsibilisation under the heading of communitarianism is too simple. There can be interesting differences between cities, regions and countries (as shown, for example, by De Leonardis who offers two variants of care and neighbourhood policies in two regions of Italy). Furthermore, responsibility cannot simply be understood as a zero-sum game, with the state first translating personal or familial responsibilities for the welfare of self and others into public policies in the formation of welfare states and then, more recently, asking citizens to pick up responsibilities that the state no longer wishes (or is able) to bear. Responsibility has to be understood as a *relational* concept. Barnes, for example, highlights the moral and ethical dilemmas that arise in the care relationship, and the different notions of responsibility offered by carers and by governments: 'The responsibility for care felt by friends, lovers and family members is evident in their stories of their lives together and the challenges they face. But the absence of an explicitly relational perspective on care within official discourse suggests very different understandings of what the responsibilities of care consist of: to undergo training to become more effective; to look after your health so that you can continue to care; [and] not to assert your own views in opposition to the person you care for'.

This omnipresence of responsibility, then, should not blind us to the tensions in this discourse. Firstly, there is a tension between empowerment (through training and development) and responsibilisation. State programmes of empowerment may be directed to training citizens to become more effective in delivering the state's objectives. Newman notes that the issue of responsibility is also present in the self-governing community and in citizenship education, each of which present themselves as forms of empowerment.

Secondly, there is a tension between individual responsibility and responsibility towards others. Anttonen and Häikiö note that in Finland, people are first and foremost responsible for themselves but at the same time called upon to be responsible for others around them. And Barnes notes the tension between the kinds of individual responsibility now required of service users and moves towards the empowerment of carers.

Third, we can identify tensions between the expansion of responsibilities in family and community on the one hand and the labour market activation policies on the other that assume that all those able to do so take up paid employment. The expanding role of women in the labour market in the UK and other countries sits uneasily with expanded responsibilities in the personal domain of household, family and community (Newman 2005, and this volume).

Finally, several chapters point to tensions that arise as responsibility is overlaid on a rights-centred discourse (see chapters on Norway, Finland and Germany in particular). For example, Anttonen and Häikiö trace how a rights-centred discourse has given way to a responsibility-centred discourse, with participation and responsibility closely interwoven themes; but citizens continue to view themselves as bestowed with rights.

The 'responsibilisation' thesis then needs to be treated with caution. Its elaboration in critiques of the emergence of neo-liberal governmentalities of the self and personal lives (e.g. Rose 1999; Cruickshank 1999) tends to be at a high level of abstraction. As such, they fail to take account of important differences between the kinds of responsibility being devolved to citizens in different services, sectors and countries (economic, consumerist, democratic, developmental). They also fail to address the dynamic ways in which responsibility is 'shared' between state and citizen, with the state often taking on additional roles in empowerment, development and regulation as well as moving towards coercion, conditionality and/or retreat. Finally, they begin from a given set of responsibilities enshrined in welfare states that are now being devolved or shed through neo-liberal or communitarian political projects, thus failing to address the relational, affective and ethical forms of responsibility inscribed in citizenship itself. It is of course the case that these relational components are being challenged by individualising concepts of consumerism and choice, considered below; but our analysis suggests that these are by no means hegemonic in citizens' own understanding of what it might mean to be an active citizen (see Anttonen & Häikiö; Barnes).

Participation

Citizen participation is viewed in many of the countries considered in this volume as a means of overcoming welfare dependency, and of ensuring that older people and other welfare users take an active part in society, thus enhancing their health and well-being. It is also viewed as a means of enhancing local democracy and overcoming social exclusion. But participation, like responsibility, cannot be considered solely as a set of governmental discourses: it also denotes a wide range of struggles for inclusion into and for the transformation of the public sphere, whether local, regional, national or transnational. Such struggles have, in part, been transformed through the rise of new media and web-based technologies.

While governmental actors now attempt to engage in such innovations, they remain on the margins of government-led public or consumer participation strategies. However, governmental actors and profes-sional workers have been very concerned to expand the range of voices that can be heard in policy and service delivery, and thus have taken measures to tolerate a wider range of forms of expression. The classic forms of participation – through representative democracy – invoke a gender-neutral sense of personhood. However, feminist critiques of the public/private distinction highlight ways in which the public sphere of participation has been one to which women have struggled to gain ac-cess. The proliferation of opportunities to participate in public service provision and public policy suggests a reframing of public and personal such that new forms of voice and new modes of expression can now be recognised. This acknowledges feminist arguments about recognition and respect (see Introduction) and means that the voicing of personal experience is now valued by public authorities as a means of assessing the effectiveness of service provision and for enhancing local involve-ment in decision making.

However, there is considerable variation in the meanings of participa-tion, as demonstrated by our contributors. First, service users are en-couraged to take an active part in the service system, either as 'co-produ-cers' of services (e.g. in the UK), as members of service user councils or forums (e.g. in Norway and the Netherlands), or as user representatives in new governance arrangements (e.g. in Germany). A second meaning of participation is the expectation that citizens will become more active and responsible members of the communities in which they live, per-haps looking out for the care and welfare of neighbours, or contributing to social solidarity and cohesion. Examples here include those of the Netherlands and the UK. The third and broadest meaning relates to poli-tical participation. This may be something that governments concerned about democratic engagement seek to foster: examples in this volume include those of the UK and France. But political participation may also be generated through activist engagements that challenge government policy, as in Norway, or that seek to extend government recognition and support, as in the UK carers' movement.

Also at stake is the form of citizenship evoked through participation, and the degree of power with which citizens are invested. Kulhmann's analysis of the German healthcare system shows how, despite the expan-sion of opportunities for participation, patients continue to be regarded as 'objects not actors'. For example, representatives of user groups are now included on the boards of the social insurance funds but remain second-class participants because of the continued power of the medical professions.

This can be contrasted with the notions of co-production and partner-ship in the UK. Tonkens traces the shift from the democratic move-ments of the 1970s in the Netherlands to the concepts of voice in health policy in the 1980s when 'without the voices and views of patients, pol-icymaking was hardly considered legitimate'. In the 1980s patient's de-

JANET NEWMAN AND EVELIEN TONKENS

mands for voice were supported by government's promotion and subsidy of patient organisations, not least as a means of expanding their responsibility for the management of cost reduction of healthcare. Voice and responsibility were brought together here in a seamless coupling, but a coupling in which democratic notions of participation were subordinated within the wider political project of communitarianism. Democratic participation remains weak, with local governments fulfilling the requirements of government to give citizens a say, but doing little more.

The weight and depth of participation in notions of active citizenship also varies between the countries considered. This variation influences who is supposed to participate and how, but also shapes who does in fact participate. In the UK, participation is very central to the idea of active citizenship, and there is an explosion of deliberative spaces creating new opportunities for voice and agency. Anttonen, Häikiö and Vabø trace the expansion of opportunities for older people's participation in Nordic welfare states, but it seems that these are primarily directed towards the users of welfare services rather than to carers: carers' participation tended to be through voluntary organisations. In Tampere, carers participated through interest organisations that made it possible to construct a collective carer identity; however, this tended to be for the purpose of maintaining social activity and capability as carers. But when there was a need to challenge decisions, this tended to be through the exercise of individual participation and rights (Finland).

This can be contrasted with the success of the carers' movement in England (Barnes). And De Leonardis points to the different possibilities of participation offered within two different modes of territorial governance. In Germany, voice is enshrined in democratic features such as the collective representation of stakeholders and the election of representatives in regulatory bodies, but the position of the service user is weak, with user participation only open to established groups.

How can we account for these differences between countries concerning the weight and depth of participation? These differences can be argued to partly reflect the issues that social movements raised in different countries and how successful they were in doing so. Also significant is the role of public authorities in supporting and enabling participation. In the UK, for example, the strong orientation towards the participation of carers can be traced back to the period after World War II and the actions of unmarried women lacking sufficient income because of caring tasks. Their later success was also partly attributable to the early impact of the demographic changes leading to increasing numbers of elderly people in need of care. There has been high-profile campaigning since the 1980s, with the slogan 'Remember you're a carer!' and in April 2009, a protest focusing on the continuing poverty experienced by carers. There are now innumerable carers' organisations operating at both the local and national levels, and these have become recognised and supported in public policy. And the territorial differences high-lighted by De Leonardis can be linked both to the place and role of social movements in each region, but also to the role of public institutions. In Lombardy the consumerist model of participation means that citizen or-ganisations 'function like companies', while in Friuli a more political moulding of active citizenship looks back to social movements and also reflects the active role of public institutions. In Germany, the influence of social movements has been limited; this may account for the weak voice of citizens in healthcare described by Kuhlmann.

From collective to individual claims-making

A common trend in the various chapters of this volume is a shift from collective toward individual claims-making. This leads to a paradoxical situation, as Newman notes: the opening up of new spaces of participa-tion outside the domain of formal politics is taking place in parallel to an erasure of space where collective claims-making practices take place. In the UK, she points to a marginalisation of collective identities in the participative process, including those based on gender and ethnicity (though organised groups of service users and carers are now regarded as stakeholders who should be consulted in policymaking and service evaluation). Enhancing participation – both of service users and of citi-zens in local communities – is a central concern of policymakers, but in the process activist notions of citizenship tend to disappear from view.

Similarly, De Leonardis points to the erosion of collective and politi-cised spaces of participation in Italy, including those of trade unions and political parties. In Norway, while enhancing local democracy was at the heart of the 1980s process of decentralisation, participation has now be-come oriented towards social inclusion rather than democracy.

Neveu's chapter provides a deeper analysis of this process of indivi-dualisation of participation, away from collective identities. She analyses how the mobilisation of citizens to participate in local decision making originated with the goals of enhancing social cohesion in 'derelict' neigh-bourhoods rather than the modernisation of social welfare. But there are important resonances: 'inhabitants were, in that period [the 1970s] and still are in large measure, perceived as immature individuals unable to act as responsible citizens'. Citizenship was thus conceived of in terms of capabilities rather than rights. More recently (from the 1990s), local participation became the subject of a series of policy imperatives that sought to promote neighbourhood councils through which residents might contribute to urban management and decision making.

These work unevenly across the categories of users, communities, ci-tizens, residents, actors or 'the public'. Neveu argues that such cate-gories are significant in that they offer 'more or less explicit concepts of them [citizens] and their role: as individuals or as organised representa-tive collectives; as political actors to be listened to or to be trained and informed; as members of a territorially defined community, or of an abstract (national) political community'. She argues that 'les habitants' is the most frequently found category of participation schemes in France: as such they can be contrasted with associations and collective organisations, and can be called on to 'bypass or at least counterbalance these collective structures considered as not being representative of the local population in its diversity'. But 'stakeholders' offer a different conception of participation, one that asks participants to be *detached* experts rather than one that summons them as *attached* to a particular place or identity. However, many scholars note that what motivates people to participate are precisely their strong attachments.

The distinctions offered by Neveu, together with her emphasis on the constitution of citizenship roles and identities by public authorities, can be helpful in revisiting the new roles offered to health and other service users as participants in the modernisation of new governance arrangements. Institutions summon up actors and constitute them in particular ways. The contrast between democratic decision making and the enhancement of the service user voice suggested by Tonkens resonates with Neveu's distinction between citizens' roles as individuals and as members of organised representative collectives. Similarly, Vabø highlights the distinction between organised campaigning and individual negotiations within the service relationship. Anttonen and Häikiö's analysis of political participation in Tampere suggests that it now offers citizens individual rather than collective opportunities. Voice is given to politicians, administrators and voluntary organisations, not to citizens and carers. So where the elderly citizens they interviewed do try to exert influence, this is just an individual action, based on individual rights-claiming within a framework of local authority. And the opportunities offered to service users to participate in policymaking forums in Germany may constitute them as attached (to a particular service experience), thus ceding power to those who can speak with the authority of the detached professional or expert.

With the shift from collective to individual claims-making, citizen participation also seems to be less activist and more adaptive. Citizen participation is viewed in many of the countries considered in this volume as a means of overcoming welfare dependency, and of ensuring that older people and other welfare users take an active part in society, thus enhancing their health and well-being. As De Leonardis suggests, these are very different forms of active citizenship from those expressed in the political mobilisations of the 1970s: militant politics has been displaced by volunteering in service provision, and the repertoires of contentious politics by involvement in the local governance of welfare policies. This reshapes the spaces through which influence can be exerted. Kuhlmann contrasts the inclusion of user representatives in new governance arrangements – legally defined, and limited to groups with high levels of formalisation – with self-help and voluntary groups committed to an older discourse of empowerment, whose discourses can be traced back to the medical counterculture and the women's health movement of the 1970s. Self-help and voluntary groups thus 'fall through the grids of new modes of active participation, or must move "sideways" to get access through nomination as a delegate from an approved user group'. Vabø, while noting the importance of governmental attempts to shape citizen identities, also shows how activist citizens may capture the policy agenda. The Norwegian elderly revolt was a public protest, skillfully orchestrated through the media, against cutbacks in services. This was a very successful mobilisation on the part of citizens, resulting in a reaffirmation of elder care as a matter of public concern. However, the protest drew attention to individual users indignant with poor quality of care rather than towards citizens concerned with the challenge to collective welfare provision. As such, it prefigured the emergence of a more consumerist orientation that paved the way for later market reforms. Nonetheless, campaigns by the elderly continue, and current modernisation agendas work uneasily across the tension between a rights-based discourse of entitlement and a market discourse based on citizens as discriminating and active consumers – a theme we develop below.

Tensions

Imperatives to enhance participation thus give rise to a number of tensions, one of them being tensions between the claims put forward by active and activist citizens and the claims recognised in policy. For example, Barnes traces how the development of a carers' movement has resulted in the elaboration of new social policies directed towards supporting and 'empowering' carers, but also suggests that the claims of social movements and the official discourse exist in an uneasy relationship. In particular, the relational notions of responsibility in the context of care conflicts with the more limited conception of consumer responsibility dominant in current policy.

Secondly, we have also traced the tensions inherent in the citizen identities that are mobilised, in particular between attached and detached identities. In some contexts attached identities are preferred, with service users invited to participate on the basis of their everyday experience and their intimate attachments to a place or to a particular service relationship. In others, citizens are invited to shed such specificities in order to take up the identity of a detached citizen, able to speak for the general good rather than from the basis of individual attachments. This is a gendered distinction in which local and particular concerns may be afforded less recognition than the abstract and strategic. Women's enhanced voice – as service users, carers, responsible members of communities and civil society – may thus not lead to enhanced power in the public domain.

Thirdly, tensions also arise between the kinds of activity that are viewed as legitimate. These operate around a distinction between activist citizens – mobilised in collective struggles – and governmental images of the active citizen, volunteering and participating in welfare governance or in the local community. The new invited opportunities for participation, whether in communities, in the service relationship or in governance, stand in curious (and sometimes troubled) relationship with other forms of political agency. Participation as active citizens has a rather oblique relationship to the strong tradition of public protest and dissent and other forms of collective agency in many western European countries. Such politicised forms of agency may be less than welcome in the new invited spaces of participation; those invited tend to be 'ordinary people' stripped of prior affiliations and interests (Newman & Clarke 2009: chapter 3), '*les habitants*' of particular localities, and the individual service user. This undermines collective attachments and relationships of solidarity. It also has the capacity to produce new lines of inequality.

Finally, we want to highlight the tensions that emerge as demands for recognition and participation as citizens became translated into emerging discourses of choice and autonomy. Both the UK and the Netherlands witnessed demands by groups of people with disabilities for recognition as full citizens, participating on equal terms rather than subject to social discrimination or paternalistic policies. The idea of active citizenship resonated with these claims and led to a focus on notions of choice and autonomy in both countries. In the Netherlands, Tonkens traces the institutionalisation through the 1980s of the patient's voice and their rights to participate in decision making, but notes how in the 1990s increasing weight was put onto the consumer role. Similar themes are evident in the UK, where issues of equality were translated and displaced through the new policy focus on choice. Even in Norway, Vabø notes that in the successful elderly revolt it was rich, well-educated people who both mobilised and benefited. These active elderly were not representative, she claims, and the needs of other groups were not recognised; such groups were not helped by consumerist claims on the part of the highly educated and influential. The issue of unequal participation in terms of class, gender and ethnicity is all too familiar, and may well be exacerbated as social movements and collective forms of mobilisation give way to consumerist claims.

Choice

Choice, as many of our contributors argue, is an ambiguous concept, open to many meanings. Different discourses of choice may also be directed towards different groups of users (with some being viewed as needing more support) and different publics (with choice being viewed as an attractive option for those wishing to free themselves from state control and professional dominance).

Most dominant in relation to the notion of active citizenship is consumerist choice. The elaboration of 'choice' as a policy concept heralds a predominantly consumerist inflection of active citizenship and the introduction of market mechanisms. The period in which this happened varies somewhat. In Norway, consumerist discourse, contracts and markets were propagated from the 1990s, linked to a promise of consumer control and consumer choice. In the Netherlands, choice was also extended in the 1990s in ways that expanded citizens' roles in 'demand-steering' in order to put pressure on insurance companies. In practice, choice was constrained and limited, mediated by contracting and tendering processes. In Finland, choice and consumerism have become central notions in elder care policy only recently. Active citizenship is now linked to increased choice and to opportunities to express preferences: for example Tampere is starting up a home-market project that promotes the citizen as a conscious consumer, albeit one who needs the help and support of care managers. In the UK, the picture differs somewhat across services and periods, with co-production and partnership discourses in some areas of health and social care in tension with those of free choice of provider in other areas. Forms of consumerism in the 1980s and early 1990s were later displaced by market models and the introduction of choice of provider in many sectors. Mechanisms of choice – in health, education, housing, social care and other sectors – continue to be extended.

Consumerism has been much less central in Germany, as Kuhlmann shows. Here, choice has long been inscribed into the pillarised system of social insurance. Free choice of provider was linked to an entitlement culture and a strong orientation towards solidarity. Freedom of choice did not lead citizens to 'shop around', acting as market subjects; as such, it did not deliver hoped-for cost containment nor did it improve the voice and agency of citizens. Such a culture is now being challenged as governments seek to redefine choice in ways that allow for greater control of both providers and users and a limit to the traditions of provider self-regulation. In contrast with other countries, while free choice of sickness funds opened the door for internal markets and competition, the emphasis now is on regulating and containing choice. Furthermore, Kuhlmann argues, the discourse of choice and competition did not really challenge the older discourse of solidarity. Turning citizens into consumers was not very successful, and cost containment has failed, not least because of the continued power of the medical professionals. In Germany, it seems that choice and contractualisation are now associated with mitigating state power rather than exercising market power. This contrasts with other countries – for example the Netherlands – where the agenda of market-based choice conflicts with the gains of democratic and liberal struggles in the Netherlands through the 1970s and 1980s.

A range of instruments are used to open up choice, including purchaser and provider splits (Norway), vouchers (Finland, Lombardy in Italy), contracts (e.g. the Netherlands), competition between providers (the UK), and individual budgets (Friuli in Italy, the Netherlands, the UK). And a number of measures are used to support and 'empower' users in the exercise of choice. These different instruments and measures offer different models of the service relationship and suggest different roles for public authorities – and for citizens. And even though there is a clear policy agenda concerning choice, consumer choice is not simply imposed: choice has often been a way of responding to demands from service users and social movements for greater autonomy (from professional and bureaucratic forms of power) and control (for people over their own lives).

Choice is inscribed through a range of policy intruments. In Norway the introduction of purchaser-provider splits heralded the rise of a more consumerist discourse, with citizens expected to be active in new ways – 'not as co-producers who collaborate on the "inside" of welfare organisations, but as consumers who act in a detached and discriminating role "outside" welfare institutions'. As such, they are supposed to act with scepticism and distrust towards service providers. Elsewhere, the main instrument to promote consumer choice is individual or personal budgets for social care service users. Access to a world of consumption and choice may symbolise entry into a public sphere of full citizenship for some groups – the disabled, people with learning disabilities and others. In Italy, De Leonardis contrasts the empowering potential of individual budgets in one region of Italy (Friuli) with the market-based models of provision in Lombardy. Newman is more sceptical, suggesting that markets and choice herald particular kinds of public domain based on relationships of exchange rather than relationships of solidarity. While empowering for some, individual budgets can serve to displace collective or public responsibility.

This suggests that it is not the instruments themselves that produce empowerment (or not) but the political context in which they take place, and the role taken by public authorities (state, municipal and professional) in reconciling consumerist demands with wider public considerations and judgements. The role of public authorities is also significant in constituting the public in new ways, seeking to foster new identifications and attachments (see chapter by Neveu). This can be consequential. Interestingly the introduction of individual budgets in the Netherlands led the Dutch patients' movements to reposition themselves in terms of consumerism, thus retaining their role as attractive partners for policymakers and expanding their role as voicing the interests of patients.

Citizens' perspectives on choice

Several chapters take us beyond policy analysis to a consideration of citizens' perspectives on choice. As the ethnographic data shows, market-based reforms do not necessarily meet the desires of citizens, carers or service users. In the Netherlands, Tonkens cites research that shows extensive resistance to choice among citizens: 'citizens appeared to be less enthusiastic about the rights and duties of choice than policymakers and patients' organisations had hoped for'. In Finland, while it seems that a minority viewed consumerism (institutionalised in a voucher system) as a good thing, overall it was viewed by carers as troublesome or deficient. Vabø shows there are few signs of consumer behaviour among the elderly in Norway, and Newman points to the low take-up of individual budgets among the elderly in the UK. To explain such resistance, Tonkens draws a distinction between steering and empowering choices – that is, between choice as an instrument to serve the aims of policymakers, who need citizens willing to make choices in a marketised system, versus choice as an instrument for citizens, who can exit providers and systems that they feel disempowered by and choose more empowering options.

In practice, choice is often limited, sometimes even more so than before. Frail elderly are marginalised in the Norwegian consumer movements, and financial squeezes in the UK and elsewhere mean that access to services – whether as a consumer or as a client – is becoming more difficult. Both Barnes and Anttonen & Häikiö note the limited impact of consumerism on carers: indeed, in focusing on the consumer role of service users rather than carers, new distinctions are opened up and the relational dimensions of care have come to receive less recognition. Barnes discusses the limited choice that carers in the UK are experiencing: consumerist forms of empowerment tend to be offered to users not carers. The policy focus on enhancing the choices available to those in need of care may deny carers the chance to experience full choice and control over their own lives.

The centrality of choice, then, may result in new inequalities in terms of who gets to choose, and who tends to be chosen by providers. In Norway, Vabø argues, the demands on the part of the active elderly that are framed in terms of consumerism are probably not very helpful for other elderly who are not so active in rights seeking but who are rather in need of receiving proper care. Here, consumerism is not empowering, she suggests, since it demands considerable capacity to navigate one's way through the system. In the case of the UK, Newman points to a paradox: government documents present choice as a means to enhancing equality, but in doing so detach equality from its social democratic roots and reinscribe it into market models. There is now an extensive body of research and criticism on the consumerist turn in the UK and the inequalities that arise, especially in schooling but also in healthcare. In the case

JANET NEWMAN AND EVELIEN TONKENS

of social care the results are more contested, with choice viewed by many as a means of empowering disabled people and offering them an adult, inclusive model of citizenship. But as we have seen, this may be at the expense of carers. While it is not possible to simply dismiss choice as a feature of neoliberalism, the extension of consumer identities produces a form of individualism and a rejection of the legitimacy of public authorities. However, such identities may well be rejected by citizens themselves (see also Clarke et al. 2007).

Choice without consumerism

A focus on choice in the marketplace of services also serves to displace attention from other meanings of choice. Firstly, there is choice in terms of autonomy over one's own life. Kulhmann notes how notions of choice in Germany were inflected through the post-war settlement which prefigured profound institutional change and greater participation in decision making: 'Choice was linked to a "happier" way of life after WW2 [rather than] being used as a policy concept – it was a means of welfare, consumption, freedom from state control and universal social security'. Vabø shows that in Norway, choice was more related to shaping one's life according to one's own views. In Nordic countries, the generous provision of state welfare gave women 'freedom of choice' to take up paid work, knowing that the care needs of their dependents would be met. Secondly, choice may concern the moral and ethical choices associated with the caring role, as Barnes notes. She argues for attention to be paid to how carers describe and negotiate the choices they face – not least in reconciling their own needs with the needs of those they care for. And she shows how caregiving staff are confronted with moral choices in deciding priorities and allocating resources. Thirdly, also neglected are the difficult choices faced by professionals and others as they are confronted with the needs of those without entitlements or rights, including some categories of migrants or asylum seekers.

The world of choice is a world of conditionalities and the proliferation of 'fine print' concerning who can choose what and in what circumstances, but the inequalities or injustices that result may be hidden from view by the dominant focus on its empowering possibilities. We conclude this section where we began, with the ambiguities of choice and in particular how its consumerist inflections are tending to displace the moral, ethical and relational choices that citizens worry about.

Alignments and articulations

So far, we have explored three different dimensions of active citizenship as distinct discourses. We now turn to the issue of how they work with and against each other, and with what consequences. We first explore how different discourses of active citizenship are articulated with each other, and which may be dominant in particular contexts. We then return to the question raised in the introduction concerning the relationship between struggles for access and inclusion – or even transformation – on the part of citizens, and new governmental discourses. We argue that the tensions that arise mean that citizenship, even in its 'activated' forms, remains the site of struggle and negotiation on (in)equality, and inclusion and exclusion. Particularly important here are the role of professionals and the negotiation of what counts as public or private, we will argue. The centrality of these two themes gave rise to two post-concluding chapters, meant to formulate stepping stones for an agenda on active citizenship that is more sensitive to issues of (in)equality and inclusion/exclusion.

One key set of articulations between the concepts considered in this chapter brings together notions of *participation* and *responsibility*. As noted above, participation carries many potential meanings in the policies traced in this volume. However, the alignment of participation and responsibility brings to the fore an emphasis on enabling citizens – for example older people – to manage their lives and to be socially active (Anttonen and Häikiö), enhancing their capacity to care for others (Barnes), to help sustain civil society and enhance social cohesion (Tonkens, Newman) and to engage in the renewal of local neighbourhoods (Neveu, Newman). The implicit coupling of participation and responsibility subordinates other potential meanings of participation, including more politicised forms of active citizenship. It thus tends to privatise active citizenship and allocate responsibility for people's (often women's) daily, seemingly private, acts – an issue further explored in chapter 12.

A second key articulation concerns *participation* and *choice*, which tends to align participative and consumerist discourses. New spaces of participation, as several of our contributors argue, are increasingly oriented towards enhancing the voice and choice of the consumer. So, just like the coupling of participation and responsibility, the coupling of participation and consumerist choice marks a shift towards individualising rhetorics and logics. For example, Anttonen and Häikiö note how in Tampere the goals of increasing users' choices and opportunities to express their preferences invoke forms of consumerist participation, and how this is framed by a focus on individual needs, demands and resources; support may well be provided through private contractors rather than by professionals in municipalities. In Norway, the elderly revolt of the 1990s and subsequent campaigns drew on a socio-liberal/consumerist discourse that, while highly effective, gave a particular meaning to citizen participation. In relation to carers, Barnes traces the tension between consumerist and citizenship-based notions of participation, and argues that the carers' strategy in England is oriented towards consumerism as the route to active citizenship. However, the dominance of the 'citizen consumer' discourse squeezes out the relational notion of caring she espouses.

These individualising rhetorics and logics produce (potential) new lines of inequality and exacerbating old ones. The discursive dominance of responsibility and choice frames participation in ways that undermine rights-based and collective attachments and identities. Also, citizens have differential access to the personal resources needed to navigate new service configurations, and different degrees of support through personal and social networks. Anttonen and Häikiö's analysis of how the emerging political discourse on active citizenship is materialised in everyday care practices brings into view questions of justice and equality: citizens as informal carers, they suggest, have very different resources at their disposal. In addition, some groups are more 'attractive' to policymakers, and some have more capacity to be vocal. Vabø traces how the consumer discourse, while empowering some groups, means that activists, usually the fit elderly in their 'third age', often fail to speak on behalf of the most frail elderly – 'they tend to stick to the powerful language of consumerism rather than to the evasive and almost poetical language of care'. So along with De Leonardis we might argue for a particular focus to be placed on research on those with the weakest voices – are they involved in choices or subjected to new disciplinary practices?

However, citizens may not perform their responsibilities or make their choices in ways that policy actors intended, and may not take up the consumer identities offered to them. They may, as in Norway and Finland, continue to regard public authorities as responsible for caregiving and continue to claim a rights-centred form of citizenship with the entitlement to services – and services of good quality – that this presumes. They may retain collective rather than individualised social imaginaries, and may – as Barnes suggests – hold relational and ethical/moral conceptions of care that conflict with notions of individualism and choice. As Anttonen and Häikiö argue, 'policy discourses did not recognise the everyday reality in which people live and consume services, and citizens did not identify themselves with positions that policy discourses offered'.

This leads us to argue that the analysis of welfare discourse alone gives an incomplete picture; also significant is the study of the enactment of citizenship and patterns of relationship and identification. Policy discourses on active citizenship have consequences: but at the same time citizens may well reject or refuse – or just not hear – the 'calls to power' by governmental actors (Clarke et al. 2007). Several chapters have highlighted the resilience of notions of justice and equality in citizens' own responses to the emergence of communitarian and neo-liberal inflections of citizenship. Finally, whether or not new inequalities are formed depends again to a large degree on the role of professionals and on the demarcations between public and private in its various forms, which are the topic of chapters 11 and 12.

The 'Janus face' of active citizenship

How far does our analysis help to answer one of the questions raised in the introduction to this volume: that is, whether new government policies on inclusion and participation, choice and responsibility, might be considered the crowning achievement of the social movements of the second half of the 20th century or whether such policies 'devoured' the political energies and potential of such movements. The arguments offered in this chapter draw attention to what Lister et al. (2008) term the 'Janus face' of citizenship: it can operate as a force for inclusion and exclusion, and can be simultaneously emancipatory and disciplinary. Activating measures are similarly ambiguous in their effects. Participation may open up new spaces of collective agency or may offer spaces of subjection as citizens become subject to new pedagogies and governmental logics. Participatory democracy seemingly offers a more nuanced means of engaging diverse publics, taking account of different interests and identity claims and connecting citizens more purposively to the institutions they encounter in a plural polity (Benhabib 2006). It also potentially offers a deeper democratic process, engaging with emotional and affective as well as rational dimensions of decision making and – if done well – enabling dialogue and debate rather than simply taking a snapshot of opinions at a particular point in time (Fung & Wright 2003). The question is raised whether forms of active citizenship in these invited spaces of governance should be understood as opening up new forms of political agency or as incorporating or accommodating new demands.

The answer to this last question depends not least on the political project in which they are situated. The techniques of participation seemingly matter less than the context in which they arise: for example, individual budgets may be viewed as individualising (in chapters by Newman and Anttonen & Häikiö) or, in some contexts, as empowering (De Leonardis). What seems to matter is the public role taken on by the state and other actors. But also significant is the extent to which participation is shaped within consumerist rationales or by logics of responsibilisation. As several chapters have shown, there are significant slippages taking place. Devolution processes open up new community-based or neighbourhood-based responsibilities to participate, responsibilities that require citizens with time and energy to manage local resources and facilities, resetting the borders between public and private. This reminds us that participation is work... and such work may be gendered, especially in contexts where local issues are viewed by women as significantly affecting the quality of their lives and those of their families. Moreover,

JANET NEWMAN AND EVELIEN TONKENS

such work often takes place in the liminal zones between public and private, an issue further explored in chapter 12.

Various facets of the Janus face of active citizenship are also revealed in different political projects. Surveying the differences between the projects of the Lombardy and Friuli regions of Italy, de Leonardis shows that 'local contexts are different, policy arenas are shaped differently, and different ways of becoming active citizens – with different repertoires of action and relative grammars of justification – can be observed'. She shows how different expressions of active citizenship – choice, responsibility and participation – are combined in different ways, producing two dynamics: one of expansion and inclusion, and one of division and selection. These reflect different political cultures and the institutional and professional practices that flow from them. The combinations of choice, responsibility and participation are unstable, she suggests: however they are 'crystallising' in particular ways in the regions she considers. This draws attention once more to the importance of the different national, regional and local political projects discussed in chapter 1. Our multi national, multi sectoral set of studies brings into view not only different scales and services but also the importance of differences produced by institutional and professional mediations – a theme developed in chapter 11.

Just like the notion of citizenship, the issue of choice is similarly 'Janus faced'. The empowering possibilities of choice depend on what kinds of choices are opened up, for whom, and in what context. The expansion of choice may have freed many service users from the disempowering and patriarchal qualities of traditional forms of service provision, but at the same time the coupling of market mechanisms and individualising discourses tends to undermine solidarities and to exacerbate inequality. Wherever choice is propagated, we need to ask who gains (often middle class, or the 'fit elderly') and who loses (those without the resources to navigate the system or to bear the newly devolved economic responsibilities).

A more nuanced response to the issue of how far the claims of social movements have become displaced or co-opted is produced when we bring citizen perspectives into the analysis. For example, Barnes's interviews with carers suggests the resilience of notions of justice in struggles around care, and the continued processes of challenge and opposition on the part of carers – both on their own behalf and on behalf of those they care for. The studies of Norway and Finland show the continued significance of a rights-based discourse of care and highlight the unresolved struggles over what is properly public, as opposed to personal or familial, responsibility.

The question is raised, then, about how far we can observe general processes of crystallisation as new discourses of active citizenship confront established cultures and practices. This metaphor of crystallization is helpful: it implies layering or sedimentation processes that may result in relatively stable institutionalisations of roles and relationships, identities and practices. However, it is an evolutionary process that may be disrupted as conditions change or as unexpected events disrupt the patterns and forms that are emerging. The results of national and local elections, of citizen movements and mobilisations, of media campaigns, and of financial crises all highlight the unpredictable dynamics of change.

However, recognising these unpredictable dynamics should not prevent us from drawing some general conclusions and formulating some general questions for future research and policy agendas on active citizenship. Throughout this volume, the issue of new or reproduced (in)equalities and inclusions/exclusions arose on virtually every page. The Janus face of active citizenship is particularly significant here: it can both reduce and reproduce (in)equalities and inclusions/exclusions. Moreover, the chapters in this volume also point to what seem to be decisive issues: professional and institutional processes of mediation, and the gender dimension of active citizenship concerning changing configurations of public, private, personal and political. These two themes are therefore further explored in the two final chapters. These should be read as post-concluding chapters, pointing to future agendas concerning active citizenship in policy, public debate and social scientific research.

References

Benhabib, S. (1996) (ed.), *Democracy and Difference: Contesting the boundaries of the political*, Princeton, NJ: Princeton University Press.

Beveridge, W. (1942), *Social Insurance and Allied Services*, London: HMA, (cmd 6404)

Clarke, J., J. Newman, N. Smith, E. Vidler and L. Westmarland (2007), *Creating Citizen Consumers: Changing publics and changing public services*, London: Sage.

Cruickshank, B. (1990), *The Will to Empower: Democratic citizens and other subjects*, Ithaca: Cornell University Press.

Isin, E. (2008) (ed.), *Recasting the Social in Citizenship*, Toronto: University of Toronto Press.

Lister, R. (2003), *Citizenship: Feminist perspectives*, 2nd edition, Basingstoke: Palgrave Macmillan.

Rose, N. (1999), *Powers of Freedom: Reframing political thought*, Cambridge: Cambridge University Press.

11 Active citizens, activist professionals

The citizenship of new professionals

Evelien Tonkens and Janet Newman

Even though chapter 10 could be read as the concluding chapter, this is not where we want to end this book. We ended chapter 10 by pointing to some agendas emerging out of this book that we thought deserved elaboration. In this and the next chapter we want to elaborate on two of these agendas: the citizenship of professionals and the gender dimension of active citizenship. This chapter is devoted to the changing power-knowledge relations between citizens and professionals (used in the broad sense, including all somewhat skilled 'public service' workers), while the next chapter elaborates on a feminist agenda of public and private.

Professionals are traditionally understood as possessing specialised training, knowledge and skills as well as a particular ethos to serve the public good or even a 'secular calling' to serve higher values such as health, freedom or development (Freidson 2001). The notion of active citizenship, however, has repercussions for what it means to be a service professional. The roles of citizens and professionals become more complicated, but they seldom get blurred. In this chapter we take up this theme of the citizenship of service professionals.

We begin by exploring the transformations in the professional-user relationship, drawing on chapters two to nine in this volume to highlight three possible 'regimes' of professional practice that may coexist in specific sectors, services and places but that suggest different kinds of ethos of professional practice. We also highlight the significance of these regimes for unpaid carers as well as paid workers. We go on to suggest some of the 'changing landscapes of power' that are reordering professional work and that govern the emergence and sustainability of specific regimes. We take up Ellen Kuhlmann's idea of 'citizen professionals', showing how professionals and other workers exercise control and influence not only in defence of their professional interests but also shaping transformations in professional practice (Kuhlmann 2006). Professionals and other workers are both activated by government to take on new roles, and also sometimes take action to transform the meanings of active citizenship discourse and to influence its outcomes on users and on the wider society.

However, this focus on the citizen agency of workers has to be set in the context of modernising pressures that produce the routinisation and regulation of professional practice, squeezing the spaces of agency. We conclude by highlighting the significance of the 'politics of mediation' that shapes the meanings and practices of active citizenship of professionals.

Professionals and users

The emergence of ideas of active citizenship took place against a background of critiques of professional power and challenges to the traditional relationship between professionals and service users. Citizens were to be 'empowered' through the extension of choice and voice; and the hierarchy of professional expertise and authority were to be transformed as the expertise of citizens was afforded greater recognition. In addition, citizens were to be respected as persons in their own right, not defined or pigeonholed in accordance with professional diagnoses of needs or conditions. But how far has this ideal led to a fundamental change in the relation between professionals and the users of social welfare services?

All the authors in this volume reported the increasing promotion of the idea that the power of citizens – as customers, consumers and users – should be enhanced. Indeed, drives towards placing their needs and demands at the centre of the service relationship underpinned the reform of services. This reflected criticisms of the power position of professionals and their supposed self-centredness in the bureau-professional regime of the welfare state, and the rise of New Public Management (NPM) as a supposedly more 'client-centred' alternative (Clarke & Newman 1997; Pollitt 2003). Many scholars, most of them from the Anglo-Saxon world, have been critical of this embrace of the user by policymakers, with the centrality of the user criticised as a 'further commodification of basic human needs and welfare' (Cowden and Singh 2007). The idea of the user as consumer of welfare services is further criticised as running 'counter to practices based on personal trust and continuous dialogue on needs' (Vabø 2006).

Despite such critique, for many decades now there have been efforts to minimise professional power and enhance the power of the service user through the key mechanisms discussed in this book: choice, responsibility and participation. To what degree do we witness such power shifts between professionals and service providers? And what can we say about the citizenship of professionals that arises out of the efforts to create these power shifts? There is an extensive body of literature that expresses scepticism about the empowerment of citizens under the banner of active citizenship: rather than a real shift in the relationship between citizens and professionals, active citizenship is charged with giving shelter to new forms of manipulation, control and boxing in (Bagott

EVELIEN TONKENS AND JANET NEWMAN

2005; Cruickshank 199; Cooke & Cothari 2001; Hodge 2005; Raco 2000; Swyndegedouw 2005; Jones 2003).

The arguments that are put forward are somewhat contradictory: some argue that participation is a sham and that citizens can only be empowered by more choice (Bagott 2005), while others argue that choice is a sham and citizens can only be empowered by proper participation (Carr 2005; Cowden & Singh 2007; Hickman 2006). Many studies also underline the many obstacles in the relation between professionals and citizens that impede the development of proper forms of participation. Factors blocking substantive changes in the relationship between citizens and users are numerous, ranging from the defensive attitudes of professions with a low professional status (Brooks 2006) to the tendency of NPM-inspired policies to aim for quick policy results rather than citizen involvement (Foley & Martin 2000). Studies also highlight the strategic use by policy actors of the argument that citizens invited into the new spaces of participation lack representativeness: an argument raised when citizens express views that are not welcomed by policymakers or professionals (Harrison & Mort 1998).

There are, however, also numerous studies showing that practices of active citizenship – especially those linked to participation – drastically change the relations between citizens and professionals and thus do empower citizens (Crawford & Rutter 2002; Dzur 2002; Leighninger 2003; Lenaghan 2002; Paddison et al. 2008). Most attach conditions to this finding, such as a well thought-out structure (Cawston & Barbour 2003; Milewa 1997; Milewa et al. 2004; Tunstall 2001) as opposed to 'laissez-faire' participation (Fung 2003, 2004), the education of citizens to engage in deliberation (Hunt 2007; Maloff et al. 2000) or the empowerment of professionals to enter into proper deliberation (Sullivan 2004).

What is at stake, then, is neither the resilience of professional power nor its demise, but a reordering of power and authority. As Clarke et al. (2007) argue, as citizens come to see themselves, and be seen as, active, competent participants in the service relationship, participative forum or governing body, so the unity and stability of the relationship between professional knowledge and power is disrupted. As a result, 'we see the relationships between knowledge and power as a tangled knot, in which many threads are wound together' (2007: 115). As we will see, the threads of this 'knowledge-power knot' may become looser or tighter in different contexts. We might conclude, then, that the idea of a shift towards greater centrality for the user and the demise of professional power is way too simple. Power between citizens and professionals is not like a ball that can be passed over from the one to the other: authority and expertise are not handed over but have multiplied and at the same time they have become more conditional. Moreover there are crucial variations in the conditionality and multiplication of that authority and expertise. It is to these variations that we now turn.

The professional-user relationship: three regimes

We can discern three regimes of professional-user relationships that can be found, often in the same country but dominating in different regions or services. Firstly, there is the continuation of a more or less *classical regime* of professionalism (Freidson 2001). The centrality of the service user is found here, but it merely means a stress on professionals working for the sake of the client or patient, as their professional vocations continue to demand. There are few signs of a power shift here. This is the case for healthcare in Germany where, as Kuhlmann argues, NPM-like efforts to break medical power were hardly successful, even though this is what the government intended. This can be understood, Kuhlmann suggests, by looking at post-war history where, as a reaction to Nazism, the state was massively distrusted but professionals were not. A more interventionist state and more citizen participation from the 1970s onwards did not replace the power of medical associations. Neither did NPM-like measures such as competition and marketisation have much influence on the position of professionals in the regulatory architecture of healthcare. Patients seem not to have played the role that the government expected of them. The idea of citizens counterbalancing service providers does not fit with the model of professional power and public control that can still be found in German healthcare. The 'knowledge-power knot' remains tightly tied. However, the history and the circumstances of German medical power are quite specific and cannot be generalised to other sectors, services or countries. Nor can the continuing power of a male-dominated medical profession be generalised to other professions.

Elsewhere in this volume we can trace an emphasis on granting citizens more power and independence, and freeing citizens from professional control. This produces not so much a handing over of power but rather the multiplication and conditionality of authority and expertise touched upon above. A new regime arises in which the professional is viewed as a *negotiator* between different parties: the user, the provider and the public authority that assesses needs and provides funding. This is very clear in the Lombardy region of Italy, where, as De Leonardis shows, the voucher system places citizens in opposition to service providers and professionals, with the freedom to choose a provider in a competitive market. It also gives professionals the responsibility of negotiating with providers, with citizens having the negative freedom of exit. In practice, De Leonardis argues, the freedom of citizens is rather limited. They do not have real contractual power; the exit option is hardly used and then only by people with a stronger socio-economic background. In addition, providers are able to choose their clients, creaming off the more desirable and less troublesome users. But nevertheless the new authority of the service user challenges the traditional power and authority of the professional.

EVELIEN TONKENS AND JANET NEWMAN

This emphasis on the power and independence of citizens was not only found in the Lombardy region of Italy but also in the UK, the Netherlands, Finland and to some degree in Norway. In each case it carries both empirical and normative connotations: citizens are both deemed as powerful and independent experts of their own situation and it is argued that they are entitled to be so, and are summoned to be so, while professionals and service providers are required to acknowledge this power, expertise and independence. The independent expert-citizen is expected to be more of a negotiating citizen. Many scholars of social policy, again mostly writing about the UK or the US, are critical of this trend, arguing that negotiation masks the continuation of power structures and inequality patterns rather than breaking them (Hickman 2006; Carr 2007). This is not necessarily a result of power plays on the part of professionals, but may be just because of a lack of competence on their part to really engage in dialogue (Brooks 2006). This again illustrates the growing conditionality and multiplication of power, rather than a power shift.

In this regime of negotiation both the knowledge and the power base of professionals shifts. Their power is invested in brokering solutions, and the expertise required to do this combines traditional knowledge (e.g. how to assess 'needs' and conditions) and new forms of expertise (about how to 'empower' users through access to information and capacity building). For example, Anttonen and Häikiö show how in Finland a new role has emerged – that of care integrators. These are part of the domiciliary care market and have become responsible for setting up service packages for each consumer and ensuring access to information. Now all the parties, including municipally based professionals, have to negotiate.

This invitation to enter into negotiation with service providers is not welcomed by all. While it is presented as a universal entitlement for all citizens, in practice it presupposes competent, clear-headed clients and carers and excludes many who are too vulnerable (sick, old, exhausted, confused) or who lack the necessary literacy, bureaucratic or negotiating skills. Comparative research in eleven European countries showed that many vulnerable people did not want to negotiate, but merely wanted to enter into caring relationships (Bastiaens et al. 2006). Other studies show that citizens tend to prefer access to proper services rather than participation (Contandriopoulos 2004). This preference requires flexible and responsive skills on the part of the professional and other workers, since they have to judge when to support, when to intervene and when to negotiate: that is, when to return to their traditional forms of expertise and authority and when to attempt to share power with newly independent and assertive users. This flexibility itself implies some loosening of the knowledge-power knot of traditional professional authority, and the weaving in of new skills and forms of power. Again, it implies that power is more conditional and multiplied.

So far we have pointed to two regimes: one in which the traditional hierarchical relationships between professionals and users remain, and one in which professionals are required to negotiate with newly independent users who are empowered through mechanisms of choice and voice. But we can also discern a third regime, of *reflexive cooperation*. De Leonardis shows how in the Italian region of Friuli the budget-for-care implies a completely different relation between users and professionals as providers. This contract does not separate citizens and providers in order to negotiate on equal terms but, conversely, it binds them together in a shared personalised project. It charges providers with the task of pursuing the improvement of housing conditions, increasing the chances for paid employment and enriching the user's network of personal relations. The power asymmetry between services and users is taken into account as a problem to be dealt with. Citizens' power is not sought through the exercise of choice but merely in voice: in participating in shared discussions about how to achieve the aims of the shared project to improve the quality of the person's life.

This model of reflexive cooperation, suggests de Leonardis, 'confounds the widespread image of active citizens arrayed against the overweaning power of public institutions'. Such a model is traceable in the expectations that users bring to their interactions with public services. For example in Finland, Häikiö and Anttonen show that some unpaid carers continue to direct themselves to public authorities whom they expect to provide care rather than entering into a negotiation. But, rather than looking back to the traditional professional regime, their expectations rather fit the third regime, of reflexive professionals and reflexive institutions. However, they are often disappointed since their relationship with professionals is contractualised, limiting the scope for responsiveness and leaving carers to fill the care gap themselves.

These variations in the interactions between professionals and citizens are widely debated among scholars who study professionalism today. The second regime of course echoes well-known and widely debated models of New Public Management and the marketisation of public services (Pollitt 2003; Clarke & Newman 1997; Noordegraaf & Steijn 2010; Brandsen et al. 2010). The third regime, however, is less often articulated and is not even known by one established name. It comes close to *civic professionalism* (Sullivan 2004), *activist professionalism* (Sachs 2000) or *democratic professionalism* (Dzur 2004; Preston 1996; Tonkens et al. 2009). These concepts imply varying efforts to articulate and promote a further democratisation of the relationship between professionals and service users, without supposing or aiming for (a simple handing over of power and thus) complete equality between professionals and clients. While some theorists of participation argue that 'traditional boundaries between expert and lay become blurred' (Cawston & Barbour 2003: 721), these various forms of active, civic or democratic professionalism maintain that professionals and citizens/clients occupy different positions, while simultaneously stressing the need to renew and particularly democratise the relations between professionals and citizens. Active professionalism retains the orthodox values of professionalism such as expertise, autonomy and altruism, but it politicises the practices in which professionals striving for these values are involved: it strives to bring together alliances and networks of interest groups for collective action to improve services (Sachs 2000).

Advocates of democratic professionalism argue that negotiation in the service relationship fails to recognise the issue of authority (Tonkens 2009) and suggests therefore that issues of authority and inequalities of power should be recognised and dealt with. Democratic professionals, then, are task sharers, not task monopolists. Such an approach requires professionals to combine both dialogue and leadership: they must 'both exercise authority and share it' (Dzur 2004: 12). This double task concerning authority is what makes democratic professionalism so complicated (Kremer & Tonkens 2006).

This offers a reframing of the knowledge-power knot, both by recognising the expertise of service users and citizens, and by addressing issues of authority in the service relationship and in everyday civic encounters. Here the idea of both conditionality and multiplication of power make sense. Democratic professionalism demands the acceptance of conditional power of both professionals and citizens that is challenged by both citizens and professionals. It also demands not a discrete body of knowledge on the part of professionals but an inquisitive, critical attitude and a willingness to acknowledge the importance of informal as well as formal relationships. There are no easy prescriptions: traces of democratic professionalism can be found in 'personalisation' strategies in the UK and elsewhere, and in new service models based on individual budgets. But the political and organisational context in which these are implemented seems to govern how possible democratic moves towards democratic professionalism might be.

Looking across these three regimes we can observe differences not only between countries and regions but also between services. With health, traditional models of professional power and the dependent relationships that follow may be resilient, but in social care we can see traces of the second and third regime. Here moves towards promoting independence, and sometimes personalisation, dominate the relations between users, professionals and those providing unpaid care. In local governance, Newman suggests that in the UK the emphasis is on interdependence rather than independence, with voluntary and community organisations drawn into partnership with the state and citizens. The extent of democratisation and power sharing in these partnerships is, however, highly variable.

These different regimes not only offer different kinds of recognition to the service user and citizen but also position the carer in different ways. In the traditional regime informal, unpaid care work is tacitly assumed but does not form a central feature of discourse; nor is the carer recognised as a responsibility of the professional. This regime is associated with a gender contract between the state, the male breadwinner and the female carer, and this unequal contract serves as a hidden backbone stabilising the finance of the healthcare sector, Kuhlmann argues in the case of Germany. In the second regime of independence, markets and choice, the growing centrality of the user as consumer tends to silence carers and to make them invisible, while at the same time they may be relied on more heavily. Because most healthcare reforms go together with tighter budgets and a reduction of service levels, so more is expected of unpaid carers while their voice in relation to professionals and service providers is reduced in favour of that of users. There is of course no logical reason to turn this into a zero-sum game: the role of both users and carers could be strengthened. But usually, strengthening the role of users implicitly means weakening the recognition given to the role of carers.

In some cases there are hints of a more reflexive model of partnership between carers, users and professionals. In Tampere, Finland, carers are taken seriously as the main actors in a caregiving situation. And in the UK, unpaid carers are recognised as 'partners' in negotiations with professionals and may receive personal development and training. They also have an entitlement to have their own needs assessed. Carers are also recognised as actors in the Friuli region of Italy. However, the recognition of informal care as valuable work is much less developed in Norway and in the Lombardy region of Italy. Even where the needs and roles of carers are acknowledged in public policy; however, carers may still struggle to be viewed as active citizen-subjects in their own right, as Barnes shows. Rather than democratic professionalism, her interviews with carers point to battles with service providers for recognition, for being listened to and for getting proper help.

The extent of recognition of carers in each of these regimes is of course also a gender (and increasingly racialised) issue. Gender and ethnicity are implicitly at stake here: there is more pressure on paid work as well as on care, which is particularly targeted at women and migrant workers, and in particular on female migrant workers. These are increasingly the ones who facilitate the combination of paid work and unpaid care for Western couples, while they themselves increasingly pay the price of seeing their paid work and unpaid care being ripped apart, sometimes thousand of miles away (as in the case of au pairs and domestic servants working in the US, Western Europe or the Middle East). The success of the Western feminist movement in achieving recognition for the importance of unpaid care has created new social tensions and problems that are 'neutralised' by displacing them onto female migrant labourers (Gottfried 2004; Lister et al. 2007). Hochschild (2003), Williams (2004) and others point to the intensification of the emotional labour of care work conducted by such migrants as they are stretched between different care worlds. And within the professions and para-professions, processes of up-skilling and de-skilling, contracting and marketisation shift the profile of both paid and unpaid care workers, changing the gendered hierarchies of the professions themselves. It is to these issues that we now turn.

Changing landscapes of power

So far we have focused narrowly on the interaction between professionals, service users and unpaid carers. These, however, take place in a wider landscape of modernisation and reform that raises a series of questions, and that may limit the capacity of professionals and providers to move towards the third regime of reflexive cooperation and democratic professionalism, even where professionals espouse its values.

First, there are serious challenges concerning the status and pay of some service professions, particularly the lower skilled ones, dominated by (migrant) women, that do not favour the development of democratic professionalism, to put it mildly. In many countries those now delivering social care and other services comprise new occupational groupings carrying out relatively low status and low paid work. At the same time, professions themselves may be becoming deskilled as information technology, new managerial rationalities and tighter regulatory processes limit the scope for the exercise of discretion and bureaucratise the work itself. Professional 'careers' may also become more fragmentary as staff turn to agency work or to becoming 'social entrepreneurs' as alternatives to an organisational career that is increasingly regulated and subject to new performance pressures. Finally, we must also take account of the ways in which the skills gap in mature welfare states are being met by migrant workers, whose citizenship status may prevent them from being trained and employed as professionals in their host country. Each of these processes creates new distinctions – and often divisions – in what were once considered to be unified and coherent professional groups, with the authority and legitimacy to assert professional values, whether 'traditional' or 'democratic'. In addition, the reordering of professional hierarchies changes the gender order, with managerial professionals – often male – situated at the pinnacle of predominantly female occupational groups.

Second, the ongoing implementation of NPM, marketisation, tendering and contracting out also complicate the development of a democratic professionalism. The relationship between professional and service user is more often carried out at a distance, with care services being delivered through contractual arrangements with a range of third-sector, private-sector or community-based providers. Sometimes, the professional-user relationship is rather intensified as professional work shifts from that of delivering services to that of supporting service users as they navigate their way through multiple and competing providers, or to that of advocacy for those in need in the context of declining resources.

The impact of New Public Management on the professional-user relationship, and on professional work itself, has been extensively documented. Rather than care work, professionals and other staff are increasingly involved in managing access to care through bureaucratised assessment and contracting processes. This was evident in some of the chapters in this volume. For example, Vabø notes how inter-professional relationships are becoming fragmented as a result of purchaser-provider splits that challenge the coherence and integration of care work from the service user's perspective. Professionals are also subject to increasing regulatory procedures that have the advantage of ensuring good practice and enhancing public accountability, but that add new layers of work in documentation and preparation for audits and inspections. Their performance is becoming subject to greater scrutiny as organisational regimes become more focused on introducing and managing performance regimes, such that professionals become subject to organisational logics that take precedence over loyalty to the wider profession and its peer-based norms (see Evetts 2009, who contrasts 'occupational professionalism' and 'organisational professionalism').

Practitioners working in the 'third sector' and in commercial organisations are also of course subject to these new logics, which become tightly codified in the contracts that govern their relationships both with public authorities and with service users. It will be interesting to see how these logics are themselves transformed as both the old hierarchical organisations and 'block contract' arrangements become subject to challenges from the more recent emphasis on the informal and highly differentiated systems of provision linked to individual budgets and personalised services. One might speculate that professionals will be sidelined further as users turn to informal sources of support, but it may also open up a space for 're-professionalisation' as workers take on the role of advocates, capacity builders and supporters of citizens trying to navigate their way through an ever more complex system of care services.

Citizen professionals: active and activated?

The binary relationship between professional (as agent of the state) and user (as active citizen) ignores and erases the citizenship of professionals. The regime of democratic professionalism conversely recognises professionals as citizens. Ethnographic studies show clearly that 'frontline' workers have themselves to be considered as citizens. They have to judge how to act in areas of ambiguity and use both their professional ethos and their political values in making such judgements (Hill & Hupe 2007). They sometimes silently subvert policy prescriptions, using their discretion to 'translate' policies to suit local contexts or to

EVELIEN TONKENS AND JANET NEWMAN

privilege particular goals. They may also use the spaces of agency to assert the values of care against the managerial logics described above.

For example, Askew (2009) shows how workers describe and enact a variety of care practices in the 'everyday performances' of human service work. Actors describe their care work as the 'real' and genuine part of their working day and express pride and satisfaction in the care that they give. They identify with the difficulties faced by the people and families they encounter, and 'frequently engage their own life experiences in guiding and shaping their interactions with community' (2009: 660). Similarly Larner and Craig (2005) highlight the new forms of 'gendered professionalism' taking place in local partnership working and the forms of activism that are pursued. In such work we can trace ways in which professionals, human service and community workers bring their own citizenship into the service relationship, using it as a resource to resolve the dilemmas raised in everyday work (Hoggett 2006) but also taking on a more expansive citizenship role.

The agency of citizen-professionals may be understood partly in terms of what Barnes and Prior (2009) term 'subversive citizenship'. More than democratic professionalism, this concept points to the activism that many professionals perform. Sometimes this happens silently, behind closed doors, e.g. in manipulating registrations in order to serve the customer instead of the financier (Buckloh & Roberts 2001; Danziger & Welfel 2001; Pomerantz & Segrist 2006). In this volume, Kuhlmann shows how the system of healthcare in Germany 'provides both users and professionals the opportunity to outflank tighter regulation'.

But there are also signs of service users and professionals becoming partners or allies in openly contesting or even subverting policy norms and prescriptions or tighter regulatory controls. As Vabø shows, in Norway protest against constraining conditions of work due to NPM reforms was not heard in the public debate until it was voiced by a person speaking on behalf of service users. The person happened to be an old labour party leader, then a 98-year-old home care recipient. His experience of the free choice model was that it did not provide sufficient latitude for home helpers to respond to his need for a small chat. He protested against what was from then on called 'stopwatch care'; he argued that free choice was a sham, as long as it did not give providers the freedom to respond to unstable and shifting needs. Until his penetrating voice was heard in the media, the problem was dealt with tacitly by the labour unions and by care staff who twisted the reform, for example by deviating from contracts or changing priorities to better fit the needs of individual users. This is an issue taken up by Prior (2009) who uses the concept of 'counter-agency' to describe various processes of revision, resistance or refusal on the part of frontline staff faced with implementing policies whose effects they see as harmful or iniquitous.

Prior (2009) goes on to argue that the space for the exercise of discretion and for autonomous judgements may be shrinking – in the terms of this volume, 'deactivating' the forms of citizenship expressed in professional ethics and political values. But professionals are also becoming activated in a completely different way. They are targeted to be not only agents but also objects in the transformations of welfare governance. As Kuhlmann shows, they are both agents of change and subject to activation policies. Professionals are implicated in setting up new forms of contracts as well as in establishing local collaborative networks. Professionals are 'activated' – through new forms of training and new policy prescriptions – to take on the negotiating and 'empowering' roles described earlier. For example in Trieste, an important city in the Friuli region of Italy described by De Leonardis, the programme stresses the territorial vocation of health service work, and social professionals were expected to be much more active and responsible for citizens' welfare. Service providers do not wait for people to come to them, but they 'go where people live'. This means of course professionals engaging much more extensively in boundary crossing work, not only 'reaching out' from the organisation but also working across different categories of knowledge and power.

Elsewhere – for example in the UK – professionals and other workers are allocated new responsibilities for monitoring and managing the service user. They are also charged with the responsibility of 'squaring the circle' of increasing care needs and declining resources. They are activated as particular kinds of agent in societies preoccupied with fear and insecurity, charged with the responsibility for managing disorder, and guarding against intolerance and abuse. They are summoned as partners in the emerging networks of organisations and agencies charged with addressing so-called 'wicked problems', whether of social exclusion, divided communities or economic decline, and of a range of problems associated with poor health and poverty.

A third factor weakening the power and independence of users in relation to professionals may be the weakening of collective citizen identities in the context of increasing individualism and consumerism. There has been a 'backlash against citizens' groups', with efforts to 'hear individuals as individuals, not as members of interest groups' (Jenson & Philips 2001: 84). Active citizenship, then, paradoxically comes with a depoliticisation of citizenship: citizenship gets stripped of its activism and collective overtones and becomes more an individual task. This leads to a contradictory move: on the one hand, citizens are summoned to negotiate, while on the other hand, the collectivist basis for negotiation is weakened as citizens are increasingly expected to just speak for themselves and not to voice views of particular interest groups or groups with certain convictions or political agendas. We pursue this theme further in chapter 12.

EVELIEN TONKENS AND JANET NEWMAN

Conclusion: active citizenship and the politics of mediation

In this chapter we have further pursued one of the agendas that arose out of the chapters of this volume: the changing power-knowledge relations between citizens and professionals (in the broad sense, including various kinds of service workers) and the citizenship of professionals. We argued that we need to pay attention to professional workers as both active and activist citizens and take seriously their responsibilities as the carriers of public values. They are confronted with new ethical and moral choices concerning their dedication to serve services users and/or the public good; to weigh conflicting demands of efficiency, cost-containment and maximising their 'production' against demands to serve the public good. This can only be done by participating with service users and other professionals and by taking up new roles as mediators.

References

Askew, L. E. (2009), ' "At home" in state institutions: the caring practices and potentialities of human service workers', *Geoforum*, 40 (May): 655-663.

Barnes, M. and D. Prior (2009) (eds.), *Subversive Citizens: Power, agency and resistance in public services*, Bristol: Policy Press.

Bastiaens, H.P., P. Van Royen, D. Pavlic, V. Raposo and R. Baker (2007), 'Older people's preferences for involvement in their own care: a qualitative study primary health care in 11 European countries', *Patient education and counselling*, 68: 33-42.

Baggott, R. (2005), 'A funny thing happened on the way to the forum. Reforming patient and public involvement in the NHS in England', *Public Administration*, 83 (3): 533-551.

Brooks, F. (2006), 'Nursing and public participation in health: an ethnographic study of a patient council', *International journal of nursing studies*, 45: 3-12.

Carr, S. (2007), 'Participation, power, conflict and change: Theorizing dynamics of service user participation in the social care system of England and Wales', *Critical social policy*, 27: 266-276.

Cawston, P.G., and R.S. Barbour (2003), 'Clients or citizens? Some consideration for primary care organisations', *British Journal of General Practice*, September 2003: 716-722.

Cowden, S., and G. Singh (2007), 'The "user": friend, foe or fetish? A critical exploration of user involvement in health and social care', *Critical social policy*, 27: 5-23.

Contandriopoulos, D. (2004), 'A sociological perspective on public participation in health care', *Social science and medicine*, 58: 312-330.

Dzur, A.W. (2004), 'Democratic professionalism: sharing authority in civic life', *The good society*, 13 (1): 6-14.

Elstub, S. (2006), 'Towards an inclusive social policy for the UK: the need for democratic deliberation in voluntary and community associations', *Voluntas: International journal of voluntary and non-profit organisations*, 17: 17-39.

Evetts, J. (2009), 'The management of professionalism: a contemporary paradox', in S. Gewirtz, P. Mahony and A. Cribb (eds.), *Changing Teacher Professionalism*, London: Routledge.

Fung, A. (2003), 'Survey article: recipes for public spheres: eight institutional design choices and their consequences', *The journal of political philosophy*, 11 (7): 338-367.

— (2004), *Empowered Participation. Reinventing urban democracy*, Princeton/Oxford: Princeton University Press.

Foley, P. and S. Martin (2000), 'A new deal for the community?' *Policy and politics*, 28: 479-91.

Gottfried, H. (2004), 'Gendering globalization discourses', *Critical Sociology*.

Hafferty, F. (2003), 'Finding Soul in a 'Medical Profession of One', in *Journal of Health Politics, Policy and Law*, 28 (1): 133-158.

Harrison, S., and M. Mort (1998), 'Which champions, which people? Public and user involvement in health care as a technology of legimation', *Social policy and administration*, 32: 60-70.

Hickman, P. (2006), 'Approaches to tenant participation in the English Local Authority Sector', *Housing studies*, 21 (2): 209-225.

Hill, W.Y., I. Faser and P. Cotton (2001), 'On patients' interest and accountability: reflecting on some dilemmas in social audit in primary health care', *Critical perspectives on accounting*, 12: 453-469.

Hochschild, A.R. (2003), *The Commercialization of Intimate Life*, Berkeley/Los Angeles/London: University of California Press.

Hodge, S. (2005) 'Participation, discourse and power: a case study in service user involvement.' *Critical social policy*, vol. 25, 164-179.

Hoggett, P. (2006), 'Conflict, ambivalence and the contested purpose of public service organisations', *Human Relations* 5 (2): 175- 194.

Hunt, V. (2007), 'Community development corporations and public participation: lessons from a case study in the Arkansas Delta', *Journal of sociology and social welfare*, 24: 9-35.

Jenson, J., and S. Philips (2001), 'Redesigning the Canadian citizenship regime: remaking institutions for representation', in C. Crouch, K. Eder and D. Tambini (eds.), *Citizenship, Markets and the State*, Oxford: Oxford University Press.

Kuhlmann, E. (2006), *Modernising Health Care. Reinventing professions, the state and the public*, Bristol: Policy Press.

Kremer, M., and E. Tonkens (2006), 'Authority, trust, knowledge and the public good in disarray', in T. Knijn and M. Kremer, *Professionals Between People and Policy*, Amsterdam: Amsterdam University Press, 122-136.

Larner, W., and D. Craig (2005), 'After neo-liberalism? Activism and local partnerships in Aotaeroa, New Zealand', *Antipode*, 37 (3): 402-424.

Leighninger, M. (2003), 'Shared governance in communities: using study circles to put citizens at the centre of the system', *Public Organization Review*, 2: 267-283.

Lenaghan, J. (1999), 'Involving the public in rationing decisions. The experience of citizen juries', *Health polis*, 49: 45-61.

Lister, R. (1997), *Citizenship. Feminist Perspectives*, London: MacMillan Press.

— et al. (2007), *Gendering citizenship in Western Europe. New challenges for citizenship in a cross-national context*, Bristol: Policy Press.

EVELIEN TONKENS AND JANET NEWMAN

Maloff, B., D. Bilan and W. Thurston (2000), 'Enhancing public input into deci-sion making: development of the Calgary Regional Health Authority Public Participation Framework', *Family and Community Health*, 23 (1): 66-78.

Marquand, D. (2004), *The Decline of the Public: The hollowing out of citizenship*, London: Wiley Blackwell.

Milewa, T. (1997), 'Community participation and health care priorities: reflec-tions on policy, theatre and reality in Britain', *Health promotion international*, 12: 161-167.

—, G. Dowswell and S. Harrison (2002), 'Partnerships, power and the 'new' politics of community participation in British health care', *Social policy and administration*, 36: 796-809.

— (2004), 'Local participatory democracy in Britain's health service: innovation or fragmentation of a universal citizenship?' *Social policy and administration*, 38: 240-252.

Paddison, R., I. Docherty, R. Goodlad (2008), 'Responsible participation and housing: restoring democratic theory to the scene', *Housing Studies*, 23 (1): 129-149.

Prior, D (2009), 'Policy, power and the potential for counter-agency', in M. Barnes and D. Prior (eds.), *Subversive Citizens: Power, agency and resistance in public services*, Bristol: Policy Press.

Prabhakar, R. (2006), *Rethinking Public Services*, New York: Palgrave Macmillan.

Preston, B. (1996), 'Award structuring: a catalyst in the evolution of teacher pro-fessionalism', in T. Seddon (ed.), *Pay, professionalism and politics*. Melbourne: ACER.

Sachs, J. (2000), 'The activist Professional', in *Journal of Educational Change*, 1: 77-95.

Swyndegedouw, E. (2005), 'Governance innovation and the citizen: the janus face of governance-beyond-the-state', *Urban studies*, 42 (11): 1991-2006.

Sullivan, W. (2004), 'Can professionalism still be a viable ethic?' *The good society*, 13 (1): 15-20.

Raco, M. (2000), 'Assessing community participation in local economic develop-ment- lessons for the new urban policy', *Political geography*, 10 (2000): 573-599.

Tonkens, E. (2009), 'Civicness and citizen participation in social services: condi-tions for promoting respect and public concern', in T. Brandsen, P. Dekker and A. Evers (eds.), Civicness in the governance and delivery of social ser-vices.

—, M. Hoijtink and H. Gulikers (2010), 'Democratizing social work', in M. Noor-degraaf and B. Steijn (eds.), *Professionals Under Pressure. Perspectives on profes-sionals and professionalism in public service delivery* (forthcoming).

Tunstall, R. (2001), 'Devolution and user participation in public services: how they work and what they do', *Urban Studies*, 38: 2495-2514.

Williams, F. (2004), 'Trends in women's employment, domestic service and fe-male migration: changing and competing patterns of solidarity', in T. Knijn and A. Komter (eds.), *Solidarity Between the Sexes and the Generations: Trans-formations in Europe*, Cheltenham: Edward Elgar, 210-218.

Witz, A. (1992), *Professions and Patriarchy*, London: Routledge.

12 Towards a feminist politics of active citizenship

Janet Newman and Evelien Tonkens

Gender has been a recurrent theme in this volume. But in order to understand the different genderings of active citizenship, we need to look at differences between the political projects involved (see chapter 1). Looking across this volume as a whole, it is evident that such political projects – however diverse – are transforming public and private responsibilities. The recurrence of this classic feminist theme of public/private throughout this volume urges us to examine more closely the gendering and re-gendering of active citizenship as a governmental construct, as well as a recurrent thread in the personal lives and choices of women.

In this chapter we trace active citizenship as a set of relationships that reconfigure public and private, personal and political. We disentangle the public-private dichotomy by elucidating four different sets of concepts that this dichotomy points to. By drawing on these we hope to elaborate a feminist politics of active citizenship.

The idea that we engage with is that there has been – and continues to be – a marked shift from public to private. This resonates with an extensive (feminist and non-feminist) body of scholarship on the rise of the 'New Right' and the transformations of welfare. For example, Mayer (2008) traces the crafting of a new conservative consensus on welfare reform from the 1970s onwards in the US. She argues that the conservative reform project displaced the previous liberal understandings of citizenship with a simultaneous communitisation and marketisation of public welfare institutions. Although there were significant differences between the reform projects of economic liberals and social conservatives, they were aligned through a common perspective on the public/private dichotomy, she argues: social interaction was understood through a conceptual separation between a public sphere of action, regulated by the state, and a private sphere 'in which individual citizens are free to exercise moral and political autonomy' (2008: 171). Welfare reform, in the US and in the countries or regions considered in this volume, seeks to rework the relations of welfare around and through this distinction, shifting previously 'public' roles, services and identities to the 'private' domain, but maintaining the conceptual separation.

However, the conceptual separation is one that has been repeatedly challenged in feminist scholarship. The argument that 'the personal is political' has led to the inclusion of issues previously considered personal as proper issues for public dialogue and debate. While the first wave of the Women's Movement in the early 20th century struggled for entry into a (male defined and dominated) public domain, second-wave feminism problematised the contours of the public domain itself in seeking to make public so-called 'private' issues such as domestic abuse, reproduction, sexuality and care. Their success is marked by care 'going public' in Nordic countries (see chapters by Anttonen & Häikiö, Vabø), and by a series of policy and legislative reforms on equality and rights, sexuality and domestic violence in the UK and elsewhere. These public rationalities are now being challenged by the rise of consumerist, individualising and personalising policies; but at the same time public policy continues to extend its reach to address issues formerly considered private or personal.

Public and private, then, are dynamic concepts whose meaning is constituted as they are placed in opposition with each other or sutured into new articulations (Newman & Clarke, 2009; Mahony et al. 2010). But despite decades of critique of the public/private dichotomy, not least from feminist activists and scholars, it remains remarkably resilient. Such resilience is perhaps because it offers a useful shorthand for both advocates and critics of welfare reform. But the poverty of the concept is revealed as we return to some of the questions and issues raised in the chapters of this volume. For example, is care a public or private matter? Do personalisation strategies offer a valuable remaking of public provision or do they serve to individualise and privatise it? How might we conceptualise organisations that are publicly funded but that both have to compete in the market and respond to public regulation? Does the market represent a public domain of exchange and action distinct from the personal domain of family and emotions, or does it serve to privatise and individualise public goods? Do new participative strategies enable more personal and affective voices to enter into – and perhaps transform – the public domain? Are spaces of community – the site in some countries of increased governmental concern and the focus of 'responsibilisation' strategies – public, private or personal?

These questions suggest that a simple public/private dichotomy is conceptually inadequate: it condenses multiple sets of relationships. In the next section we trace the contours of some of these relationships and their gendering. We then go on to assess the implications of our analysis for the wider project of developing a feminist analysis of active citizenship.

Remaking (and rethinking) public and private

This section opens out the simple public/private distinction into a number of relational categories: state/market, collective/individual, public/personal and personal/political. Each offers a specific way of under-

JANET NEWMAN AND EVELIEN TONKENS

standing welfare reform, and opens out a different dynamic in the remaking of citizenship. Each, we suggest, is also implicitly gendered. Indeed it is by thinking through gender that these multiple dynamics are
brought into view, offering a way of understanding active citizenship not
simply as a formal relationship between individual and state but 'as a
total relationship, inflected by identity, social positioning, cultural assumptions, institutional practices and a sense of belonging' (Werbner &
Yuval-Davis 1999: 4, cited in Hobson, Lister & Siim, 2002: 23). In what
follows we will elaborate on each of these relationships and how this
volume contributes to the analysis of its reconfiguration. What we are
concerned with is how each of these relational categories is already gendered and how their gendering is shifting in the course of the reforms
and developments traced in this volume.

State-Market

This set of categories signifies the allocation of powers and responsibilities between sectors. It does not work as a 'pure' binary: most typologies
recognise the significance of civil society, the so called 'third sector' and,
in some feminist work, family. However, state and market currently
form the institutional enactments of current discourses of public and
private. Across this volume we have highlighted a number of different
marketising logics, including contracts, vouchers, purchaser-provider
splits and outright privatisations of public services. Some have also suggested how the publicness of public institutions is challenged as market
logics and rationalities are brought deep inside the public sector, and as
so-called 'third-sector' organisations become subject to commercial logics as providers of formerly public services. Several contributors have
highlighted the potential inequalities produced by marketising reforms
(e.g. De Leonardis; Newman). They have also pointed to the impoverish-
ment of relationships produced by the marketisation of services, not
only between citizens but also between citizens in their roles as users
and providers of services (Vabø), or between carers and those cared for
(Anttonen & Häikiö, Barnes). One common theme highlighted in the
different studies is the transformative potential of active citizenship –
how it prepares welfare systems for marketisation and makes managerialism somehow more acceptable (see in particular Kuhlmann, Vabø).
The retreat of the welfare state and the shift to market mechanisms impact on women as both users of welfare services and, as we saw in chapter 11, as workers and professionals.

However, the state/market binary, and oscillations between these categories in public policy, fails to acknowledge the complexity of the new
configurations that are emerging that cross and complicate the binary. It
has been argued elsewhere (Newman & Clarke 2009) that state and market have become increasingly entangled in new hybrid forms of organisation, and that private and public authority are assembled and overlaid

in complex ways. For example, as contributors to this volume have shown, while public provision may be in retreat, the state is taking on new regulatory roles, whether in the quality assurance schemes of elder care in Norway or the legislation designed to enhance the accountability of social insurance schemes in Germany. Individual budgets serve to open up new markets, with service users as commissioners of services, but do not divest the state of responsibility, at least in the case of Friuli discussed by De Leonardis.

The proliferation of new organisational forms that work across the categories of state and market (e.g. public private partnerships or social enterprises) tend to make it more difficult to see precisely what is public about new service configurations. The proliferation of new hybrid forms means that it becomes questionable how far it is possible to assure public values or to inscribe public governance rationalities: questions of value tend to be subordinated to matters of efficiency and effective delivery.

Collective-Individual

Collective/individual is often mapped directly onto state/market, but refers not to sectors but to cultural patterns of identification and action. What matters about active citizenship is who citizens think they are: the identifications that are sought, encouraged and tutored, and those that are discouraged, rendered part of a vilified past of dependence and powerlessness. Such identifications govern the form and shape of the actions encouraged by discourses of active citizenship. A dominant argument here is that the reorganisation of state services around market logics brings with it a transformation of the discourses through which identities are summoned, with collective universalism shading to individualised consumerism.

The introduction of consumerist logics has tended to be viewed, in the country-based chapters of this volume, as having a number of malign consequences. One is the increasing tendency towards citizenship being viewed in individualistic, rather than solidaristic, terms; as consumers rather than as participants, as an individual rather than a relational subject (Newman, Vabø, and De Leonardis on Lombardy). This serves to degender the citizen, detaching her conceptually from families and relationships and the implicit forms of support these offer. As such, it offers entry into a kind of public sphere as a de-gendered citizen-subject. A second is that the active citizen subject in social welfare is constituted as an individual rational chooser rather than a moral or ethical subject: moral and ethical judgements and choices tend to be subordinated to consumerist logics (Barnes; Anttonen & Häikiö). Overall we can see the constitution of new citizen subjects as individualised knowing consumers, with the state seeking to ensure access to information (to support choice) and to 'empower' the consumer (e.g. by dismantling producer dominated services). Individual consumers can of course also organise themselves to form new collectives, taking on the identity of consumer activists. This is more present in some fields – e.g. those of the environment and food – but is also present in health and social welfare, as demonstrated in the chapters by Tonkens and Vabø.

However, the consumerist narrative can easily overstate the shape and direction of change, flattening complexity and rendering invisible the personal and political commitments of those implicated in such relationships. Such commitments were highlighted in each of the chapters that drew on ethnographic data on citizen perspectives (those by Vabø, Anttonen & Häikiö, Barnes, De Leonardis, Tonkens). Of particular importance are the identifications of professionals and other staff (as we saw in chapter 11). Even those working in contracted out or privatised services may hold on to collective sensibilities as part of a distinctively public form of provision, or bring wider notions of the public good to their judgements on individual service encounters. This is not to romanticise their role, but they do mediate the collective/individual dynamic and must themselves be considered as active (and sometimes activated) citizens.

Public bodies and public service staff, then, can play important roles in summoning, constituting and supporting collective solidarities. They may also contribute to more individualising logics. For example, Neveu notes how different kinds of participation fora elicit different kinds of roles and performances from participants (see also Barnes et al. 2003, 2007, on the constitution of the publics of public participation). Publics may be summoned as individual users or consumers, detached from political or social solidarities and from the networks that might sustain or foster collective identities. They may, in contrast, be summoned in ways that sustain and nurture solidaristic attachments. Both Neveu and De Leonardis go on to highlight the role of public bodies in constructing territory as public space – space in which participation can take place on issues of a collective interest. De Leonardis contrasts Milan in Lombardy – in which the process of territory making serves to displace public authority – with Trieste in Friuli, where citizen involvement in collective issues takes on a public character and 'acquires the features of political participation'. Public authorities, she suggests, have key roles in constituting and managing both publics and politics; the results can be exclusionary and disciplinary or inclusionary and empowering.

However, De Leonardis, Newman and Neveu's work suggest that new territorial configurations of governance may displace what might be considered to be collective and moral areas of judgement – including judgements about how to balance needs and resources – onto local residents or those on the 'front line' of localised welfare services. This is consequential in accounting for some of the differences traced across this volume: as De Leonardis notes, in shaping different trajectories and their consequences, 'the position and action of public institutions are not extraneous: rather, it is through the interface between public institutions and citizens that new forms of active citizenship are translated and enacted'.

Personal-Public

Throughout this volume we have emphasised the shift of responsibility from public to personal as welfare states have divested functions and roles to individuals, families and communities. Three foci of this new entanglement of personal and public are particularly significant for our argument.

The first is care. Barnes notes how care was transformed from a personal to a public policy issue – and how the participation of carers 'unsettles the distinction between the supposedly private values of care and the public values of citizenship'. The attempt to make care a public issue, it might be argued, has been quite successful, as not only paid care but also unpaid care remains high on the political agenda of Western welfare states. The claims by particular groups – disabled people, people with learning difficulties and carers themselves – for recognition by care services as citizens rather than 'dependents' have had considerable success (Tonkens, Barnes, this volume). Nevertheless, the question can be raised whether this agenda empowers carers and care receivers. Despite decades of public care services, their funding has remained precarious and social care is currently the site of attempts to 're-privatise' it to personal and familial domains. Rather than empowerment, we may witness, in some countries at least, a process of handing over responsibilities from governments to carers, families, communities and to citizens themselves as choice makers and commissioners. This narrative is of course uneven, with different trajectories of change in each of the nations we have examined. And what is at stake is often not simply the handing over of public responsibilities and government withdrawal; governments may shift their role from service provision to service stimulator. But overall we might conclude that there has been some kind of shift from public provision to personal responsibility.

A second area of entanglement between public and personal is the strategy of personalisation in the service relationship. This too is ambiguous: it tailors services around individual needs, but as Anttonen and Häikiö note, services tend to be negotiated case by case, thus potentially deepening existing inequalities. Personalisation also invokes new forms of partnership between service users and providers. Such partnerships supposedly share responsibility but also open up a relationship in which the capacities of individuals to take their share of those responsibilities can be enhanced, and in which new forms of contractualisation can be fostered.

This shades into the third focus of new entanglements of personal and public, as the personal may be the focus of new governmentalities of the self and personal lives. The active citizen here is not necessarily set free from bureaucratic or professional control but is to be tutored, empowered and supported. Responsibility to participate in personal plans or in deliberative spaces has opened up a concern with capacities and competencies, and led to the proliferation of new pedagogical practices. The responsible citizen, it seems, is not abandoned to exercise her responsibilities as she sees fit but has become subject to an array of new governmentalities. The personal, then, is not just a matter of individual, private lives but is also the focus of political and cultural practices (Barnes & Prior 2000). Governments, voluntary bodies, the professions, faith organisations and other actors are keen to transform the ways in which personal lives are lived, changing behaviour, teaching personal and life skills, fostering good parenting, 'nudging' people to eat healthily, and so on. This suggests a new morality, or form of soft paternalism, that may be displacing the old paternalism of welfare states (Pykett 2010; Newman 2010).

Personal lives, then, are entering the public domain as objects of scrutiny, pedagogy and behaviour change strategies. And rather than the retreat of the state, or a shift from public to personal, we might point to the enlargement or extension of state concern with how personal lives are lived – how people can be 'nudged' towards appropriate behaviours, how disabled people can come to view their lives in terms of work and well-being rather than dependence, how carers might be 'developed' not only to provide good care but also to look after themselves properly, how mothers should best look after their children, how older people can be mobilised to forms of activity that will keep them fit and independent for as long as possible, and so on. While those to be tutored are not exclusively women, women are often addressed not as citizen-subjects but as mothers, paid and unpaid carers, and 'empowered' members of communities.

But it is not only the state that is concerned with personal lives. With the turn to 'civil society' as a resource for welfare provision, religious groups and faith organisations are becoming increasingly significant players (Dinham et al. 2009). The increasing place of religion in public life and of faith groups in welfare provision means that notions of responsibility are being reworked. This is particularly significant in the UK and US, where faith organisations are not only active citizens in their own right but also inflect notions of responsibility in specific ways. This opens out new lines of contestation around both 'race' and gender. Faith appears as a new inflection of multiculturalism: one which however fragments the values of a tolerant, liberal public sphere into a series of different – and potentially conflicting – enclaves. When summoned as service providers, potential recipients may be required to conform to the values of a particular faith, and the sexuality and moral behaviour of workers subjected to disciplinary practices. The rise of faith discourse also has significant implications for the remaking of gender settlements. Such settlements rested on secular values, and such values – especially those that relate to issues of sexuality – have been strongly resisted by the Christian church. The eruption of 'faith' into public culture has thus led to a number of hard-fought disputes over the territorial boundary between religious and secular principles for public life. This boundary continues to be most contested where issues of gender and sexuality – specifically the control of women's bodies – are at stake.

The public-personal relationship thus brings into view ethical and moral choices that cannot be contained in the economic rationalities of market choice. At the same time, it exacerbates many of the hard choices that citizens – especially women – have to make. This takes us to the fourth set of categories: personal and political. These relate to the opening up or closing down of the spaces in which personal lives become the focus of political agency, and thus perhaps of public action; but also draw attention to the 'depoliticisation' of politics itself.

Personal-Political

In the same way that public and private are defined in and against each other, rather than being absolute categories, so 'political' has tended to be defined as the antithesis of 'personal'. In this opposition, the personal is framed as 'outside' of and a barrier to politics. This concerns firstly, questions of style: what way of talking and deliberating is considered legitimate in the sphere of politics? Politics itself is supposed to be conducted in a rational and impersonal manner. Delegates and participants of the numerous public participation forums mentioned by our contributors (and elsewhere – see Barnes et al, 2007; McDermont et al. 2009) are asked to leave their personhood and individuality behind and to become the 'abstracted' citizens noted by Neveu when they engage in political debate. Furthermore, the debate itself is expected to be conducted without undue expressions of emotion and without recourse to anecdotes about personal experience (Barnes 2008). What is political, it seems, cannot be personal, and the personal – with all of its unruly passions and disruptive emotions – is to be kept out of politics.

These efforts to separate the personal and the political have of course been widely critiqued by feminist thinkers and many other activists groups – including movements of carers, patients and service users. Feminists have argued not only that 'the personal is political' but also that a focus on detached rationality serves to exclude experiences – and often the experiences of women and marginalised groups, including older people, disabled people, mental health service users, children, from the decision making process (Phillips 1995; Young 1990). The (feminist) politics of everyday life challenges definitions of what is properly a personal matter and what is a matter for public debate and collective provision, drawing attention to the public value created by informal labour in family, civil society and community.

Paradoxically it is precisely this set of transformations that have led governments to pursue projects of state modernisation and reform that seek to draw on or capture this value. Policy discourses on active citizenship as a set of practices associated with responsibilities in home, community and civil society, it seems, both amplify and transform informal sources of agency and power. This has led institutional actors in some countries to seek out and enrol the 'authentic' experiences of 'ordinary people' in order to enrich the decision making process. They have embraced the idea that the personal is political but twisted its meaning in a populist manner (see Newman & Clarke 2009; Clarke 2010 for elaboration and critique of this point). The recent rise of populist forms of discourse and politics has of course further confounded the opposition between personal and political styles of operating. For populist politicians, anecdotes as well as explicit expressions of emotion are integral to their message. The paradox noted above is deepened further in the populist logic that ordinary people are supposed to voice the views of 'The People', while the notion of ordinary people is itself highly racialised and exclusionary.

The articulations of populist politics and market logics underscore the move from collective identifications to individual preferences. Both imply a preference for individual persons rather than those linked to collective entities. Both potentially strip the person from social identifications beyond the service encounter or locality, including social identifications that might become the focus of collective forms of agency. With public participation and political renewal having become governmental priorities, a paradox presents itself: while public participation is proclaimed, it is individual participation that is favoured. This paradox underscores the importance of analysing the ways in which the publics of public participation initiatives are constituted. The chapters of this volume raise questions about what forms of agency are deemed legitimate, who gets to speak, in which modes and styles of expression.

The contributions of feminist research and analysis

Such discussions lead us back to questions that have long been contested and debated amongst feminist scholarship. In the preceding chapters we have hinted at some of the contours of how a feminist analysis of active citizenship might proceed; here we try to draw these together, while acknowledging their incompleteness and lack of coherence. Feminist work on citizenship points to struggles over the meanings and practices of citizenship as well as inclusion into already defined categories and statuses.

But there is of course no one feminism and so no single frame of analysis. From the standpoint of feminist political economy, questions are raised about the effects on women of the withdrawal of state funding and state services, especially for women in poverty. This is certainly significant: but the 'total' relationality of citizenship suggested at the outset of this chapter suggests that we also need to draw on feminist ethics (including work on the ethics of care – e.g. Sevenhuijsen 1998, 2000; Tronto 1993), feminist psychological and psychoanalytic approaches on difference and identity (e.g. Wetherell et al. 2007; Lewis 2000), feminist work on citizenship (e.g. Lister 2003; Siim 2000), space (e.g. Massey 1994; Staeheli 1996), governance (e.g. Cooper 2004), publics (e.g. Fraser 2008) and feminist inflections of post colonial studies (e.g. Bhasin 2010). Furthermore the increasing body of feminist research on 'race' and ethnicity serves to trouble existing traditions of work on citizenship itself, which often remain framed by residues of a liberal, rights-based conception of citizenship as status (see Lister 2003; Isin & Nielsen 2008 for critiques).

Engaging with these different bodies of theory would be a huge undertaking and we cannot hope to do justice to the richness and subtlety of this ever-expanding body of scholarship. Our aim is more modest: that of drawing on our work in and beyond this volume in order to highlight some of the different dimensions of what a feminist sensibility might offer. Throughout we have highlighted the implicit gendering of taken-for-granted concepts. We have, in Neveu's terms, explored the significance of certain keywords – citizen, care, community, public, personal, and responsibility, participation and choice – showing not only how each is already gendered, but also how their gendering changes as the meaning of the concepts slide in the context of new public policies and political projects. For example, choice was a mantra of the women's movement and many of the movements that followed – including movements of disabled people. But such struggles have tended to become accommodated within market models. As such, we have shown how the meaning of choice in public policy has displaced or silenced moral and ethical choices, and asserted the hegemony of market choice. In shifting from relational to transactional inflections of choice, the experiences, preferences and concerns of many women are sidelined. However, as the ethnographic studies we have cited show, dominant meanings may not exclude other perspectives.

Similarly we noted that 'responsibility' is of course already gendered, not least because of the gendering of responsibility for care work. However, the extension of 'responsibility' to encompass developmental, economic, community based and other dimensions both expands the responsibilities of women while also apparently offering more gender-neutral conceptions of personhood. The historical ambiguities around women's roles in the public sphere have apparently been resolved by the proliferation of service user and community-based spaces of participation. However the 'habitant' versus detached categories offered by Neveu suggests a gendered distinction between the everyday, prosaic and the

JANET NEWMAN AND EVELIEN TONKENS

strategic, political – a distinction that may reproduce the already gendered boundaries of the public domain.

This feminist concern with highlighting the gendering of apparently gender-neutral concepts appears to be still necessary and fruitful. From this, four more specific points arise that are related to the four pairs of concepts discussed in the first part of this chapter, all enwrapped in and constitutive of the public/private dichotomy. The first returns us to the state/market binary, and directs attention to the continued need to analyse the gendered consequences of welfare state reform. This volume takes forward previous comparative work, e.g. that of Siim, who contrasted forms of politics and agency in France, Britain and Denmark from feminist perspectives, and the (2007) study by Lister et al. exploring gendered citizenship across Europe. But it departs from attempts to categorise gender orders in terms of institutional and policy regimes. Welfare regime theory takes us back to the problems of methodological nationalism discussed in chapter 1. It also tends to privilege the relationship between women's paid work and the care of young children, neglecting other forms of care, other areas of responsibility and other dimensions of citizenship. This body of work is reviewed in Orloff (forthcoming), who criticises the falsely universalising (implicitly masculinist) analytical frames that have undergirded all comparative studies of welfare states, including Esping-Andersen's.

In drawing out the gendered dynamics of active citizenship, our contributors have tended to avoid the commodification-decommodification approach of labour market analysis and welfare policies. Rather they have focused on the gendered dimensions of choice, responsibility and participation. Several chapters offer research by women on (mainly) women's lives and experiences in programmes of welfare reform that shift responsibilities between market, state and civil society. The research that the chapters of this book build on takes as its starting point citizens' own perspectives, issues and questions, and includes research from the standpoint of service providers and professionals as citizens themselves. This has enabled contributors to highlight the experiential and subjective dimensions of active citizenship alongside more 'objective' accounts of policy shifts. Such forms of analysis have enabled us to analyse the gendered consequences of welfare state transformation beyond the commodification-decommodification nexus. This does not mean that paid work – and labour market activation – are not at the centre of new governmentalities of active citizenship (see Newman, this volume). But it does open up other dimensions that are not brought into view. Similarly, we have looked beyond the analysis of state policy, exploring ways in which it is mediated and enacted in diverse settings.

Implicit in these endeavours is a feminist agenda of active citizenship that we want to make explicit in this final chapter: to analyse the gendered consequences of welfare state reform in terms of everyday life experiences of (women and men as) citizens, clients and professionals. Instead of starting with grand models of welfare states in the tradition of Esping-Andersen, we have drawn on ethnographic accounts of how welfare state reform is felt and experienced by citizens. We do so not in order to make alternative models of welfare states, but in order to develop a shared language of new ideals such as active citizenship as a travelling concept.

Second, we return to the collective/individual binary. There is now a huge amount of feminist literature challenging the notion of a unitary self and highlighting the complexity of identity and belonging. As we have seen through the research cited in this volume, citizens can hold multiple identities: they can be at the same time citizens and consumers (Newman), service users and activists (Vabø), individuals and members of a public domain of belonging and action. They may be dependent and independent, want rights as well as express needs, and may phrase their demands as both individual want and as part of a wider collective good. Similarly, professionals and other workers may view themselves as individuals, subject to individual risks and performance pressures, and as part of a wider collective entity, whether a profession, a public organisation or a generalised notion of citizenship. Such forms of analysis complicate overarching narratives concerning the demise of solidarity and the rise of individualism and consumerism, while not bracketing away the significance of the political projects that seek to reframe attachment and belonging around notions of the 'active citizen'. The implicit feminist research agenda here concerns the analysis of shifts in the meaning and shape of (new) attachments, collectivities and solidarities against the background of bigger changes such as rising consumerism and individualism.

Third, the dynamic of public/personal offers a view of active citizenship as encompassing ethical and moral, emotional and affective dimensions. We have hinted at some of the multiple spaces in which ethical and moral acts of citizenship take place, and how the contours of such spaces are changing. This includes the restructuring and reform of welfare states, but also encompasses prosaic practices and experiences of citizenship. Much feminist work on welfare states has remained focused on the state and state (or sometimes EU) policies, most critically policies on the relationship between work and care. Several of our contributors draw on such scholarship, conducting critical analyses of policy texts or providing accounts of the evolution of policy. But the volume as a whole also looks beyond the state, adding a focus on the significance of territory in mobilisations of active citizenship and highlighting a range of mediating practices through which state policies are enacted. We have also highlighted the proliferation of the spaces in which citizens are summoned (to be active) and invited (to participate in service design and in welfare governance), and the prosaic practices through which new identities of citizenship are negotiated. A feminist agenda here underlines the meaning of these more prosaic practices: of how big changes such as welfare state reform and governance shifts are experienced, received and given (new) meaning by actors involved in mundane practices such as organising, giving and receiving care, education, community building and so on – most of which is performed and partly also received by women.

Finally, in exploring the personal-political dynamic, the volume has offered a view of politics as transcending personal and 'big P' politics. This raises the question of how far the collapse of the political into a concern with the personal, traced earlier, erases the possibility of political agency and the formation of collective solidarities. Such a narrative is now common in contemporary accounts of the relationship between feminism and neo-liberalism (e.g. Fraser 2009; McRobbie 2009; Eistensen 2006). However, other feminist literature has pointed to the mobile and self-reflexive ways in which women organise (e.g. Fincher & Panelli 2001) and to the significance of the 'liminal spaces' between public and private in which women's acts of citizenship often take place. 'Community' as an ambiguously public and private place may be particularly significant here. Staeheli (1996) argues that women's collective action can break down boundaries between public and private, but the fact that it is often 'placed' in the private sphere operates to their advantage in giving them 'shelter' to develop strategies that may not be visible. Jupp (2010), among others, demonstrates the significance of the 'contact zones' in which personal resources are mobilised for public projects, and demonstrates the ambiguous 'public' potential of the liminal spaces in which public, private and personal are entangled. For example, 'empowerment' and 'development' strategies open up forms of agency that may not accord with the intentions of policymakers (see Sharma 2008). The feminist agenda here points to the analysis of liminal spaces and contact zones; such liminal spaces are particularly interesting for the way meanings of active citizenship in the context of welfare state reform and new governmentalities are created and contested.

In taking forward thinking about the relationship between active and activist forms of citizenship, we might engage with current work that offers a very different understanding of the 'active' of active citizenship. Isin and Neilsen (2008) propose a shift of analytical focus from citizenship as status to citizen acts. Such acts are not the everyday, mundane practices of everyday life that reproduce societal forms but are collective or individual deeds that *rupture* social-historical practices. While perhaps reproducing a gendered distinction between active (doing the everyday work of citizenship) and activist (rupturing the taken for granted, the given), this is also helpful in that it enlarges the meaning of the political: acts of citizenship can be simultaneously political, ethical and aesthetic, and can embrace cultural and social interventions alongside more formally public acts. As such, the focus on acts of citizenship potentially collapses the distinction between the public domain and private selves: it is through acts of citizenship that citizenship itself is produced, rather than being a pre-constituted status. And – elaborating on this perspective in ways that may not be acceptable to its authors – we might suggest that the forms of citizenship that are produced through citizen acts might be gendered, aged, racialised and sexualised, thus challenging the image of the citizen as a disembodied individual and of citizenship as a universal status free of particularities and untainted by modalities of difference. The overarching feminist agenda points to the analysis of citizenship acts, in liminal zones in between public and private, collective and individual, personal and political or state and market. It is here that (gendered) demands on citizenship are experienced; it is here that they may be protested and modified.

This is of course a selective view of what a feminist project might be. It is different from the extensive body of work on the gender dynamics of welfare state reform, structured around questions of the relationship between work and care, with labour market activation as the key dynamic. While many of our contributors have not claimed an explicit feminist perspective, their analysis has consistently been grounded in a focus on the 'everyday' and 'personal' experiences associated with the transformations of citizenship – a focus strongly linked to feminist scholarship (e.g. Smith 1987). They have illuminated citizenship as experience as well as status; and helped us to see how rights and responsibilities are not separate categories but are lived together in everyday practice. We think then that this volume makes a contribution to ongoing interdisciplinary debates and conceptual development. By exploring active citizenship from perspectives that privilege gender, a number of paradoxes are revealed that might shape future research and analysis.

Conclusion

In this volume we have shown how the reform of welfare states around the notion of active citizenship both acknowledges and responds to the political struggles of feminism and other social movements while also potentially closing down and depoliticising the spaces they opened up. We have nevertheless seen, in the preceding chapters, how citizens, activists and professionals continue to forge new spaces for political and social action. The power of the new governmentalities of self and community to constitute active citizens as compliant, responsible, consumer-oriented individuals seems to be limited; other notions of rights, responsibility, choice and participation continue to circulate. We have suggested the contained and diminished focus of the 'active' of active citizenship but also shown that this does not necessarily map on to the identifications of citizens and their everyday acts of citizenship.

We have also traced the 'Janus faces' of active citizenship. It seems to produce both the possibility of empowerment while subjecting citizens to new governmentalities of responsibility, choice and participation. The person who becomes the focus of new governmentalities of the self is an apparently gender-neutral person, but the increase of familial and community responsibilities are highly gendered. Active citizenship, then, may be both emancipatory and disciplining, inclusionary and exclusionary. What seems to matter is how it is translated and enacted in the context of specific political projects, whether of nation states, regions or localities; and how active citizens themselves seek to transform the meanings of both 'active' and 'citizenship' in social and political struggles to come.

Our focus in this volume has been on tracing emergent dynamics rather than providing a picture of a completed set of political projects. What then of the future? We cannot say, but do want to highlight some issues that we think warrant further investigation and collaborative research. The most immediate is the likely consequences of the global financial crisis on the policies and strategies of welfare states. The limits of markets became startlingly revealed, and we saw some reassertion of the role of public authorities – including states – in managing the consequences of unbridled markets. In 2008-2009 there was a marked change in tone concerning programmes of marketisation in some countries as well as the rise of new regulatory practices. But we can now anticipate the exacerbation of inequality as the squeeze on welfare expenditure tightens eligibility criteria and as more responsibilities are devolved from states onto citizens, both responsibilities for care and responsibilities to support charities and non-state-funded services. Here the focus on the consequences for existing citizens of specific welfare states is limited, taking us back to the problems of methodological nationalism discussed in chapter 1. The global recession is already having consequences for patterns of migration, a further rise of political parties of the far right, and intensifying areas of conflict between the global north and south.

This opens up questions about how notions of active citizenship are racialised and ethnicised. Asylum and migration policies are now very influential in shaping the dynamics of active citizenship, governing who gets to speak, in what arenas, who carries rights, and how issues of belonging are negotiated (Lister & Pia 2008; Modood 2009; Kymlicka & Bashir 2008). As Lister et al. (2007) note, a distinction needs to be made between legal rights of entry to a nation state and the internal policies that specify the rights and obligations of those who have already entered legally. But this distinction is increasingly difficult to sustain, not least because of the multiplication of categories of legality and illegality within the nation. Such categories produce difficulties for those seeking to engage citizens as participants (how can the voices of the 'sans papiers', overstayers, illegal migrants, asylum seekers awaiting a decision, those held in 'holding centres' and others be heard?). They also produce problems for those delivering health, education, housing and care services: should those with no formal right to a service be excluded from it, even when presenting extreme need? National public policies increasingly stretch across national boundaries, producing new ways of framing questions of social justice and human rights. This complicates issues of citizenship and also shifts the territorial understanding of the arenas in which active citizenship is exercised.

This takes us to a related question: how far active citizenship as a travelling idea (see chapter 1) might travel, and with what consequences. Our study has been limited, not least since it reflects the standpoint of those working against the background of the expansion and subsequent reform of western European welfare states. The dynamics elsewhere are likely to be very different. As Ute Gerhard suggests, 'The pioneering role Scandinavian countries played in the establishment of women's rights of citizenship seems to be particularly due to the shared political platform of the labour movement and the women's movement during that period. Completely new and different questions are raised by the juxtaposition of East and West. Here Western feminism cannot be taken as a role model' (2002: 312). Similarly Western feminism, and a preoccupation with the fate of 'mature' welfare states, can offer little to the analysis of new formations of citizenship in the global south (e.g. Kabeer 2005).

How, then, will active citizenship as a travelling idea intersect with the very different political projects of central and eastern Europe (especially post communist and transition countries), and 'modernising' nations in the global South? Our challenge to methodological nationalism has been only partly realised in this volume: much more work needs to be done on how ideas flow and on the complex rescaling of both welfare and of politics. Attention also needs to be paid to how the identities and practices of citizenship work across different scales, from the home through local and national politics to more 'cosmopolitan' understandings; or to an engagement with issues of global concern, from environmental degradation to the degradation of the human rights of others. These all form arenas for active citizenship; and indeed for the kinds of 'citizenship acts' that seek to transform the polity.

References

Barnes, M. (2008), 'Passionate participation: emotional experiences and expressions in deliberative forums', *Critical Social Policy* 28 (4): 461-81.

—, and D. Prior (2000), *Private Lives as Public Policy*, Birmingham: Venture Press.

— (2009) (eds.), *Subversive Citizens: Power, agency and resistance in public services*, Bristol: Policy Press.

Bhasin, G. (2010), 'Mediating publics in colonial Delhi', in N. Mahony, J. Newman and C. Barnett (eds.), *Rethinking the Public: Innovations in research, theory and politics*, Bristol: Policy Press.

Clarke, J. (2010), 'Enrolling ordinary people: governmental strategies and the avoidances of politics', *Citizenship Studies*, 14, 6: 637-650.

Dinham, A., R. Furbey and V. Lowndes (2009) (eds.), *Faith in the Public Realm: Controversies, policies and practices*, Bristol: Policy Press.

Eisenstein, H. (2006), 'Scouting parties and bold detachments: towards a post-capitalist feminism', *Women's Studies Quarterly*, 34 (1-2): 40-61.

Fincher, R. and R. Panelli (2001), 'Making space: women's urban and rural activism and the Australian state', *Gender, Place and Culture*, 8 (2): 129-148.

Fraser, N. (2008), *Scales of Justice: Reimagining political space in a globalizing world*, New York: Columbia University Press.

Gerhard, U. (2002), 'Introduction: women's movements and feminist research', in C. Griffin and R. Braidotti, *Thinking Differently: a reader in European women's studies*, 311-312.

Hobson, B., J. Lewis and B. Siim (2002) (eds.), *Contested Concepts in Gender and Social Politics*, Cheltenham: Edward Elgar.

Isin, E., and G. Nielsen (2008) (eds.), *Acts of Citizenship*, London: Zed Books.

Jupp, E. (2010), 'Private and public on the housing estate: encounters among small community groups and the local state', in N. Mahony, J. Newman and C. Barnett (eds.), *Rethinking the Public: Innovations in research, theory and politics*, Bristol: Policy Press.

Kabeer, N. (2005) (ed.), *Inclusive citizenship: Meanings and expressions*, London: Zed Books.

Lister, R. (2003), *Citizenship: Feminist perspectives*, 2nd ed. Basingstoke: Palgrave Macmillan.

Lister, R., F. Williams, A. Anttonen, J. Bussemaker, U. Gerhard, J. Heinen, S. Johannson, A. Leira and B. Siim (2007), *Gendering Citizenship in Western Europe*, Bristol: Policy Press.

McDermont, M., D. Cowan and J. Prendergrast (2009), 'Structuring Governance; a case study of the new organisational provision of public service delivery', *Critical Social Policy*, 29 (4): 677-702.

Mahony, N., J. Newman and C. Barnett (eds.), *Rethinking the Public: Innovations in research, theory and politics*, Bristol: Policy Press.

Massey, D. (1994), *Space, Place and Gender*, Minneapolis: University of Minnesota Press.

Mayer, V. (2008), 'Crafting a new conservative welfare consensus on welfare reform: redefining citizenship, social provision and the public/private divide', *Social Politics*, summer: 154-181.

McRobbie, A. (2009), *The Aftermath of Feminism: Gender, culture and social change*, London: Sage.

Newman, J. (forthcoming), 'Soft paternalism and the politics of publicness', *Political Geography*.

Newman, J., and J. Clarke (2009), *Politics, Politics and Power*, London: Sage.

Pykett, J. (forthcoming), 'The emerging geographies of soft paternalism', *Political geography*.

Ruppert, E. (2006), *The Moral Economy of Cities: Shaping good citizens*, Toronto: University of Toronto Press.

Sevenhuijsen, S. (1998), *Citizenship and the Ethics of Care: feminist considerations of justice, morality and politics*, London: Routledge.

Sevenhuijsen, S. (2000), 'Caring in the Third Way: the relation between obligation, responsibility and care in *Third Way* discourse', *Critical Social Policy*, 20 (1): 5-37.

Siim, B. (2000), *Gender and Citizenship: Politics and agency in France, Britain and Denmark*, Cambridge: Cambridge University Press.

Smith, D. (2005), *Institutional Ethnography: a sociology for people*, Lanham, MD: AltaMara Press, Rowan and Littlefield pub.

Staeheli, L. (1996), 'Publicity, privacy and women's political action', *Environment and Planning D: Society and Space*, 14: 601-619.

Tronto, J. (1993), *Moral Boundaries*, New York: Routledge.

Werbner, P., and N. Yuval-Davis (1999), 'Introduction', in N. Yuval-Davis and P. Werbner (eds.), *Women. Citizenship and difference*, London, Zed Books: 221-45.

Wetherell, M., M. Laflèche and R. Berkeley (2007) (eds.), *Identity, Ethnic Diversity and Community Cohesion*, London: Sage.

About the editors and contributors

Anneli Anttonen is a professor in the Department of Social Research, University of Tampere, Finland. Her research interests cover welfare state change, care services for children and older people, care regimes and social services.

Marian Barnes is Professor of Social Policy and Director of SSPARC, the Social Science Policy and Research Centre at the University of Brighton, England. Her research has focused on user and citizen involvement, user and carer movements and new forms of public participation. She has worked with carers, mental health- and older people's service user groups as an ally in their campaigning and in carrying out collaborative research.

Liisa Häikiö is a post-doc researcher of the Nordic Centre of Excellence: Reassessing the Nordic Welfare Model and working in the Department of Social Research, University of Tampere, Finland. She is interested in citizenship and citizen participation in urban governance, the dynamics of welfare state change and discursive formations of power.

Ellen Kuhlmann currently deputies the Chair of Social Policy and Social Structure at the Goethe-University in Frankfurt, Germany and is Senior Lecturer in the Department of Social and Policy Sciences at the University of Bath, UK. Being trained as a nurse, she also has extensive clinical experience. Her main areas of research are the modernisation of healthcare, the health professions, and gender mainstreaming policies in healthcare.

Ota De Leonardis is full Professor of Sociology of Culture and Director of the Research Centre Sui Generis on Sociology of Public Action at the Department of Sociology and Social Research, University of Milano Bicocca, Italy. Her teaching, supervision and research activities concern the normative and institutional changes within the 'new spirit of capitalism' and are presently focused on the contractual citizenship taking shape in welfare transformations, especially regarding healthcare, social and urban policies.

Catherine Neveu is senior researcher at LAIOS (Laboratoire d'Anthropologie des Institutions et des Organisations Sociales), IIAC, CNRS-EHESS, Paris. As an anthropologist, her research centres on citizenship processes in Europe, with specific attention to participatory practices, representations and practices of citizenship in public engagement, and issues of nationality and ethnicity.

Janet Newman is Professor of Social Policy and Director of the Public Research Programme within the Centre for Citizenship, Identities and Governance at the Open University, UK. Before becoming an academic she worked in local government for some 20 years and was actively involved in the women's movement and other political mobilisations. Her research centres on questions of new formations of governance, professional and organisational change, and the transformations of notions of publics and publicness. Her most recent book is *Publics, Politics and Power: remaking the public in public services* (with John Clarke: Sage 2009).

Evelien Tonkens is Professor of Active Citizenship at the Department of Sociology and Anthropology of the University of Amsterdam since 2005. She is also a weekly columnist for the Dutch daily newspaper *de Volkskrant*. She was a member of parliament for the Green Left between 2002 and 2005. Her research focuses on changes in the interactions between citizens and professionals that result from new social risks such as globalisation, welfare state restructuring and meritocracy. Her most recent book is *Understanding Citizenship in Multi-ethnic Societies* (with Menno Hurenkamp and Jan Willem Duyvendak: Palgrave 2011)

Mia Vabø is Senior Researcher and Research Director at NOVA – Norwegian Social Research. She has participated in several Nordic and international research projects and is currently involved in the Nordic Centre of Excellence in Welfare Research: Reassessing the Nordic Welfare Model. Her current research interests include the transformation of care systems in an ageing and diversified society and in particular the political and institutional changes associated with shifting modes of governance.

Index

Personal/public dichotomy 222-224, 228
Personalisation 113, 167, 170, 222
Pillarised (health) organizations 46-48
Pillarised welfare system 32
Place *see* territory
Policy discourse 61, 67ff., 89, 197, 108ff., 195ff.
Policymaking boards 48
Political citizenship 128, 217-232
Political projects 11, 21, 24, 107-108, 149-150, 185, 198-199, 217
Politics, depoliticisation 224-225
Populism 225
Power 119, 131, 134, 186; *see also* consumer power; discretionary power
Private insurance 46, 53
Professional associations 36-37
Professional mediations 20, 40-41, 199, 201-213
Professional network 60
Professional/user relationship 11, 201, 204, 209-210
Professionals 47ff., 109, 121
Professions 24, 36, 40ff., 201-213, *see also* citizen professionals; medical profession
Protest movements 107; *see also* social movements
Psychiatric health 51, 54, 61, 127, 132
Public goods 68, 132, 141, 201, 213, 218, 221
Public health 45ff., 139
Public housing *see* housing
Public participation 23, 67, 71, 76, 112, 115, 120, 225; *see also* participation
Public/personal dichotomy *see* public/private dichotomy
Public/private dichotomy 10, 12, 14-16, 68-69, 74, 137-138, 141, 162, 176, 180, 186, 217ff.
Public private partnerships 74, 131, 220
Public services 33, 38, 45ff., 69, 79, 88, 90, 99, 133ff., 221; *see also* health services; social care
Public space 135ff.

Public values 22, 137, 167, 220, 224-225
Publics 148ff., 221
Pyjama days 57

Quasi-markets 50, 94

Race 113-118, 226, 231; *see also* ethnicity; migration
Recognition 16-17, 57-59, 81, 118, 120, 135, 161, 167, 186
Redistribution 16-17, 120
Regional planning 50
Regions 130; *see also* territorial governance
Relational models of care 161ff., 190
Representation 37, 41, 51-52, 149, 152, 157
Representative democracy 151, 186
Respect 16, 49, 55, 96, 186
Responsibilisation 10, 14, 55, 61-62, 70-72, 183
Responsibility 10, 13-15, 45ff., 113, 118, 168-170, 179-184, 196, 226
Rights and duties 10, 45, 47, 49-54, 62, 194

Scale 20, 232
Self-criticism 47
Self governance 115
Self help groups 17, 38-40, 92, 112
Self-management 54, 138
Self organising 14, 128-129, 139; *see also* self governance
Service user movements 107, 112-113, 161; *see also* user groups; social movements
Service users 40-41, 52, 71, 75-76, 102, 129; *see also* patients; carers; consumers; citizens
Sexuality 10, 14, 182, 224
Social care 11, 45-62, 67ff., 90-91, 102, 192-195; *see also* care
Social care services 45ff., 69ff., 161ff.
Social cohesion 9, 22-23, 54, 58, 62, 120, 147, 180, 182, 188, 196
Social contracts 31-36, 41, 171; *see also* gender settlements
Social entrepreneurship 128-129